T5-AWJ-588

FOUCAULT

Foucault

Historian or Philosopher?

Clare O'Farrell

*Lecturer in the Department of
Education Studies
Brisbane College of
Advanced Education, Australia*

St. Martin's Press   New York

© Clare O'Farrell, 1989

All rights reserved. For information, write:
Scholarly and Reference Division,
St. Martin's Press, Inc., 175 Fifth Avenue, New York, N.Y. 10010

First published in the United States of America in 1989

Printed in Hong Kong

ISBN 0–312–03463–6

Library of Congress Cataloging-in-Publication Data
O'Farrell, Clare.
Foucault : historian or philosopher?/Clare O'Farrell.
p. cm.
Bibliography: p.
Includes index.
ISBN 0–312–03463–6
1. Foucault, Michel.   I. Title.
B2430.F724043   1989
194—dc20   89–33424
                                                  CIP

B
2430
.F724
043
1989

Contents

Preface   vii
Abbreviations   xii

1   A New Generation of Thinkers   1
2   The Same, the Other and the Limit   20
3   Discontinuity and Order   44
4   In Search of the Limit   65
5   The Limits Forgotten   91
6   The Return of the Limits   113

Notes   131
Bibliography   153
Index   182

Preface

Why write about Foucault? Just ten years ago, an English-speaking writer might have felt obliged to provide a detailed answer to this question, in terms of Michel Foucault's prestige in France and the intrinsic historical and philosophical interest of his work. Nowadays, this same writer could dispense with these lengthy introductions, and reply quite simply that it is not least because everybody else is writing about Foucault. In the vast literature Foucault's commentators have produced, certain questions appear again and again in one form or another: Unity or Fragmentation? Eternity or History? System or Difference? Philosophy or History? Jacques d'Hondt unwittingly sums up this discussion in a rather alarmist article about structuralism: 'Certain ages ruminate with a gloomy delectation over the question, to be or not to be. Times have changed! Our contemporaries pose quite another alternative: to break or not to break.'[1] In the present book it is this alternative that is posed in terms of an opposition between history and philosophy. In other words, this is a question of an opposition between a world view based on the belief that we are discontinuous and continually changing historical beings, and a world view which posits a small number of general principles valid for all times and places.

Which view or which combination of these views most accurately describes the reality of existence? Foucault's own solution to this problem was to write a *history of the limits*, of that edge between the orderly and historical systems societies impose upon the world (the Same), and that which is outside, or beyond that order (the Other). He often changed his mind about how this project should be carried out, but it was the constancy of a philosophical quest and a philosophical vision which led him to make these constant changes, shifts in emphasis, and reinterpretations of his work. Thus, during the 1960s, Foucault proposed a number of different limits which, each time, he thought finally explained the relation of the Same and the Other. During the 1970s, perhaps disappointed with his failure to find the final limit, he proposed a system in which the Same and the Other were mutually coextensive, locked in an endless power-struggle. This vision changed again in 1982, when power disappeared from his analysis to be replaced by the idea that, as 'free beings' living in history, we must continue to work on the limits and ourselves.

Although most of Foucault's work will be discussed here, two writings in particular will act as a focal point for discussion. The first of these is *Histoire de la folie*, written at the beginning of Foucault's career and the second is 'What is Enlightenment?', written right at the end. The empirical details of Foucault's historical interpretations will not be discussed: this has been done elsewhere by a host of specialists. Neither will 'power' and related notions form as important a part of this study as they do in many other current English-language studies of Foucault's work. In general, Foucault's work will be dealt with in philosophical terms, as a historical, philosophical and ethical reflection on the 'limits' of history, society and culture.

At the same time, however, this work will be situated in its intellectual context, and extensive reference made to its reception in French and English. Such is the volume and the sheer diversity of the writing on Foucault, not to mention the fact that it spans several cultures, that its analysis poses complex difficulties, not least of classification and categorisation.

As Foucault himself remarked with a certain ill-disguised glee concerning merely his political classification:

> I think I have in fact been situated in most of the squares on the political checkerboard . . . as anarchist, leftist, ostentatious or disguised Marxist, nihilist, explicit or secret anti-Marxist, technocrat in the service of Gaullism, new liberal, etc . . . None of these descriptions is important by itself; taken together, on the other hand, it means something. And I must admit that I rather like what they mean. It's true that I prefer not to identify myself and that I'm amused by the diversity of the ways I've been judged and classified.[2]

In consequence the examination of the secondary literature will be limited in a number of ways. First of all, only French and English-speaking literature, which forms the main body of writings on Foucault, will be dealt with. This will also provide an opportunity to look at some of the similarities and differences between the French and Anglo-Saxon intellectual mentalities.[3] Secondly, questions of empirical and specialised application will be put aside and a series of recurrent and important issues relating to philosophy and history will be addressed. In addition, the treatment of literature produced before Foucault's death in 1984, will be more comprehensive than the treatment of the literature after that date. To remain entirely up to date with every small element of this massive and ever more rapidly growing industry would be an impossible task that would fully occupy the most willing of writers, to the exclusion of time for their own considered contribution to discussion. Finally, in the context of a literature which is not, in the English-speaking world, particularly noted for its clarity or simplicity, there has been a consistent attempt to avoid certain types of jargon popular amongst 'foucaldians'. It is used only where it is absolutely unavoidable.

I am extremely grateful to the many people and institutions that have helped make this book a reality. Needless to say, as the cliché properly has it, any shortcomings that are apparent are entirely my own responsibility. I owe a very large debt, first of all to Paul Foss and Professor Randall Albury at the University of New South Wales, who originally introduced me to the work of Foucault. Over the years, Professor Albury's encouragement and discussion have been essential in seeing this project to its final completion. Also at the University of NSW, I would like to thank Professor Jarlath Ronayne and Professor Jean Chaussivert, members of the French Department, and Dr Patricia Brown for their support in various ways. A Postgraduate Research Award from the Australian Government and the Australian National University in Canberra made it possible to undertake research. And in Canberra, Professor Eugene Kamenka, and Dr Robert Brown of the History of Ideas Unit and Professor Genevieve Lloyd were the source of much help in refining and clarifying my ideas.

A French Government scholarship also provided me with the opportunity to conduct research in Paris. While I was there, many people gave me all sorts of practical and intellectual assistance. I owe a great deal, to begin with, to Michel Foucault himself who kindly agreed to talk about his ideas with me. I also wish to record my considerable debt to the late Professor François Châtelet whose firsthand knowledge as a participant in recent French intellectual history and whose incisive and enthusiastic discussion of ideas were of the utmost assistance. Also in Paris, Professor Judith Robinson-Valéry provided invaluable practical help and advice. During my most recent trip to Paris, and since my return to Australia, I have greatly benefited from discussions and correspondence with Professor Pierre Bourdieu. He has also generously made his most recent publications available to me. In addition, I would like to thank François Ewald, director of the Centre Michel Foucault, whose invitation to an international conference on Foucault in January 1988 afforded me the unique opportunity of participating in a very stimulating and remarkable intellectual gathering.

At the University of Queensland, Dr Rod Girle and the other members of the Department of Philosophy and also members of the French Department, were particularly helpful, as were my students in the Department of Philosophy whose enthusiasm and questions were greatly appreciated. A Research Fellowship at the University of Melbourne has made it possible to complete the book and I wish to thank Dr Margaret Rose, in particular, for all her discussion, help and encouragement during the final stages. Professor Rod Home of the Department of History and Philosophy of Science has also been generous with his support. At other institutions, I am grateful to Professor Jean-Claude Guédon of the University of Montreal for his most enlightening comments, and to Dr Paul Patton for a number of lively and informative conversations.

Research for this book was undertaken at a range of libraries: the Bibliothèque Nationale and the well-stocked municipal lending libraries of Paris were especially useful. In Australia, the libraries of the Universities of NSW, Queensland, Melbourne, Sydney and the Australian National University as well as the Australian National Library and the State Library of Victoria have all become familiar territory. Thanks are also due to the Department of Immigration and Ethnic Affairs in Canberra for their generous study-leave provisions whilst I was in their employment. And I am indebted to Dianne Manning and the other typists at 'The Typist' in Canberra and to Robyn Keely and Lorraine Beck at the Melbourne Word Processing Centre who typed the manuscript very efficiently through many revisions and to impossible deadlines. Angela Feery also kindly helped with proof-reading. Finally, I cannot thank my friends enough for all their unfailing support, especially Sally Hone, John Delaney and Michelle Walker, who by dint of various means of persuasion, encouragement and discussion saw me safely to the end of a long and difficult task. And of course, all of this would have been quite impossible without the essential and constant support of my family.

If this list of acknowledgements seems long and large, it nonetheless does no more than brief justice to the contribution of others to the life and labours of something of a 'wandering scholar'. Those medieval persons carried with them dedication and happiness, and the quest for true knowledge. I hope this work, pursued and compiled in many places, will be, however humbly, in that tradition.

CLARE O'FARRELL

Note: The publishers have tried to contact all holders of copyright material, but in cases where they may have failed will make the necessary arrangements at the first opportunity.

Abbreviations

A number of abbreviations have been used to refer to frequently cited works by Foucault. They are listed here in chronological order. Full references are included in the list of works cited at the end of the book.

MMP	*Maladie mentale et psychologie.*
FD	*Folie et Déraison: Histoire de la folie à l'âge classique* 10/18 1961, abbreviated edition.
HF (1972)	*Histoire de la folie à l'âge classique*, edition including two annexes.
HF	*Histoire de la folie à l'âge classique*, 1976, edition without annexes.
M&C	*Madness and Civilization.*
NC	*Naissance de la clinique.*
BC	*Birth of the Clinic.*
MC	*Les Mots et les choses.*
OT	*The Order of Things.*
AS	*L'Archéologie du savoir.*
AK	*The Archaeology of Knowledge.*
OD	*L'Ordre du discours.*
SP	*Surveiller et punir.*
VS	*La Volonté de savoir.*
UP	*L'Usage des plaisirs.*
SS	*Le Souci de soi.*
PK	*Power/Knowledge*, ed. Colin Gordon.

When references to these texts have been made (with the exception of *Power/Knowledge*) the abbreviation has been included in the main text in brackets. For example (AS:32) refers to *L'Archéologie du savoir*, p.32.

All translations are my own except where otherwise stated. Except in a few cases, I have generally consulted only the original French versions of Foucault's work.

1
A New Generation of Thinkers

In 1966, the year that Michel Foucault first became a star on the French philosophical scene, he remarked that he and the generation who were under 20 during the war: 'very suddenly and apparently without reason . . . noticed that we were very very far from the preceding generation; Sartre's and Merleau-Ponty's generation'.[1]

It is well known that structuralism and other related forms of thought popular during the 1960s and early 1970s were a reaction to the forms of 'nineteenth-century' thought that preceded them: 'that ill-fated nineteenth century, where you are banished in order to be discredited', as Jean-François Revel wrote caustically in 1971.[2] Much of Foucault's philosophical and historiographical reflection can in fact be seen as an effort to provide an alternative to this 'nineteenth-century' legacy. However, before examining Foucault's own works and period, it might be useful to cast a brief glance over the political, social and intellectual conjuncture from which he and others of his generation emerged and which they rebelled against. There have already been several excellent articles and books written about the social and political prehistory of structuralism in France, so it is not necessary to give more than a flavour of the period here. If there is a certain emphasis on the Marxist intellectual experience during the 1950s in the following discussion, it is because as François Furet remarks, structuralism developed in the same intellectual circles that had been Marxist after the war.[3]

At the end of the Second World War, the Right emerged totally discredited by the Vichy experience. Few intellectuals of note were tempted to think within its confines any longer. As Furet suggests, 'ideological elaboration became . . . a quasi-monopoly of the Left.'[4] On the other hand, the French Communist Party, the 'Party of the Resistance', emerged with flying colours, even if these colours had been delicately retouched: it was conveniently forgotten, for example, that the PCF had in fact been pro-German in 1939

1

and 1940.[5] However, this worried few people at the time and a
large number of intellectuals found the Communist Party the
answer to their desire to become politically engaged, in a society
which seemed to have lost its direction, and its sense of values.
Even Jean-Paul Sartre, the dominating intellectual figure of the
time, who had made his opposition to Marxism quite clear before
the war in his existentialist work *L'Etre et le Néant*, changed his
mind. He began to declare his wholehearted, but by no means
always appreciated, support for the Communist Party. This sudden need amongst the intellectuals for political 'engagement' after
the war can also be explained by a certain sense of guilt about
having been born into the bourgeoisie and not the working class.
Political activity seemed a suitable act of penance to make up for
this and Sartre, perhaps more than any other intellectual, was
tortured by this sense of guilt to the point of obsession. His case is
representative of the itinerary of many other intellectuals during
this period. Simone de Beauvoir in the third volume of her
Mémoires says that it was Sartre's experience in the Resistance and
as a prisoner of war that helped him understand the meaning of
history and action. As a result of this experience, he became
interested in the Communist Party towards the end of the war. She
explains that although it was true that until then he had always
considered the proletariat as the 'universal class', he had thought
it possible to reach the absolute through literary creation and had
thus considered his relations with fellow human beings (his
'being for others') or politics as secondary. She continues:

> With his historicity, he had discovered his dependence; no
> more eternity, no more absolute; the universality to which he
> aspired as an intellectual, could only be conferred by those men
> who were its incarnation on earth. He already thought what he
> was to express later: the real point of view is that of the most
> disinherited . . . It was through the eyes of the exploited that
> Sartre would learn what he was: if they rejected him, he would
> find himself imprisoned in his petit-bourgeois individuality.[6]

The Cold War was also another factor in contributing towards
the increase of the Communist Party's influence. Emmanuel Le
Roy Ladurie mentions that although immediately after the war,
Communists were not much in evidence at the famous Ecole
Normale Supérieure in the Rue d'Ulm, the new 'Post-Resistance'

Cold War generation of 1948 to 1949 were much more open to Stalinist doctrine.[7] During this period we find, for example, Foucault as a card-carrying member of the Communist Party, 'ghost-writing' in the Communist journal *La Nouvelle Critique* for authors such as the well-known Party prop Jean Kanapa. However, Foucault (never an excessively zealous Stalinist) left the Party in 1950, somewhat earlier than most, when a number of Jewish doctors were tried in Russia for alleged treason.

But, Marxism and Communism were by no means the sole refuges of postwar intellectuals, although this school of thought (or dogmatism) was by far the most significant. If Sartre attempted an uneasy marriage between Marxism and existentialism, there were also the important currents of Catholic existentialism and personalism as well as Camus' non-Marxist and atheist version of existentialism. There was also a number of dedicated Gaullists such as the writer François Mauriac (who was to transfer his allegiance to the Left during the Algerian war). In addition, one must not forget the school of phenomenologists inspired by the ontological theses of German philosophers such as Jaspers, Heidegger and Husserl.

Nonetheless, it was almost impossible to be an intellectual worthy of respect without a political commitment. Maurice Merleau-Ponty writing in 1961 comments: 'One thing is certain, that there was a political mania amongst philosophers which produced neither good politics, nor good philosophy.' It was from politics that the solutions were supposed to come. 'Every political anger became a holy anger, and reading the newspaper every morning . . . the philosophical morning prayer.'[8] Althusser makes some similar observations about the 'philosophers without works that we were . . . turning every work into politics, and slicing the world, arts, literature, philosophy and sciences, with a single blade – the pitiless division of classes.'[9] This reverence for the political could extend to the most banal and everyday level. Le Roy Ladurie recounts that a militant organising a meeting with some young people dealt with a complaint about the lack of chairs by replying: 'Comrades, if you want these chairs politically, I am certain that you will succeed in finding them.'[10] One of the early opponents of this dogmatism, Claude Lefort, although still a Marxist, describes the 'ideological terror' which the Communist Party exercised over the Left and the massive adhesion of pro-gressivist writers to Stalinism.[11] Le Roy Ladurie also mentions that 'intellectual terrorism' was not only exercised against anyone who dared criticise Stalinism, but also within the Party itself.[12]

Fortunately, in 1956, this state of affairs began to change, and indeed the years 1956–60 were to mark the end of one way of thinking and the beginning of another. With the close links of philosophy, the humanities and even scientific thought with politics, it was in fact a number of political events which precipitated this transformation of ideas, producing a move away from politics and existentialist and humanist philosophies.

In January 1956, a Centre-left government was voted into power. In March, this government decided to step up 'pacification' measures in the colony of Algeria which had been becoming more and more restless since 1954 under French administration. These measures meant not only increasing the length of military service, but sending 400 000 French soldiers into Algeria at the end of April. Amongst the 455 deputies who voted in favour of this policy were the Communists, and the fact that the Communist Party could pronounce in favour of the suppression of a colony caused enormous moral problems for some Communist intellectuals. Sartre, in an indignant article, attacked Guy Mollet's government, accusing it of betraying its allies, its electors and in general all French people.[13]

In June, *Le Monde* published the translation of the Khrushchev report which had been delivered in February. This report, which condemned Stalin's regime, produced two distinct reactions; disbelief and shattering disillusion. *L'Humanité*, the official organ of the French Communist Party, referred to the report as 'attributed' to Khrushchev, and quite a number of Communists simply did not believe the reports of atrocities, although for many others it came as a brutal disillusion. However, this was by no means the first news that had filtered through of the excesses of Stalin's regime. Arthur Koestler had already written on the subject, as had Claude Lefort, Cornelius Castoriadis and other Trotskyists in their journal *Socialisme ou barbarie*. But, on the whole, French Communists simply remained deaf to anything remotely resembling a criticism of Stalin's regime.[14] Le Roy Ladurie reports, for example, that Jacques Le Goff, then a pupil at the ENS in the Rue d'Ulm, after a visit to Prague in 1948 and 1949 returned with stories of police repression in the universities, but 'the Communist students . . . received his word, and remained deaf to his arguments. "They have ears and they do not hear".'[15] Even if the reports of concentration camps and purges were believed, they were explained away as being necessary for the progress of socialism: reactionary or ignorant elements had to be re-educated for their own good. In any case, all in all, the USSR was definitely in the forefront of the struggle against exploitation. In 1977, Cornelius Castoriadis reports Sartre's rather surprising persistence in his 'error', saying that Sartre 'wrote recently that *Socialisme ou barbarie* was right at the time but wrong to say so (thus, Sartre was right to be wrong). The walls haven't collapsed, and paper will bear anything.'[16]

If the Khrushchev report was not sufficient to disillusion a number of Communists, the suppression of the Hungarian Revolution in November 1956 produced a further exodus from the Party in France, especially as the leadership of the PCF insisted that this revolution was nothing more than a fascist uprising and not the legitimate struggle of workers against Russian tyranny, as many Communists in France had believed it to be. Probably many felt as did Le Roy Ladurie on hearing the news of the entry of Soviet tanks into Budapest: 'I had read and believed the newspapers of the Party with too much faith when they said "white" to swallow their new lie whole, when without warning, they suddenly decided to say "black".'[17]

Out of the fiasco came a new anti-dogmatic, ex-PCF, but still Marxist journal, *Arguments*, founded by François Châtelet, Henri Lefebvre, Kostas Axelos, and Pierre Fougeyrolles. Although the dream of the USSR as the embodiment of socialism was destroyed, it still did not occur to the intellectuals involved in the journals *Socialisme ou barbarie* and *Arguments*, so critical of the way Marxism was put into practice, to criticise the *theory* of Marxism; to ask, for example, was Stalinist tyranny made possible by something in Marxism itself? The socialist dream was gradually transferred to the Third World: Cuba (where Fidel Castro arrived to organise the guerilla network in December 1956), China and Africa.[18]

In 1958, the process of destalinisation was given an additional push, as De Gaulle's accession to power contributed further to depoliticising intellectuals. The Communist cell of philosophy students at the Sorbonne was also dissolved as the chiefs of the PCF considered it far too critical of the Party line. As a result, there was a general exodus from politics towards research. Many young intellectuals turned away from literature and the humanities, which had been until then the preferred mediums of philosophical and social reflection with the ascendancy of Sartre and Camus.

More 'exotic' or 'scientific' subjects, apparently free from ideological overtones, such as epistemology, ethnology, psychoanalysis,
linguistics and the human sciences in general, began to find
favour. 'The end of dogmatism produced a real liberty of research',
remarks Althusser.[19] Disenchanted and bored with the endless
and increasingly sterile humanist and political litany, intellectuals
at the end of the 1950s became interested in 'things' and 'systems'
rather than 'Man' and the problems of the 'subject'. They also
abandoned the grand continuities and progress of History for
'anti-historical' studies such as ethnology. François Furet, writing
in 1967, suggests that this historical disillusionment may have
been partially occasioned by the intellectuals' feeling that France
had lost its historical mission: 'This France, expelled from history,
found it all the more acceptable to expel history', he says. However
it was probably more a case of *reculer pour mieux sauter.*[20]

Another factor contributing to this transfer of interest was the
tremendous advances being made in the human sciences and in
technology. In October 1957, the first Sputnik was sent into space
and television began to appear in some households. The first
primitive computers had appeared and there seemed to be little
that science could not promise, or could not explain. The economy
was expanding, as was bureaucracy, and the consumer age was
just coming into its own. The era of 'the end of ideologies', of
'structuralism' was ushered in. The new generation of thinkers
vigorously defended their ideas against the combined forces of
existentialism, Marxism and humanism and in an interview which
one critic described as ringing 'like the manifesto of a new school',
one of the most famous of these new thinkers, Michel Foucault,
met the challenge head-on.[21] Humanism, he announced, 'pretends
to resolve problems it cannot pose!', problems such as happiness,
artistic creation, reality and the relation of man to his world, and
'all those obsessions which are absolutely unworthy of being
theoretical problems'. 'Our *system*' he proclaimed enthusiastically,
would have nothing to do with these unworthy obsessions: 'it is
the "human heart" which is abstract, and it is our research which
wants to link man to his science, to his discoveries, to his world,
which is concrete.'[22]

Michel Foucault began his career in the mid-1950s and his first
book, *Maladie mentale et personnalité*, was published in 1954 and
appeared in a revised and retitled edition in 1959 as *Maladie*

mentale et psychologie. But it was his second book, *Folie et déraison: Histoire de la folie à l'âge classique,* that distinguished him, quietly at first, as one of a new generation of thinkers. This book (and *Maladie mentale et psychologie,* which is similar in content) constitutes a philosophical and historical treatment of madness and the problem of the 'Other' in Western civilisation. There are two versions of *Histoire de la folie,* the original of almost 600 finely printed pages, and an extensively abridged pocket version of 300 pages. Unfortunately the translation available in English is that of the shorter version with a few additions from the unabridged work. In the second edition of 1972, the original preface is also suppressed and replaced by another shorter and less illuminating preface, consisting mainly of rather abstruse remarks on commentary (indirect references to the reception of the first edition) and ending on a rather flippant note about the shortness of the new preface. Later, in 1981, Foucault declared himself willing to reinstate the first preface, saying that he had in fact returned to some of his earliest preoccupations.

Although *Histoire de la folie* is now to be found in the bibliographies of most works on the subject of the history of madness or psychology, when it was first published it did not attract much widespread attention. In later years Foucault complained about and even exaggerated this lack of interest.[23] Nonetheless, Georges Canguilhem, the noted historian of science, helped in its presentation for a *doctorat d'état* and Philippe Ariès, whose own brand of history was considered marginal at the time, managed against considerable opposition to get Foucault's text published in the collection which he was directing at Plon.[24] Michel Serres, Roland Barthes and the novelist Maurice Blanchot gave it enthusiastic reviews and Fernand Braudel praised it in *Annales: économies, societés, civilisations.*[25] Across the Channel, a sympathetic review by Richard Howard, the future translator of the book, appeared in *The Times Literary Supplement.*[26] But it was not until after the enormous success of *Les Mots et les choses* in 1966 that it began to sell well. Indeed, such was the subsequent increase in sales after five years of initial obscurity that the editor of Payot editions, Jean-Luc Pidoux, uses the example of the career of this book to condemn current trends in France which obstruct the publication of young unknown authors.[27]

It was not only the success of *Les Mots et les choses* that contributed to the interest in Foucault's earlier work, but the growth of the anti-psychiatric movement, which particularly in the Anglo-Saxon world, fastened on to (and distorted) some of Foucault's theses to provide support for its cause. The English translation, *Madness and Civilization*, was published in Britain in a collection edited by the noted anti-psychiatrist R. D. Laing, with a controversial and somewhat inaccurate preface by David Cooper that annexed Foucault's book to the anti-psychiatry movement. In actual fact, Foucault's critique of the science of psychiatry was undertaken from an angle that diverged widely from that of the anti-psychiatrists, even if he did identify himself with their activities during his 'political' phase in the 1970s. Later, in 1984, Foucault also remarked that he had shared 'no community' with Laing, Cooper and Basaglia when he wrote *Histoire de la folie*, even if all their work was to later form the basis of a 'community of action'.[28] In France his work also attracted a tremendous amount of attention from the psychiatrists. In 1969, much to Foucault's dismay, a group of eminent psychiatrists met to discuss and criticise his work.[29] Another psychiatrist seems to have taken Foucault's remarks on the nineteenth-century reformer Pinel as a personal insult and after a disagreement with Foucault on the radio on the occasion of Pinel's centenary, launched a series of attacks on Foucault as the 'incompetent' 'father of . . . anti-psychiatry in France.'[30]

But there was yet another reason for the sudden increase in popularity of *Histoire de la folie*, and that was the growth of a tremendous and widespread interest in all kinds of social 'margins' after 1968. The subject of Foucault's book, its historical analysis of the origins of the division between the normal and the pathological, made it of eminent topicality. So much so, that Foucault was to complain in 1977 that he was embarrassed and even distressed by the fact that after all those years of difficult and lonely work carried out by himself and a few others, interest in notions concerning madness, delinquency, children and sex was nothing more for some people than 'a sign of belonging', being on the 'good side', the side of madness and so on – a cheap way of buying a social conscience.[31] Quite apart from all this, *Histoire de la folie* is a quite fascinating blend of history, philosophy, social comment and indignation at the plight of madmen, written in a beautiful, often difficult and idiosyncratic poetic style. It reads like a subtle and gripping Gothic drama, mazed with intricate subplots and arcane details. Small wonder its readers have been alternatively fascinated, bewildered, frustrated and even enraged by it.

Foucault's next book, *Naissance de la clinique*, published in 1963, was a historical and epistemological study of the foundations of French clinical medicine at the end of the eighteenth century and the beginning of the nineteenth century. In 1972, at about the same time that Foucault deleted the first preface of *Histoire de la folie*, he revised *Naissance de la clinique*, a revision which consisted of the elimination of some of its 'structuralist' terminology. The word 'discourse' was substituted for 'language' in some places, and phrases such as the 'structured analysis of the signified' were rewritten as 'the analysis of a type of discourse'.[32] In spite of this, 'language' and 'structure' remain frequently-used words in the text, leading many critics to describe it as Foucault's most 'structuralist' book. Although the history of medicine has not acquired the public appeal that questions relating to madness have acquired in the past twenty years, *Naissance de la clinique* has become something of a classic in its own right. In a collection on the history of medicine published in 1982, for example, most articles include references to Foucault.[33]

In 1963, Foucault also published a rather obscure book on the even more obscure French surrealist writer Raymond Roussel. An anonymous reviewer in *The Times Literary Supplement* remarked that the book 'seems addressed to an audience of *cognoscenti*, which must be exceedingly small in France and can hardly number more than two or three here.'[34] However, the book did not go unnoticed by the new novelists in France, and Alain Robbe-Grillet saw Foucault's 'fascinating essay' as one of the signs of a growing interest in Roussel, but it remained an interest that was not widely spread beyond certain circles.[35] In the period between 1960 to 1965, Foucault also published a number of articles of literary criticism, essays on language and prefaces to an assortment of books, and translated texts from German. Much of this work, like *Raymond Roussel*, is poetic and obscure and not always easy to understand on a first reading.

In 1966, Foucault published the book that was to become an instant bestseller: *Les Mots et les choses*. This was a 'history' of the origins of the human sciences: economics, linguistics and biology, and became notorious for its declarations concerning the death of Man and the end of humanism. With this book, Foucault was dubbed one of the 'gang of four' of the new 'structuralist' movement and a famous cartoon drawn by Maurice Henry depicted Foucault, Lacan, Lévi-Strauss and Barthes sitting in a jungle dressed in grass skirts. A tremendous amount has been written about structuralism, both for and against, and the issue of whether Foucault is or was a structuralist, and what relationship his work bears to this disparate movement is still being discussed. Unfortunately for the English-language critics, the preface to the English translation of *Les Mots et les choses* put them in somewhat of a quandary, since in this preface Foucault insisted on depriving them of this useful label to fit his work.[36] As a result, there was a division into two schools of opinion: one which argued that Foucault's views on the matter were irrelevant, and that some, if not all, of his work was manifestly structuralist, and one which accepted Foucault's rejection of the label with an almost religious faith. 'With customary perversity', argues one critic, 'Foucault insists that he is not a structuralist, but the label persists, justifiably, in sticking.'[37] Later English-speaking critics eagerly defended Foucault from any charge of structuralism, and for many of them, as Colin Gordon points out about two particular writers, 'the very activity of "structuralist" thinking constitute[d] a moral error.'[38] On the other hand, French commentators in the late 1960s and early 1970s, before structuralism went out of fashion in Paris, were more concerned with describing first and foremost their own views on what structuralism was, than with seeing how far Foucault's work could be accommodated under this label.

In the final analysis, perhaps, 'structuralism' is simply a convenient label which describes a diverse series of researches often performed quite independently, but having a certain number of traits in common. For the sake of simplicity, let us characterise the so-called 'structuralists' as representing the antithesis of the postwar philosophies. First of all, they espoused a rigorous anti-humanism and anti-'subjectivism'. In ethnology, Claude Lévi-Strauss, often seen as the 'father' of the structuralist movement, argued that 'in a certain way myths think amongst themselves' without being consciously formlulated by individual subjects.[39] The psychoanalyst Jacques Lacan decentred the subject in the unconscious ('ça parle'). Louis Althusser renovated Marxist epistemology, declaring that history was 'a process without a subject . . . a process which has no real subject or goal(s)' and that Marx was definitely an antihumanist.[40] Roland Barthes declared the death of the author in literary criticism: 'it is language that speaks not the author'.[41] At the same time the new novelists such as Nathalie Sarraute, Philippe Sollers and Alain Robbe-Grillet dissolved the subject and the narrative form in literature. It was also a style of thought which emphasised every form of 'break' and discontinuity. Structural linguistics provided the methodological model, and epistemology, the history of sciences and the human sciences were the preferred areas of enquiry; and of course the words 'structure' and 'system' appeared everywhere with monotonous regularity. It was a mode of thought which, to use the linguistic terminology of the time, favoured synchrony over diachrony. Anti-historicism was the order of the day, which many mistakenly saw as an attempt to 'kill history'.

This was the intellectual climate in which Foucault's book appeared. As the synthesis of many of these themes and with its provocative and stylish statements on humanism, Marx, the human sciences and epistemes, it created a tremendous stir. In the first week after its publication 3000 copies were sold and more than 50 000 were sold in the months that followed. A copy of *Les Mots et les choses* on the coffee table, as Michel de Certeau commented in 1967, had a certain snob value, even if, like Jean-Luc Godard – who poured scorn on the fashion for this book in his film *La Chinoise* – the owner had only read the first chapter.[42] The amount of discussion around this book was tremendous as can be seen by glancing at Michael Clark's annotated bibliography of Foucault.[43] It was both extravagantly praised and extravagantly damned. Jean-Paul Sartre in particular, attacked Foucault's views on history, saying that he had replaced 'cinema by the magic lantern, movement by a succession of immobilities', adding that this attack on history was, 'of course', an attack on Marxism.[44] In fact, what Foucault was really trying to do, according to Sartre, was to constitute 'a new ideology, the last rampart that the bourgeoisie can still erect against Marx.' Of course, Sartre's pronouncements caused considerable comment, since Foucault was generally seen to be the most likely candidate to succeed him as *the* star philosopher in France. The irony was, as Foucault himself pointed out, that it was not so long ago that Sartre had himself been defined by the Communists as the 'last rampart of bourgeois imperialism'.[45] This did not prevent a host of critics (especially Marxist critics) from rushing forward to repeat Sartre's remarks in order to give the weight of authority to their own arguments. Finally, in a masterful summing up of Foucault's crimes one critic indignantly remarked that not only did Foucault 'totally reject Marxism' but also 'proclaim[ed] the death of man and the end of history'.[46]

In fact, three distinct groups of French writing on Foucault began to emerge in the late 1960s after the success of *Les Mots et les choses*. The first group consisted of the writings of 'star' intellectuals such as Sartre, Raymond Aron, and Roland Barthes, or other leading intellectuals such as Michel Serres, Georges Canguilhem, or François Châtelet and leading journalists. The second group of writings consisted of violently polemical reactions to Foucault's work: this group included the writings of many Marxists, an important voice in French intellectual life, the existentialists (both atheist and Christian), and establishment psychiatrists. The third group was made up of the writings of those 'secondary' intellectuals, including journalists, who enthusiastically seize upon and follow whatever the latest Parisian fashion happens to be. This last group included what could only be described as intellectual 'gossip columnists' who keep the reader up to date with all the latest fads and scandals amongst the Parisian intelligentsia.

In all three groups, writers used Foucault as a starting point for their own discussion and reflections, in such a way that it is difficult to know where Foucault ends and the commentary begins. This practice of using other writers' work as a forum for one's own opinions is a common one in French writing, as opposed to the usual Anglo-Saxon practice of a 'neutral' exposition followed by the author's comments. There are numerous and complex reasons for this state of affairs. Some of them relate to the smallness of the Parisian intellectual 'village' and the role of the media in diffusing their works. The Parisian intellectual is expected to have read the most recent works of his colleagues in his own field as well as in other fields. And since everybody knows everybody else in the Parisian intellectual milieu, this is good public relations if nothing else. The newspapers, journals, radio and television provide a forum for discussion of these works as well as diffusing information about the latest publications and fashions (which they also help to create). The tendency is to carve out one's own domain in reference to all this. Hence the wealth of what appears to the English-speaking reader to be obscure allusions and excessive polemicising in French intellectual work. Not only does the writer assume his readers are aware of what he is talking about, but he may not wish to offend an opponent he will be seeing on the Parisian circuit by naming him too directly. In addition, he wants to make sure that his own individual position is quite clearly distinguished (even if only infinitesimally) from the rest of the field.[47] This system has its drawbacks, mainly the creation of intellectual 'tyrannies'. 'One does not reflect on an interpretation, one rallies to an argument' remarks Jean-François Revel.[48] The sociologist Pierre Bourdieu also comments at length on the 'terrorism' of fashion in Paris which reduces people who do not conform in the eyes of their judges to the right way of being and doing things, 'to ridicule, indignity, shame and silence'.[49] The dogmatic hold of Stalinism in the 1950s is perhaps an extreme example of this kind of intellectual tyranny.[50] Similarly, older systems are condemned to oblivion by the philosophy of the moment: 'structuralism wrenches the limelight away from existentialism, Lévi-Strauss banishes Sartre to the museum; because the bad habit has caught on, one does not discuss, one occupies the whole stage. "To think is to terrorise".'[51] Or, as Revel remarks,

> To entirely renew the basic themes of thought, to be the author of an intellectual revolution . . . these are fundamental philosophical necessities, at least in the presentation. No philosopher could present himself as a candidate for historical existence simply as a continuer.[52]

Another consequence of the close involvement of the media with the intelligentsia, as well as of the celebrity status of intellectuals (much envied by their Anglo-Saxon counterparts) is the frequency with which intellectuals are interviewed in the written, spoken and visual media. In particular, the written interview is a form far more commonly found in France than in English-speaking countries. These interviews serve a useful purpose in encouraging intellectuals such as Foucault, whose works are often quite difficult, to clarify their ideas and make them more accessible to readers of widely circulated journals such as *Le Nouvel Observateur* and *La Quinzaine Littéraire*.[53] These interviews also provide a forum for public discussion between the author and his readers. In the months that followed the publication of *Les Mots et les choses*, Foucault was interviewed in several magazines and journals. As in subsequent interviews, he explained quite clearly what could only be read between the lines in his books.

Foucault also used interviews to state his current position: 'my problem is . . .', 'the task of philosophy today . . .' are two phrases that constantly recur in these interviews.[54]

In 1969, in response to numerous enquiries about his method, Foucault published *L'Archéologie du savoir*.[55] This book set out a historiographical methodology which claimed to do away with some of the disadvantages of the traditional discipline of the history of ideas. It did not entirely explain what had been done in previous books, although it had much to say on what Foucault was *not* doing and what he thought he *ought* to have done. So much so, in fact, that Jean-François Revel suggested that *L'Archéologie* could be described as the negative of Kierkegaard's book *Either . . . or* and would have been more suitably titled *Neither . . . nor*.[56] Other critics found it excessively arid or difficult to read. However, for those who appreciate intricate formal geometric structures in thought and method, it is a compelling book. It offers many useful methodological hints to the historian who wants to avoid historicism, and has in fact been extensively used to this end. Nonetheless the rarefied abstraction of this work did not lend itself to a place on the bestseller lists.

Foucault's next book was *L'Ordre du discours*, the text of his inauguration speech delivered at the Collège de France in 1970. It introduced the concepts of 'truth' and 'power' which he was to develop and discuss at length in his work until 1982. At the same time his analysis of these notions during this period created an exponential growth industry in the secondary literature, particularly in America. The beginnings of this industry can be seen in the early 1970s, when a small but growing number of English-speaking critics and intellectuals began to become aware of Foucault's work. *Les Mots et les choses* was published in translation in 1970 and *L'Archéologie du savoir* and *Naissance de la clinique* in 1972 and 1973 at about the same time that some of the more radical francophiles began to abandon 'existentialism' for 'structuralism'. English-language writing on Foucault at this time (and in the 1960s) was fairly evenly divided between a popular journalism, aimed at explaining a 'French phenomenon', and serious essays in specialised reviews. These critics could be divided into camps for and against. Those against were usually advocating sound Anglo-Saxon empiricism against airy French nonsense, whereas those in favour often as not completely misunderstood the content and context of Foucault's ideas and praised them for quite the wrong reasons, although there were, of course, exceptions to this general rule. But for most, whether for or against, Foucault's works taken out of context and judged by the standards of a different intellectual tradition were mysterious and bizarre objects indeed.

During the early 1970s, Foucault went into a temporary alliance with the Maoists, adopting a rather extreme form of 'revolutionary' rhetoric in some interviews and articles. At the same time he actively participated in committees with other intellectuals against racism (*le Comité Djellali*), and for the rights of patients and new forms of institutional relations in the area of health (*le Groupe Information Santé*). The best known of the committees in which Foucault participated as a founding member was the famous *Groupe d'Information sur les prisons*, whose aim was to provide a forum for prisoners to speak and act at a time of great unrest in the prisons. According to some, Foucault and the GIP played a major role in engineering the prison riots at Toul in 1972.[57]

Also in 1972, a discussion between Foucault and Deleuze on intellectuals and power, which has since attracted much comment, was published. Foucault also produced two small books on the artists Magritte (1973) and Fromanger (1975). The former is a most amusing text, although it is difficult to judge whether this is intentional or not. In 1973, Foucault, in collaboration with Blandine Barret-Kriegel and others, published the confessions of a nineteenth-century parricide, Pierre Rivière, a text which attracted the attention of many historians and sociologists. A film was made of this book in which Foucault played a small part as a judge.[58] At the same time, Foucault continued to deliver his courses at the Collège de France from January to March every year. Attendance at these lectures which dealt with power and prisons, was *de rigueur* amongst a certain 'intellectual-mondain' set, and they became quite an event. A journalist offers a colourful, but fairly accurate description of the atmosphere at these courses:

As for a Gala performance, there was a crush outside the doors some two hours in advance. Inside, emissaries reserved places and it was a fight to the death to find a perch on the edge of a quarter of a folding seat. Women from the most exclusive neighbourhoods of Paris came decked out in their best designer clothes. And on stage, right in the middle of an interminable waxed desk, his uneven skull shining under the subdued lighting, surrounded by a thousand microphones, antennae attached to as many tape recorders, and with a flock of ecstatic young men wrapped around his feet, Foucault spoke.[59]

In 1975, Foucault published *Surveiller et punir*, a history of the prison and punishment and the growth of the 'disciplinary society' covering the period from the mid-eighteenth century to the mid-nineteenth century. In this book, the notions of 'power' and 'discipline' came to occupy a central position in Foucault's thought. It was a book that immediately created great interest amongst criminologists, an interest that quickly spread to sociologists and historians. *La Volonté de savoir*, the first volume in a *Histoire de la sexualité*, appeared the following year in 1976. In this methodological introduction to a proposed six-volume study, Foucault argued that far from repressing sexuality, Western culture has done nothing but produce endless discourses on sexuality since the nineteenth century. The critical reception of this book was less enthusiastic than for *Surveiller et punir*, as not only was it slight in volume and in empirical content, but lacked on the whole those brilliant and unusual insights that distinguished his earlier books.

In 1977, France and the world suddenly became aware of the 'new philosophers'. *Time* magazine gave them front-page coverage with the slogan 'Marx is dead', and in Russia the literary journal *Litteraturnaia Gazieta* condemned this 'lost generation of 1968'. Michel Foucault, Roland Barthes and Jacques Lacan were the '*maîtres à penser*' or the 'gurus' of this new movement. Maurice Clavel, dubbed the 'uncle of the new philosophers', in prophetic tones heralded Foucault as the 'new Kant', and based his somewhat apocalyptic Christian philosophy on Foucault's formulation on the 'death of man'.[60] Clavel's books (especially *Ce que je crois*) were immensely popular and introduced Foucault to an audience who might not otherwise have become familiar with his ideas. In these books Clavel displayed a seemingly endless capacity for repetition and self-quotation as well as 'prophetic' exaggeration. When he died in 1979, Foucault, a friend with whom he had engaged in many militant activities since the 1960s, wrote an obituary in *Le Nouvel Observateur*.[61] The younger 'new philosophers', the ex-Maoists André Glucksmann and Bernard-Henri Lévy, adapted Foucault's theories on power to fit their pessimistic conceptions of a modern all-powerful repressive Gulag-State.[62] Although initially Foucault supported the efforts of André

Glucksmann, he did not pursue this line as it became increasingly apparent that the intellectual quality and the political implications of the works of the so-called 'new philosophers' left much to be desired.[63] Their work stirred up a tremendous amount of controversy and was almost universally condemned by the intellectual establishment, who claimed that it did not even satisfy the minimum standards of intellectual scholarship and led to a right-wing if not 'fascist' politics.

At about the same time, the Anglo-Saxon intellectual world began to take more notice of the work of Foucault. Up until 1977, Foucault had remained the property of a fairly exclusive coterie, but with the translation of *Surveiller et punir* in 1977 and *La Volonté de savoir* in 1978, the steady trickle of writings turned into a flood. These books appeared at a time when a number of problems had become apparent in American prisons and when an interest in margins and relations of power within bureaucratic societies obsessed many people. Two more groups of writings on Foucault came into evidence in English-speaking criticism. The first was ardently francophile: either structuralist – or when this ceased to be respectable – interested in power or a 'non-totalising' approach to theory. For this school, Foucault could do no wrong, and every word that flowed from his pen was treated as though from an oracle. Early on in 1968, a French critic had already foreseen the danger that would be posed by ' "foucauldians" if ever there are any' and a little later in 1974, George Huppert noted the risk of some of Foucault's theses 'more or less vaguely understood . . . becoming articles of faith among intellectuals'.[64] Indeed, in their enthusiasm, the new school of 'foucauldians' erected what they saw as Foucault's lack of theory into a full-blown theory. Writers in this group vied with each other to be more imposingly obscure than the next, and direct transliterations from the French and enormous sentences following French stylistic practice, were a feature of their style. In addition, nothing was ever explained, and only those 'in the know' and with a good knowledge of French language and culture could hope to decipher these daunting texts. The second new group of writings, although these were already beginning to come into evidence in the 1960s, particularly in relation to the anti-psychiatric movement, were scholarly articles of academic research which had either used Foucault's methodology, one or two of his ideas and concepts, or alternatively used his work as a historical source. Of course, the earlier camps

continued their activity, but their self-confidence was seriously
undermined and some critics previously outraged by Foucault
became quite favourably disposed towards his writing. The
amount of clear, useful and accurate writing on Foucault began to
increase as well. Translated collections of Foucault's shorter
writings began to appear in the late 1970s to cater for this growing
audience.

Greatly affected by the poor reception of *La Volonté de savoir*,
Foucault took a year of sabbatical leave from the Collège de France
to travel to America. He then lapsed into a prolonged 'silence',
although interviews, articles, comments on political events and
edited collections of obscure documents continued to appear. The
quality of this work is variable. It includes endless divagations on
the themes of truth and power and much highly rhetorical writing
on intellectual and political events, many of which have long since
faded from public memory. As a new book still did not appear,
references to Foucault's 'silence' and apparent unwillingness to
commit himself to new ideas began to appear in the literature.
Pariscope remarked dryly in 1983: 'Each year now for the past
seven years, it has been announced that he is going to break his
historic silence. Does he have anything to say?'[65]

But in 1981 and 1982 a noticeable change began to take place in
Foucault's thought. His course at the Collège de France in early
1982 was titled *L'Herméneutique du sujet* and abandoned his
favourite Classical Age for the Ancient Greek and the early
Christian period. The word 'power' all but disappeared and it
became a question of Socrates' 'concern for self' and 'philosophies
of spirituality', then 'subjectivity'. At last in June 1984, just before
the final silence of death overtook Michel Foucault, two new
volumes of his *Histoire de la sexualité* appeared: Volume 2, *L'Usage
des plaisirs* and Volume 3, *Le Souci de soi*. In the introduction to
L'Usage des plaisirs, Foucault explains both his long silence and
why he had abandoned the original project outlined in *La Volonté
de savoir*, saying he had been forced to change his whole way of
thinking. These two new volumes, which constitute a radical
change in the style, content and form of Foucault's thought,
examine the history of sexuality in Antiquity and during the early
Christian period. Foucault, after reassessing his past work, asks
why sexual behaviour has become the object of moral preoccupation in history, and at the same time examines various historical
techniques of self-constitution.

It is a testimony to the remarkable extent of Foucault's influence that his death was reported in newspapers around the world. In France itself, the Prime Minister and the Minister for Culture expressed their regret at his passing. His death was front-page news in *Le Monde* and *Le Figaro*, which also devoted several short articles to him by well-known intellectuals. The now prestigious left-wing newspaper, *Liberation*, which counted Foucault as one of its founding members in 1972, devoted ten pages to him. Since his death, his influence has not ceased to grow, as was more than amply demonstrated by a three-day international conference on his work held in Paris in 1988. On this occasion, a star-studded collection of intellectuals from all over the globe and from a wide range of disciplines packed into a theatre on the Champs-Elysées, to discuss his work in an atmosphere of suitably dramatic controversy. The liveliness and the variety of discussion were quite sufficient to indicate that Foucault's work will continue to make an impact for some time to come.

2
The Same, the Other and the Limit

1. HISTORIAN OR PHILOSOPHER?

Even a brief survey of the literature produced on Foucault's work reveals an overwhelming interest in the question of how his work is to be classified. What 'discipline' can it be annexed to? What use can be made of it? What sections of the library can we find his books in? Alan Sheridan spells out quite well the kind of puzzlement a great many readers feel when they open Foucault's books. He also spells out the reply of a certain kind of commentary:

> 'Is he some kind of philosopher?' 'Well, yes in a way', one answers. 'Then why does he write not about Plato, Descartes and Kant, but about the history of madness and medicine, prisons and sexuality?' 'Well, he is more of a historian than a philosopher, though his approach to his material is very different from that of a historian.' 'Ah, a historian of ideas!' 'Well, no . . . . In fact it was to distinguish what he was doing from the history of ideas that he coined the term 'archaeology of knowledge'.[1]

Although some critics, English-speaking ones in particular, may now scoff that this question is irrelevant or demonstrative of the worst excesses of Anglo-Saxon empiricist smallmindedness, they do not solve the problem by saying that Foucault's work is archaeology or genealogy because that is what he says it is. One is simply led to ask then what archaeology or genealogy is. And, as Pierre Bourdieu remarks in relation to art and literature, debates over genres and disciplinary classifications are more than mere struggles over words, they are struggles for 'symbolic domination, that is, for power over a particular use of a particular category of signs and, as a consequence, over a vision of the natural and social world'.[2] Thus the issue of how Foucault's work should be described is a very important one, for it addresses a wide range of questions, questions that not only relate to the very heart of what Foucault is actually doing in his books, but to the most general effects they have had, and to important general philosophical, historiographical and epistemological problems. It is an issue that also draws attention to important differences between the French and Anglo-Saxon intellectual mentalities. One may ask, for example, do Foucault's works provide interesting new insights for the historian in his continuing struggle to understand the past and present, or are they philosophical speculations on man's place in the cosmos and his destiny? Or again, are they anarchist tracts inviting us to overthrow a corrupt society?[3] Foucault's works are, in fact, all of these things (and others as well), and what puzzles some critics is how these elements can co-exist in a single work and indeed whether they should. Another source of irritation and surprise is the sheer diversity of the subject matter: medicine, literature, art, economics, linguistics, biology, to name only a few of the areas Foucault looks at. One might even ask, as has been asked many times by English-speaking readers, whether Foucault's works are not just the idiosyncratic product of a different intellectual tradition and as such are unclassifiable, indeed incomprehensible, outside it. One writer goes so far as to suggest that Foucault's following 'must consist largely of masochists and those who can admire while they do not understand, for Foucault though ultimately intelligible is flamboyantly difficult. He is the soul of panache and perversity.'[4] Claude Lévi-Strauss makes some interesting observations on the subject of this difference between two traditions in the Introduction to *Anthropologie structurale*:

Several of my articles had been written directly in English, so I had to translate them. Now, while I was working on them, I was struck by the difference in tone and composition between texts conceived in one or the other language . . . . This difference can probably be partially explained by sociological causes: you do not think or argue in the same way when you are addressing a French or an Anglo-Saxon audience.[5]

It is the English-speaking critics who have the most to say on Foucault's interdisciplinarity and the difficulty of fitting him into any one discipline. They complain that Foucault's work 'defies classification', is 'difficult to categorise', is outside 'the conventional grids of disciplinary classification', or that it is difficult to 'decide what *kind* of books' Foucault is writing.[6] On the other hand, French writers do not complain that Foucault is difficult to categorise. They may have a range of suggestions as to what he is doing. He might be questioned on why he chose particular disciplines, or even criticised for making mistakes in different specialised areas. But there are few complaints about the difficulty of classifying his work. Even in the debates that have raged over whether Foucault is a historian or a philosopher, the difficulties that have been discussed all relate to the epistemological, methodological and ontological questions raised by Foucault's work and not to whether he should make up his mind and join either a history or a philosophy department. This difference between the two different debates over classification is a difficult one to define, and raises complex problems. In addition, with the acceptance and dissemination of Foucault's work in recent years in the English-speaking world, the problems over classification have diminished dramatically, and have largely been reduced to the issue of whether Foucault is a historian or a philosopher: by far the most interesting and most discussed problem in the debate over classifications.

At the risk of massive generalisation, one could say that in general, the tendency on the Continent is towards a unified approach to knowledge, towards formulating a satisfactory abstract and all-explaining theory which encompasses science, history, and metaphysics, whereas the empirical Anglo-Saxons prefer 'facts', and in general more fragmentary, more patiently empirical, approaches to knowledge, each discipline and science being content with its own area. In French thought, disciplinary divisions tend to be subordinated to this overriding interest in general principles. As Jean-Marie Domenach remarks perceptively, 'In France, science and politics always turn into metaphysics. This is our privilege – and sometimes our ridicule.'[7] No form of knowledge is exempt from critical enquiry. Even debates on doing away with metaphysics eventually turn into metaphysics, something which most Anglo-Saxon commentators generally fail to take into account, as it is so foreign to their own practice. It has long been the prerogative of the French 'intellectual' or philosopher to address himself to a vast range of issues in the

sciences, humanities and socio-politico arenas, and to engage in a certain type of 'journalism'.[8]
The difference is also apparent in attitudes towards science. Modern Anglo-Saxon philosophy regards itself as secondary in relation to the sciences; it is the sciences that are considered to have privileged access to reality. Therefore it makes sense that all other disciplines should follow the methods of science. This style of thought tends to assume that the world and reality can ultimately be described by the painstaking collection and categorisation of 'neutral' and 'true' 'facts'. In the final analysis, perhaps, all this knowledge could be pieced together to form a true picture of reality, but unfortunately this is showing no signs of happening. Instead, a specialisation and fragmentation of knowledge as the only means of dealing with and organising an enormous and increasing number of 'facts', has become more and more apparent. The 'secondary' position of philosophy is demonstrated by a citation from Bertrand Russell which many Anglo-Saxon philosophers and commentators would still make their own:

> It is science that is beginning to make us understand ourselves
> . . . . It is science that has taught us the way to substitute
> tentative truth for cocksure error. The scientific spirit, the
> scientific method, the framework of the scientific world, must
> be absorbed by anyone who wishes to have a philosophic
> outlook belonging to our time, not a literary antiquarian phil-
> osophy fetched out of old books . . . . An hour with Galileo or
> Newton will give you more help towards a sound philosophy
> than a year with Aristotle.[9]

This 'scientism' extends to literary style as well. Any efforts to write in an interesting or 'poetic' style are immediately condemned as 'unscientific' or 'unphilosophical'. For example, G. S. Rousseau writing about *Les Mots et les choses* says:

> those who respond to poetic talent diffused over a vast panor-
> amic verbal spate will regard this book as gospel truth heralding
> a 'breakthrough'; they will consider him the new seer in a long
> line of high priests extending from Blake and Nietzsche to
> Camus and Sartre. But the others who appeal for less verbiage
> and greater proof, who prefer to look for truth to Harvey and

Newton, Russell and Wittgenstein, Namier and Godel, Quine and the logicians, will be sorely disappointed at this necromantic performance.[10]

Continental philosophy, however, is not prepared to accept this secondary position and sees itself as being just as concerned with reality as the sciences; indeed would go so far as to say that it is dealing with an even more fundamental reality.[11] The Continental mode of thought remains sceptical about the 'scientific' neutrality of the observer, and of whether it is ever possible to perceive a 'neutral fact' independently of history, culture or subjectivity. As a result, all knowledge, all disciplines and action are based on this uncertainty, with correspondingly less emphasis on the rigidity of disciplinary distinctions.[12] French philosophers, therefore, see no reason why they should look to the sciences (natural, human or mathematical) to provide an ultimate verification for their findings (although these sciences might well provide a useful framework of analysis).

A magnificent example of the confrontation of these two styles of philosophy is to be found in an article by Jacques Bouveresse, 'Pourquoi pas des philosophes?' Bouveresse is a French university philosopher working in the Anglo-Saxon philosophical tradition. He quotes Wittgenstein, Russell, Popper and Quine, lamenting the overriding interest of contemporary French philosophers in history and politics, their visibility in the media and their literary style. He also condemns their lack of interest in the latest scientific developments and in such elite and unpopular areas as modal logic, intuitionism, linguistics, thermodynamics, information theory and artificial intelligence. In voicing these criticisms, he is also voicing the criticisms of many of his Anglo-Saxon colleagues when faced with French philosophy. Nonetheless, Bouveresse does not entirely succeed in avoiding a very French style of polemics, but then, as he complains wearily (and ironically) at the end of his article, he was only writing 'out of a sense of duty, and not in the hope that this will really be of any use'.[13]

Bouveresse also draws attention to and exemplifies a longstanding rift in French intellectual life between the 'positivistic university' intellectuals and 'avant-garde' intellectuals. The university intellectuals accuse *avant-garde* intellectuals such as Foucault, Barthes and others of catering too much to public fashion and airing their wares in public in the media, a sure sign their work cannot be of serious intellectual quality. On the other hand, the avant-garde intellectuals accuse university intellectuals of being excessively dry and positivistic and generally impervious to new ideas.[14] Bouveresse, who boldly declares that he is a 'university intellectual' and 'sees no reason to be either ashamed or proud of it', is highly critical of the relationship between philosophy and the media, an issue which, as he quite correctly points out, has been a 'recurring problem for a long time' in France.[15] Indeed, leaving aside the period before 1960, it is a problem which seems to recur every ten years or so in French thought. Each time the same observations surface, namely that the noble purity and rigour of philosophy can only be compromised by its flirtation with the media, and that the appearance of philosophy in the media is a marvellous and new phenomenon indeed. In the late 1960s, with the era of structuralism and the 'events of May', there was an enormous amount of debate around the issue. Again in 1977 and 1978, with the media 'marketing' of the new philosophers, almost the entire intellectual establishment went into print on the matter and since then a steady trickle of books exposing the scandalous iniquities of the Parisian intelligentsia and their links with publishing houses and the media has found an eager readership. Finally, in 1986, 1987 and 1988, the media coverage given to controversies surrounding 'post-modernism'[16] and also to the resuscitation by Victor Farias of the old scandal of Heidegger's adherence to Nazism has caused renewed comment on the appearance of philosophy in the media.[17]

If the mere association of avant-garde philosophers with the media was not bad enough during the 1970s, the former insisted on making things even worse by declaring virtually *en masse* that they were not philosophers or even intellectuals for that matter. This attitude was succinctly illustrated by a cartoon in the popular literary magazine *Lire*. This cartoon depicts a man knocking at the door of an 'Intellectuals Club'. The bouncer asks whether he is an intellectual, to which the man replies: 'Well, it depends on your definition of the word "intellectual" ' an answer which gains him immediate entry.[18] The anxiety about the status of the intellectual which was the subject of so much furious intellectual debate in France during the 1970s and early 1980s was due to a number of factors. Firstly Marxism: Marxists were continually denigrating philosophy which Marx was alleged to have surpassed and rendered impossible with his science of historical materialism. After 1970, Althusser's structuralist attempt to reinstate philosophy fell into disfavour and a violently nihilist and anti-intellectualist Maoism was adopted by avant-garde intellectuals. In a return to the Sartrian self-abnegation of the 1950s, intellectuals cursed themselves for being born bourgeois and not proletarian. Politics had come back into fashion, and as inhabitants of the world of ideas and not of the world of 'action' or the 'real' and material world of the oppressed and the marginal, intellectuals felt obliged to justify their activities somehow.

The second current that helped promote the fashion for intellectual anti-intellectualism was a leftist anti-establishment movement. Institutions of every sort, including the university, were attacked as the embodiment of repressive power, and professors were servants of the state imposing their sinister learning on unsuspecting young people, in order to train them to serve the system, while at the same time maintaining the illusion that they were subverting it.[19] A rather extreme example of this attitude, one which is founded on a certain type of Marxism, is to be found in the text of an uncharacteristic address by Foucault:

> Gentlemen,
> I cannot call you comrades, being myself worthless . . . . The merchandise we professors produce is an erudite lie. It is what *the State pays us for* . . . . We are thinkers authorised by the State, but I must say that our most worthwhile voluntary action over the past fifty years has been to hide the real history of the workers' movement from the young generations.[20]

Thus Marxist and post-1968 ideologies combined to promote a fashion for disassociating oneself from the accusation of being a philosopher or an intellectual. Hence the decrease, especially amongst radical commentators, in the use of the word 'philosophy' to describe Foucault's activities, during the late 1970s and early 1980s. Instead Foucault became a 'genealogist'. However, in recent years, now that the political and identity crises of intellectuals have burned themselves out in futile arguments, many commentators in both French and English are quite content to describe Foucault as a philosopher once more.

If a number of historians had followed Foucault's work with interest during the 1960s, it was not until the publication of *L'Archéologie du savoir* and later *Surveiller et punir* that he began to attract their serious interest. Of *L'Archéologie*, Jacques Revel remarks that 'the first two chapters . . . are in fact a veritable eulogy to history and the historians of today, I must say they surprised a certain number of historians.'[21] With the general growth of interest in history during the 1970s, the interest of the historians in Foucault's work was well publicised. Several interviews with Foucault conducted by noted historians appeared, and a number of articles on his historiographical method were published. In particular, Paul Veyne devoted a long article titled 'Foucault révolutionne l'histoire' to the usefulness of Foucault's methods and ideas for historians. A round table conducted in 1977 with some of France's best historians (Philippe Ariès, Michel de Certeau, Jacques Le Goff, Emmanuel Le Roy Ladurie, and Paul Veyne) discussed Foucault's work at some length.[22] All these historians agreed that Foucault was a *philosopher*, but a philosopher who was at the same time a great historian. Philippe Ariès, for example, describes Foucault as 'one of our best historians, who is nonetheless a philosopher . . . . Born a philosopher he has become a historian in order to remain a philosopher.'[23] Fernard Braudel likewise praises the efforts of 'the non-historians, the philosophers (who) first among them, the most brilliant and most likeable, Michel Foucault, are the ones who speak out on history with the greatest vehemence'.[24] But if Foucault's work was the subject of sympathetic and enthusiastic discussion and indeed application in avant-garde historical circles in France during the 1970s, it was far less well received by certain 'university' philosophers who were less than happy about the 'historicisation' of philosophy, of the encroachment of their territory by 'history'.[25] In recent years protests against the 'historicisation' of philosophy and the 'relativism' of values this allegedly leads to have increased considerably in strength.

The debate in English over philosophy and history is one that bears only a remote resemblance to French discussions. Most writers who conclude that Foucault is a philosopher also insist on denying that he is something else, just to make sure that boundaries are clearly defined. For examples, Peter Kemp argues that Foucault is not a 'politician' as some other critics would claim, but a 'philosopher as much as Sartre and Lévinas',[26] and Peter Dews holds that

Foucault is not a historian in the conventional sense but a spinner of philosophical allegories; much of the fascination of his work derives from the tension between its density of historical reference and an underlying philosophical purpose.[27]

English-speaking critics feel that they have to *prove* that Foucault is a philosopher rather than something else. The French, who have a broader conception of what constitutes suitable material for philosophy, do not put themselves to all this trouble, and those who describe him as a philosopher do not consider it is necessary to prove this classification. On the other hand, English-speaking critics are more willing to describe him as a historian – even if a somewhat unorthodox one.

In recent years there appears to be a growing myth about a 'lack of interest' or 'rejection' of Foucault's work by historians. Wuthnow and his co-authors assert, for example, that Foucault's books are 'unacceptable to conventional historians' and have 'rarely been reviewed in the historians' professional journals.'[28] Historians (particularly in France) are, in fact, some of the biggest consumers of Foucault's work but as many of the references to his ideas appear in highly specialised articles (notably in the *Annales: ESC*) or books, rather than in discussions specifically about his work, this interest tends to go unnoticed by the sociologists, philosophers or literary critics who are prone to making such comments. It is certainly true, nonetheless, that in the Anglo-Saxon world it has been sociologists rather than historians who have taken up Foucault's work with the most enthusiasm, which is not to say he has been ignored by English-language historians by any means.

What all these debates would seem to indicate, is that in the past twenty years there has been a certain *rapprochement* of history and philosophy – a process in which Foucault has played a large part. Philippe Ariès, commenting on Foucault's brand of history, says:

> We are now beginning to guess that man of today is asking from a certain history what he has always asked from metaphysics and only yesterday from the human sciences: a history which takes up philosophical themes and reflection, but situating them in time and in the obstinate rebirth of human endeavour.[29]

Jacques Le Goff, in a discussion with his colleagues, remarks that the modern consumer of history seems to be asking of history the questions, 'where are we, where do we come from, where are we going?' Paul Veyne rejoins, 'in my day we asked those questions of *L'Etre et le Néant*.'[30] In any case, traditional philosophy or metaphysics (the rational search for knowledge of 'absolute being', the causes of the universe and the first principles of knowledge) has more than ever been called into question in a post-Kantian, post-Nietzschian, post-humanist age. The injunctions of Kant, Hegel, Marx and Nietzsche against philosophy and metaphysics, which they themselves did not take to their logical conclusion, have been more than ever in the forefront of reflection. With the famous crisis of values and systems of belief, traditional philosophy for many people has a tendency to become bogged down in frustrating circularities and infinite regressions, in the rush to eliminate all 'unprovable', unempirical and therefore 'metaphysical' assumptions.

The human sciences, after offering great hopes at first, have been little better at offering solutions to the perennial problems of existence, identity and difference, and the relation of knowledge to reality. The crisis of humanism and the subject (which in fact the human sciences fostered) undermined their claims to explanation, as the essence of man they originally hoped to discover receded further and further into the mists of the unconscious or into more and more fragmented and finely grained social structures. In recent years, it would seem that the study of history has taken over from philosophy and the human sciences as a popular mode of explanation. As Peter Burke remarks, 'over the past fifty years, history has claimed sectors of human activity which were formerly considered to be changeless.'[31] There is a certain concrete 'reality' about history which is lacking in traditional philosophy, and in the absence of values of our own, we study those adopted in past ages to see how they worked and in order to study the present constitution of our own society and to see how it differs from the past. Paul Veyne comments, 'the people who buy our books want to know who they are. Exactly as the buyers of a psychology journal . . . want to know who they are, and as a consequence, who they are not', and Jacques Le Goff also describes this 'passion for history' as the 'need for identity'.[32] This new kind of approach to history, far from reinstating the classical empiricist approach as might have been expected,[33] has resulted in a blurring of the line between fact and interpretation, resulting in what the American historian Oscar Handlin calls 'faction – a combination of fact and fiction'.[34]

Foucault's work has been situated at the hub of these debates. His work has both crystallised and influenced a new way of looking at both history and philosophy. Foucault himself, throughout his career, depending on his humour or current interests, shifts between defining his work as history or philosophy. By far the most useful and most accurate self-description occurs in *L'Usage des plaisirs* where he describes all his books as being 'historical' studies by virtue of their subject matter and references. He is at pains to point out, however, that they are not the works of a 'historian', as they were embarked on as a 'philosophical exercise'. The object of this exercise was to see how far the examination of history could expose some of the unspoken assumptions and foundations of thought, and enable people to think in some other manner (UP:15).

2.   A THOUGHT OF THE LIMIT

But how exactly are philosophy and history related in Foucault's works? Why has this issue been the subject of so much controversy? At the most obvious level, the reader is immediately struck by the existence of reflections of a philosophical nature in books which purport to be histories, or conversely the use of history to prove philosophical points. For example, in *Naissance de la clinique* Foucault relates the medical discoveries, political events, and laws that led to the institution of clinical medicine in France, using the dates, proper names and documents that usually characterise historical writing. But he opens his work by saying that 'in this book it is a question of space, language and death', and then goes on to discuss the problem of language and its relation to things, and the problem of the subject of knowledge (NC:v). He concludes his work with a discussion of the attitudes formed towards death and man's finiteness in the new clinical medicine, and the role they played in the formation of the modern individual and his relation to knowledge and truth.

But, the presence of philosophy in Foucault's work is not simply restricted to the occasional appearance of the odd philosophical reflection on his historical material. In fact, his very choice of history is philosophical and is used as a means of approaching philosophical problems, such as the relation between the Same and the Other, or Identity and Difference, the relation between words and things, and the nature and the value of human knowledge and experience.

Foucault attempts to describe the relation between the 'Same' and the 'Other', and to provide a concrete description of the point at which they interact. The 'Same' and the 'Other' are concepts more commonly found in European than in Anglo-Saxon philosophy. In existentialist, phenomenological and other subjectivist systems of thought the Same often refers to the individual subject, or subjective experience, whereas in structuralist or post-structuralist thought the Same often as not refers to systems, concepts, or an accepted mode of institutionalised discourse. Indeed, depending on one's own metaphysical inclinations, one can describe these categories in a number of ways, for example, as Being and Nothingness (Sartre), Man and God (Lévinas) or Man and Woman (de Beauvoir and Irigaray). Perhaps the Same could be simply defined as that which is known, familiar or ordered, and the Other as that mysterious unexplained 'something' that lies outside and defines the limits of the known, that which is exterior and foreign.[35] The relationship between the Same and the Other is an important one because, as Althusser points out, identity or consciousness, whether it is individual or social, cannot accede to the Real through its own internal development but only 'by the radical discovery of what is *other than itself*'.[36] But if Althusser is referring to Hegel here, it must be emphasised that for Foucault the interaction of the Same and the Other, is free from 'dialectical reconciliation'.[37] Foucault, in an interesting discussion on the event, makes this quite clear. He criticises the dialectical approach to history because it

> does not liberate the different; on the contrary, it guarantees that it is always recuperated. The dialectical supremacy of the Same allows it to exist, but only according to the law of negation, as the moment of non-being. You think that you are seeing the subversion of the Other declaring itself, but in secret, contradiction is working for the salvation of the identical.[38]

Foucault's whole work can be seen as an attempt to define where the lines of demarcation between the Same and the Other lie, and how these lines are drawn in history. He also examines the historical systems of order whose extreme points are marked by these lines. Foucault thus proposes a thought of the 'Limit'.

According to Foucault, it was Kant who originally opened up this possibility before it was closed up once again by his own introduction of an anthropological foundation for critical thought, and by Hegel's introduction of the dialectic of Reason with its successions of totality and contradiction. Together, Foucault says, they contributed to more than 150 years of a 'mixed dialectical and anthropological sleep'.[39] And as Raymond Aron remarks in his book on the philosophy of history, 'without a historical science whose existence is indisputable, we must substitute the search for *limits* for the search for foundations'.[40] It is this mode of investigation which Foucault adopts. He says: 'thought should not be directed towards establishing a kind of central certitude, but should be directed towards the limits, the exterior – towards the emptiness, the negation of what it says.'[41] The thought of the 'Limit', or 'margins', only really began to come into its own at the end of the 1950s and during the 1960s with the collapse of humanism, and with Foucault (following Heidegger) as one of its most vocal champions. Foucault remarks that if Kant was concerned with defining the limits that knowledge should not cross, today it is a matter of a 'practical critique that takes the form of a possible transgression'.[42]

What a 'thought of the limit' means is this: if instead of looking at totalities, the 'edge' (limit) which separates the Same and the Other could be analysed and described, perhaps an insight into the reality or truth of the Same and the Other could be gained. Such a system of thought in which 'transgression', that which crosses the 'Limit', plays a vital role, has both critical and ontological value in Foucault's view. Its critical status lies in the fact that it is able to study the Same (finitude) which lies within the limits of empirical knowledge. As for the ontological requirements, these are met by 'transgression' in its lightning movement across the Limit separating the Same and the Other; 'transgression' indicates where the limits lie.[43] This is because transgression can only exist where there is a limit to cross. Likewise we cannot know of the existence of a limit which is not transgressed. A thought of the Limit makes it possible to resist the dreary pressure of the Same and to actively seek out the limits and go beyond them. As Foucault says, this kind of thought 'is seeking to give a new impetus, as far and wide as possible to the undefined work of freedom.'[44] By inviting us to expose the limits of our way of thinking, Foucault hopes to enable us to see beyond them and to constantly embark upon new ways of thinking. But how is one to 'think' a thought of the Limit, how can it be given a concrete form and practical expression? The answer for Foucault, is 'history': history is both a reality determined in experience and the arena where those two absolute limits, birth and death, beginnings and ends, appear with monotonous regularity. Foucault notes his debt on this score to Jean Hyppolite, saying of his work: 'Is not history the privileged place where philosophical finitude can appear?'[45] At the same time, he remarks in relation to *Histoire de la folie*, that 'limitations . . . are not historical because they are constitutive of all possible history.'[46] Limits exist at the very edge of history and are both part of historical order and beyond that order. Limits are also present in history in the form of 'events', which although they can sometimes be seen to form part of a universal system, are not totally encompassed within that system, because they represent a change, even if infinitesimal. A variation and a tension exists between the 'regularities' that can be found in history and the constant stream of events. In 'events', we see the confrontation between the Same (the system or identity) and the Other (that which is different) on the most minuscule scale.[47] Each human being also takes part in this confrontation. The individual is both an intrinsic part of his own particular society and history, and at the same time has the capacity, no matter how small, to modify that mode of belonging.[48] This precarious situation of the limits, both as part of the order of history and outside that order, leads to a system of thought that balances on a tightrope between the historical and the ahistorical: it is neither a nihilistic historical relativism, nor a study of metaphysical essences. The trick is not to overbalance into either extreme, and Foucault does not always entirely succeed in maintaining the balance, occasionally adopting an almost flippant nihilism, or alternately his own metaphysics of identity.

In choosing history, Foucault departs from the Kantian model. Although, like Kant, he is interested in defining the conditions of possibility leading to the construction of objects and structures of knowledge, he situates the *a priori* in history. It is at this point in Foucault's thought that the influence of Nietzsche and his critique of historicism and Hegelianism come into play.[49] As he says in a later interview, he is in a very real sense writing a 'historical ontology'.[50] In particular, in his choice of history as a way of avoiding 'metaphysics' and as a 'thought of the limit', Foucault is led to reject all forms of historicism, particularly as they have been inherited from Hegel and other nineteenth-century German philosophers of history.[51] In so doing, Foucault goes further in the direction indicated by Nietzsche, and by Heidegger's reading of Nietzsche, and joins the general movement of the late 1950s and 1960s which rejected historicist modes of thought. Indeed in an interview conducted in 1984, Foucault explained that although he had written very little on Nietzsche and nothing on Heidegger, these two authors had exercised a considerable influence on his work.[52] As there is considerable disagreement over the use of the term historicism – the term often being used in ways which directly contradict each other – it might be useful to provide some preliminary definitions before looking at Foucault's rejection of this approach.

Karl Popper sees historicism as:

> an approach to the social sciences which assumes that *historical prediction* is their principal aim and which assumes that this aim is attainable by discovering the 'rhythms' or the 'patterns', the 'laws' or the 'trends' that underlie the evolution of history.[53]

If, as Hegel says, 'the history of the world is a rational process, the rational and necessary evolution of the world spirit', and if the nature of this spirit is 'always one and the same', then it follows that by studying that rational process which is history, one can deduce possible directions for the future.[54] Thus, although historicisms such as humanist Marxism reject the charge of fatalism, and lay considerable emphasis on the role of action by subjects in history, this action can only speed up the inevitable process of historical progress and change. To be a good revolutionary one must follow the direction indicated by History at any given moment. As Popper remarks, 'all the thoughts and all the activities of historicists aim at interpreting the past in order to predict the future'.[55] Although historicists claim that all is subject to continuous change, and that all truth is relative to one's historical position, the *mechanism* of change itself does not change, and society moves through necessary and predetermined stages. World history from its very beginning constitutes a rational whole, a 'progress of the consciousness of freedom', the awareness that 'man is by nature free, and that freedom of the spirit is his very essence.'[56] In other words, the self-conscious and rational but preprogrammed realisation of man's liberty is the end and essence of history. All history leads to the present in an inexorable progress from ignorance to truth. As Philippe Ariès points out in a discussion about Marxist history, this approach 'destroys the otherness of history'.[57] History is reduced to the perpetual realisation of the Same. Whatever the variations, historical time does no more than reveal essences, such as Reason, Man, Freedom and so on, which remain unchanged throughout history.[58] Indeed, a certain conception of history and a certain conception of Man go hand in hand: as Althusser remarks 'in many circumstances humanism and historicism both rest on the same ideological problematic.'[59] However, as ideas in history *about* these things are constantly changing, some historicists adopt a relativist position, arguing that it is impossible to ever know which view is true, and that all views are equally true – or untrue.

Foucault writes in direct opposition to these ideas. In his view, to resort to traditional explanations of historical change relying on notions such as influence, causality, traditions, development and evolution and 'mentality' or 'spirit of the age' is merely to invoke quasi-magical metaphysical entities.[60] As he explains somewhat vehemently in an interview in reply to criticisms:

> There is a sort of myth of History for philosophers . . . a kind of great and vast continuity where the liberty of individuals and economic or social determinations are all tangled up together . . . . When one of these three myths is interfered with, these worthy people start to cry that History has been raped and murdered. In fact, it is quite some time since people as important as Marc Bloch, Lucien Febvre, the English historians, etc., put an end to this myth of History . . . . This philosophical myth which I am accused of killing, well, I am delighted if I have killed it, because it is precisely that myth I wanted to kill, not history in general. You can't kill history, but as for killing History for philosophers – absolutely – I certainly want to kill it.[61]

And to 'kill' this myth of history, to do away with the 'abstract, general and monotonous' explanations of change it proposes, Foucault upholds a principle of *discontinuity*. This principle of

'discontinuity, rupture, threshold, limit, series and transformation',[62] remains constant throughout Foucault's entire career,
even if his terminology varies and the principle is applied differently to a variety of objects and situations.

Indeed, Foucault argues that the very idea of history presup-
poses discontinuity, as the past can only be an object of study if it
is discontinuous and different from the present. But discontinuity
is a paradoxical notion because, as Foucault points out in
L'Archéologie du savoir:

> it is both an instrument and an object of research and because it
> defines the field of which it is the effect. It allows the historian
> to individualise areas of study, but can only be established
> through the comparison of those areas. It is a paradoxical notion
> because, in the final analysis perhaps, it is not simply a concept
> present in the discourse of the historian, but something that the
> historian secretly supposes to be there. In fact, how else can he
> speak except on the basis of that rupture which offers him
> history – and his own history – as an object? (AS:17, AK:9)

Philosophy today, continues Foucault in an interview, should
'diagnose the present, describe how our present is different, and
absolutely different, from that which is not it, in other words from
our past'.[63] This separation of the past and the present runs
directly counter to the historicist approach, based as it is on
the historical continuity of essences between past and present.
Jacques Léonard remarks: 'Foucault's originality consists in his
refusal at any price of the Hegelian totalising view, which
integrates opposites and provides a positive justification for
everything that has happened up till now.'[64]

Discontinuity also appears in the way Foucault structures his
own historical writing. At the most general level he posits a series
of discrete historical 'periods': for example, the Renaissance, the
Classical Age, and the Modern Age. Secondly, he deliberately sets
out to reject all historicist notions of historical change based on
continuity: such as cause, influence, tradition, development, evolution, origins and teleology, 'mentality' or 'spirit of the age'.
Thirdly, he questions traditional ways of organising texts into
disciplines (such as medicine or psychology) or according to
authors, works or entities such as the 'great man', the 'genius' and
so on.[65] All of these notions imply *essences* such as a unifying or

unchanging subject of history, or unities of 'truth' (clinical medicine has always existed, even if previous ages were too ignorant to be aware of it (NC:53–4)). Once all these unities have been dissolved (if this is ever possible in reality) one can draw out different relations and patterns, discover different lines of 'rupture', unity or change in our past. Later in Foucault's career, during the 1970s, discontinuity came to serve as a methodological basis for his political theories (strategies of power and resistance, the 'specific' versus the 'universal' intellectual, 'local' struggles versus the Revolution).

The same rejection of a certain type of history, a rejection which was often characterised as anti-history, is also to be found in quite a number of the writings of the 'structuralist' school during the 1960s. Even the Annales school of historians who had quietly begun to investigate 'structures' before the general rush, were accused of writing a kind of anti-history. But as André Burguière commented in 1971, 'structural analysis' had long been familiar to historians and that the 'previous life of structuralism was part of the history of the Annales school'.[66]

The historians, however, as we have seen, took up Foucault's work with enthusiasm, for they recognised in it a way of salvaging history from the general attack on their discipline and elevating it once again, in renovated form, to its former position as queen of the human sciences. The anti-historicists of the 1960s, Foucault, the structuralists and the Annales school thus sought to eliminate a kind of history that tended to adopt the 'legislative and critical power of philosophy'.[67] However, in so doing, they in fact reinforced history's philosophical pretensions, but in a form more acceptable to today's tastes and requirements. Indeed history and philosophy have become far more closely related than they ever were.

Although Foucault's anti-historicist history differs from that of traditional historians in quite a number of respects, it must be noted, as he himself makes clear, that he is continuing historiographical work begun by the Annales school of historians, by historians of science such as Gaston Bachelard and Georges Canguilhem, and by the historian of comparative religion and myths, Georges Dumézil. He says: 'I am not all sure that I have invented a new method . . . what I am doing is not so different from many other contemporary American, English, French and German endeavours. I claim no originality.'[68] Foucault is perhaps being unduly modest here, but his work has certainly had the advantage of drawing attention to these hitherto unjustly neglected intellectual enterprises. Paul Veyne, the Annales historian, says that if initially he thought that 'Foucault was simply a philosopher who had discovered our ideal and realised it with more talent than others, and that was all', it was not until later that he 'understood the vaster nature of the enterprise'.[69] In addition, Foucault has made a considerable contribution of his own in developing certain historiographical ideas, and such has been his influence, as well as his ability to anticipate trends, that in recent years historians have been starting to adopt those very procedures that previously distinguished his work from their own. Still, one would perhaps not go so far as Lawrence Stone, who believes that 'Foucault's work has had an enormous and disturbing influence upon traditional views of recent Western history . . . . It is he who has set the agenda for the last fifteen years of research.'[70] But certainly most of Foucault's 'innovations' are now to be found in varying proportions in the work of the new generation of Annales historians, writing what Jacques Le Goff calls 'the new history'.[71]

However, Foucault's choice of history is not simply a philosophical one, it is an ethical one. He hopes to do away with the idea of 'eternal' and 'universal' truths and with a certain form of calm self-righteous morality. As Foucault says late in his career, 'the philosophical ethos appropriate to the critical ontology of ourselves [is the] historico-practical test of the limits that we may go beyond, and thus work carried out by ourselves upon ourselves as free beings'.[72] What Foucault means in this rather difficult statement is that by studying history we can see the *limits* within which men of past ages thought and acted, as well as the slow formation of ideas, objects and sensibilities that we currently take for granted and which appear to have existed from all time. As Paul Veyne remarks in a discussion about Foucault's work:

> It is certainly a curious thing, quite worthy of intriguing a philosopher, this capacity that men have for being unaware of their limits, their *rarity*, for not seeing that there is emptiness around them, for believing every time that they are comfortably established in the plenitude of reason.[73]

People have not always thought the same way throughout history, Foucault argues, and if certain institutions and ways of thought and values have changed, it is not through some form of historical necessity, but through the far more haphazard channels of human activity: ambition, blunder, and any number of historical accidents. The aim of Foucault's history is to show that our present is not the result of some inevitable historical necessity. It is instead the result of innumerable and very concrete human practices, and as such, can be changed by other practices.[74] In studying history and historical limits, we can reflect upon our own limits and try to move beyond them. The knowledge of their existence means we are less determined by them, and can try to devise ways of thinking something else. As Foucault explains in *L'Usage des plaisirs*, his histories are written in an effort to examine how far thought can be liberated from 'what it silently thinks and allowed to think otherwise' (UP:15). He wants to 'produce a shift in thought so that things can really change'.[75]

Thus in exposing the not always 'respectable' historical origins of institutions such as asylums and prisons, and of disciplines such as the human sciences, or of attitudes towards sexuality, Foucault hopes to shock people out of their complacency, thereby provoking them into changing systems, institutions, and ways of thinking. During the 1970s when Foucault decided to cast his work in 'genealogical' and vaguely 'political' terms, this aim of his histories became immensely popular and has remained so, particularly in America. This is due, no doubt, to the fact that such a project casts a revolutionary aura around the foucauldian historian or genealogist. He becomes, as a result, at minimal cost, the author of 'radical critiques' or damning indictments of the current status quo.

If a certain emphasis has been placed up till this point on the logical coherence of Foucault's overall project as a philosophy, history and ethics of the limits, it is now time to draw attention to the apparent contradictions in the realisation of that project, contradictions that have provided endless fuel for discussion in the secondary literature. If Foucault started with histories which ignored the subject, individual choice and the ethical reflection that informed these choices, in 1984 he admits that he had to resort to 'slightly rhetorical' methods to exclude this dimension.[76] Nonetheless this level always existed at an *implicit* level in Foucault's work. As a study of the collective results of individual behaviour, Foucault's histories finally have implications for the study of individual subjectivity. Related to the subjective dimension is the question of freedom and limits. In the 1960s Foucault declared (no doubt to distinguish his position from Sartre's) that 'man does not start with freedom but with the limit, the line of the uncrossable.'[77] During this period, although Foucault rarely, if ever, mentioned the word freedom, associated as it was with Sartrian and existentialist thought, ultimately the end-result of his argument is that our freedom is exercised by being aware of, and crossing the limits. If limits restrict our freedom, the transgression of limits is an expression of our freedom. If Foucault's later interest in subjectivity and freedom prompted critics such as Peter Kemp to compare his ideas with those of Jean-Paul Sartre,[78] Foucault carefully distinguishes himself from the latter. He argues that if, in theory, Sartre avoids the idea of self as something given to us, with the notion of 'authenticity', he in fact returns to the true essential self. Instead, says Foucault, 'from the idea that self is not given to us, I think there is only one practical consequence: we have to create ourselves as works of art.'[79]

In the work Foucault produced up until 1966, there was an insistent emphasis on the existence of a rather mysterious confrontation or dialogue between the Same and the Other in history.[80] But at the same time, he was unable to decide at which point, at which limit, this confrontation emerged most clearly. In *Histoire de la folie* he was convinced it was madness, in *Naissance de la clinique*, it was death and in *Les Mots et les choses*, it was the 'being of language'. In addition to this interest in the outer limits, Foucault was also interested in the way the Same was ordered. Hence we find two parallel discussions in this work, one concerning historical structures or patterns of intelligibility, and the other concerning the limits of that order. But after *Les Mots et les choses*, perhaps disappointed with his inability to define the limits once and for all, Foucault abandoned his enthusiastic search in this direction and tried to concentrate his energies on the description of the order of the Same, at the same time feeling obliged to relocate the Other within the 'time of our own thought' (AS:21).

It is this abandonment of the limits which marks the beginnings of a profound change in Foucault's work. Much has been made of a change that occurs in his work in about 1970, so much so in fact, that in recent years some critics have begun to express their exasperation at this 'conventional wisdom'.[81] There are good reasons, however, to retain the idea that there is a difference that occurs roughly around 1970 in Foucault's work, even if not for the usual reasons put forward. These reasons generally relate to Foucault's 'discovery of politics' after May 1968 – an impression fostered by Foucault himself, who claimed that it was not possible to 'pose the problem of power' before 1968 – and the introduction of Nietzschean genealogies of power into his analysis.[82] Edward Said, for example, posits a 'major shift' in Foucault's work in 1968, a change which consists in 'reconceiving the problem of language not in an ontological but in a political or ethical framework, the Nietzschean framework'.[83] *L'Ordre du discours*, which Foucault himself describes as a work he wrote at a 'time of transition', is usually taken to be the key turning-point in this process.[84] But in fact the beginnings of a 'change' occur far earlier – in 1966 – and concern the rejection of the exterior limits rather than the adoption of power.

During the 1970s, Foucault gradually constructed a vision of society and history in which the Same and the Other were totally coextensive and indeed interchangeable, inextricably bound together in their movement, locked in a life-and-death struggle which had no end, and no meaning but its own inevitability. No dialogue was possible in this world, and even this hopeless contest was doomed to annihilation: 'A day will dawn when all that disparity finds itself effaced. The power which will come to be exercised at the level of everyday life . . . will be made up of a fine, differentiated, continuous network.'[85] To put it another way, the Other would be totally controlled or dominated by the Same in the infinite reproduction of a power so finely differentiated that we would no longer be aware of the Other.

During this period, which lasted until about 1982, Foucault's work abounded with images of struggle, fragmentation and isolation, which at the same time existed paradoxically within a totalising system. This was because although the Other was not reduced to the Same, as is the case with the Hegelian dialectic, it was totally coextensive with the Same. At the same time, however, Foucault was manifestly uneasy about the marvellously logical and watertight view of modern society he had constructed, and invited people to select any ideas they found useful in his books in order to smash systems of power, including his own books if necessary.[86] He also repeatedly insisted that history was not determined, that transcendental unities should be done away with and that we should be aware of the historical origins of ideas or institutions we thought eternal. Unfortunately these exhortations, although met with enthusiasm, were merely to become items for dogmatic repetition by Foucault's followers.

But then abruptly in 1981 the limits reappeared in force in Foucault's work. If during the 1960s, Foucault had sought to discover *the* limit, this time he came to the conclusion that we will never have 'any complete and definitive knowledge of what may constitute our historical limits . . . we are always in the position of beginning again'.[87] New objects are constantly emerging in history and it is only too easy to assume that these objects have existed for all time, and have been true for all men (even if they remained in ignorance of them). The struggle to understand our historical limits is an ongoing and difficult one, but necessary if we are not to fall into the traps of complacency and self-assured intolerance.

The critical ontology of ourselves has to be considered not, certainly as a theory, a doctrine, not even as a permanent body of knowledge that is accumulating; it has to be conceived as an attitude, an ethos, a philosophical life in which the critique of what we are is at one and the same time the historical analysis of the limits that are imposed on us and an experiment with the possibility of going beyond them.[88]

Generally, three points can be made concerning these developments in Foucault's work: first of all, the relationship of the Same and the Other changes: from one that is to be found at the limits of history (a history which also possesses its own order), to a relationship situated within the order of history itself, then finally to a relation to be found at the personal or 'subjective' level. Secondly, different historical points of contact between the Same and the Other such as madness, death, language, penality and sexuality assume varying amounts of importance at different stages of Foucault's career. Thirdly, the construction of certain historical objects, such as the human sciences and the individual, are constantly reformulated in terms of Foucault's changing views on the limits.

These complexities have provoked an enormous amount of discussion, not only because they constitute internal variations and contradictions within Foucault's own work, but because they reflect and crystalise wider preoccupations within contemporary society. These preoccupations concern the question of how far a person is determined by his historical, biological and cultural situation, and how far he may escape the range of determinations weighing down upon him. It is also a discussion about the relative merits of a world view based on ahistorical essences and continuity and a world view firmly grounded in history, in limits, difference and discontinuity – a philosophy that is a history. In short, we are dealing with a debate about our modernity and the best method of thinking it through and creating new bases for action. As Philippe Ariès notes, historian and public alike, are caught in a sort of a dialectic of the present and the past in a quest to understand our modernity – a modernity which is no longer 'a kind of ideal aim' as it may once have been, but an urgent problem that needs to be thought through now.[89]

3

Discontinuity and Order

If the critics were undecided as to how to classify Foucault's work, they were also undecided as to what to make of its constant changeability. In this chapter and the ones that follow, Foucault's work will be looked at as a constantly changing body of historical and philosophical reflection. At the same time, attention will be drawn to certain structural constants which give more cohesion to his work than would first appear to be the case. In order to emphasise different aspects of Foucault's development, the analysis has been divided into four sections. The first two deal mainly with Foucault's earlier work, beginning with the way Foucault orders his histories and his treatment of the 'interior limits' of a culture,[1] and then going on to the more difficult question of the relation of the Same and the Other and limits in his work. The third section is concerned with Foucault's later work, in which the exterior limits disappear, and in which his analyses of order and his ontological theses merge. The fourth section deals with his final writings, which reintroduce the question of the limits.

There have been a large number of comments about Foucault's propensity to change his mind. For obvious reasons more comments of this type are to be found towards the end of Foucault's career than at the beginning. 'Foucault is not easily imitated', declares James Clifford:

> His well-known stylistic excesses, his confusing redefinitions, abandonments of positions, and transgressions of his own methodological rules may well be aspects of an ironic program designed to frustrate any coherent formulation, and thus ideological confiscation of his writing. Foucault's work will not occupy any permanent ground, but must attack, pervert and transgress the grounds of truth and meaning wherever they become formulated institutionally.[2]

Another writer says that 'he seems to take a perverse pleasure in shifting his stance' and complains that 'things seem to shift in the

44

course of the writing . . . by the end we seem to be reading about something else.'[3] Neither of these critics, incidentally, appears to be able to decide whether to find Foucault's tactics an admirable attack on great 'systems of truth', or simply frustrating. Many other English-speaking critics react to Foucault's changing ideas with the same infuriated mixture of admiration and frustration. It does not seem to occur to them, however, that Foucault's 'shifting stance' might be more than simply a perverse desire to change for the sake of change, or to 'subvert totality' at absolutely any cost. It is certainly true that on occasions Foucault did make flippant remarks to this effect. 'Why change?' Maurice Clavel asked him earnestly one day. 'Just to change!' replied Foucault. 'From everything to everything?' rejoined Clavel. 'From everything to nothing!' was the reply. 'I then called him jokingly a dandy, a dilettante of Nothingness', adds Clavel.[4] But from the enthusiasm with which Foucault adopted each of his new positions, it would seem more likely that they represent a search to find what he felt to be a more accurate and more 'true' or 'useful' way of thinking through our present relation to the world, and the way people constructed reality in the past. The frequency of the changes in Foucault's work reflect not only the rapidity with which he could see the limitations of what he had already proposed, but a certain, and on occasions perhaps excessive, attention to what others were saying about his work, and the vagaries of French intellectual fashion (particularly in the 'political' arena).

French critics have equal problems with Foucault's 'shifting stance', but in a culture where it is a habit amongst some intellectuals to publicly and noisily change intellectual or ideological allegiance every few years or so, and where the word 'intellectual' is a cover-all for a vast range of activity, Foucault's activities were greeted with some degree of tolerance but not always of sympathy. This habit of changing ideology, in fact, became almost an obligation during the 1970s. As Jacques Bouveresse remarks sardonically in his article about the 'new philosophers':

> What a pity, one is tempted to say to oneself today, that one was never Stalinist, Lyssenkist, Althusserian, Maoist, etc! What prestige and what advantages can be drawn from the fact of no longer being these things today! What a prodigious effort of thought, truly worthy of the greatest of admiration, did it not require of some to arrive at where they are today, after all that![5]

Apart from the new philosophers, other examples of this kind of activity are to be found in the persons of Jean-Edern Hallier, Philippe Sollers and Roger Garaudy. Jean-Edern Hallier, a journalist 'intellectual' nicknamed by some *'fou-à-lier'* (a pun on his surname meaning 'completely crazy') and described as an 'ideological vagabond' (*'clochard des idéologies'*) has long been the source of amusement on the Parisian intellectual circuit, as much for his extravagant behaviour as for his changes in ideology. In recent years, he has been a Maoist, a new philosopher, a member of the New Right, and a Catholic. Philippe Sollers, one of the new novelists and leading light of the *Tel Quel* group, is also noted for his changes in sympathy from structuralist, to Maoist, from Catholic to a variant of 'feminist'. As for Roger Garaudy, Benamou and Pudlowski sum up his career: 'Communist, Christian, Muslim . . . . When will the next conversion be?'[6] Foucault's own changes, therefore, although they were not exclusively located in the political arena, were perhaps taken more for granted by French critics, and we do not find to the same extent the utter exasperation on this point that is sometimes evident in the English-speaking criticism.

François Ewald does point out, however, that many French critics (particularly after 1968) were annoyed by Foucault's refusal to specify from 'where he was speaking'. He notes that Foucault refuses to occupy an 'assignable place in the categories of our knowledge' and that he practises a 'certain art of the sidestep, with irony and gay science. Present everywhere, he is always elsewhere, where he is not expected. Elusive and fleeing.'[7] Roger Pol-Droit, in an obituary, remarks that 'the name of Michel Foucault is not synonymous with historian or philosopher – it is not even synonymous with "Michel Foucault". Never identical to itself. A sign of contradiction'.[8] But, if nothing else, it was a relief to know that these contradictions might be intentional, and one of the favourite passages of these critics in both French and English is one taken from *L'Archéologie du savoir*. At the risk of appearing monotonous, this 'dialogue' is worth citing again:

Aren't you sure of what you are saying? Are you going to change again, to shift your ground, to say that any objections are not really aimed at the position you are speaking from? Are you getting ready to say, yet again, that you have never been what you are accused of being? Are you already arranging a way out, which will allow you to suddenly reappear somewhere else in your next book and jeer, as you are doing now: no, no, I am not over there where you were waiting for me, but over here laughing at you.

The answer to all these questions is, of course, yes, but that would perhaps be too simple. Foucault ends his reply to his imaginary interlocuter by saying: 'I am probably not the only one who writes in order to become faceless. Don't ask me who I am, or tell me to stay the same: that is the bureaucratic morality, which ensures that our papers are kept in order. It ought to let us be when it comes to writing'. (AS:28, AK:17).

It has already been mentioned that the basis of Foucault's historiography was a principle of *discontinuity* (the methodological equivalent of the limit), a discontinuity which also underlay his political and ethical views. This principle, however, changed considerably in appearance throughout his career. Beginning with discontinuity on a large historical scale, discontinuity shrank to a smaller and smaller scale to re-emerge in a highly complex series of transformations. In the 1970s, he changed the entire focus of his discussion on discontinuity from the arrangement of historical events and 'discourse' to the arrangement of 'theory', 'power', and the role of the intellectual. By this stage, the particles of discontinuity had become so fine as to almost produce the effect of continuity. In this chapter, however, we will concentrate on Foucault's discussion of historical discontinuity prior to 1970, focusing particularly on his famous notion of the episteme.

The changes in Foucault's approach to discontinuity can be seen by comparing the following quotations. In *Les Mots et les choses* he declares: 'sometimes in a few years, a culture ceases to think as it had done up to that point, and begins to think something else, and in quite a different manner'. (p. 64).

Three years later in *L'Archéologie du savoir* quite a different view emerges:

Nothing would be more false, than to see in the analysis of discursive formations, an attempt at totalitarian periodisation: that starting from a certain moment and for a certain time, everybody would think in the same way, and despite surface differences, would say the same thing. (pp. 193–4).

Further, in 1977 Foucault expresses bewilderment at the fact that the *Petit Larousse* describes him as a 'philosopher who founds his theory of history on discontinuity' and goes so far as to say, in 1978 that 'no one could be more continuist than I am'.[9] These statements, particularly the last two, which contain a certain degree of rhetorical hyperbole, do not mean that Foucault has gone from the most extreme form of discontinuity to the most extreme form of continuity. As a number of critics have remarked, Foucault on occasions shows a marked tendency towards rhetorical exaggeration particularly when he 'is saying something that runs counter to received opinion'.[10] What his statements on discontinuity do point to, however, is the development in his thought away from the idea of large, unilateral historical discontinuities, to the notion of a multitude of ruptures at a series of different levels. At the same time, Foucault also moved away from a purely historiographical application of discontinuity to a more 'political' one during the 1970s.

Let us now go on to examine Foucault's methodological discontinuity as it emerges in his periodisation, his views on historical change, and certain categories in history such as the 'object', the 'document' and the 'discipline'. With the exception of his last writings, Foucault's histories tend to be divided into four or five periods: the Middle Ages, the Renaissance, the Classical Age, the Modern Age and finally the contemporary period (from about 1950 to the present). However, the dates marking the beginnings and ends of these periods vary from book to book. This is because in each of his books Foucault is examining a different problem or limit in his search to understand modern Western society. And, as he explains in an interview in 1967 after he had already changed his mind several times about the most important problem or limit in our recent history, different levels and types of history call for different periodisations and different points of rupture.[11] Hence in *Histoire de la folie*, where madness is the ultimate limit, the boundary dates between each period are selected in relation to fundamental changes in man's relation to madness. The end of the Middle Ages is marked by the disappearance of leprosy from Europe in the fourteenth century which left a social 'space' later to be inherited by madness. The period that follows, the Renaissance, comes to an abrupt end at about the time of Descartes. Foucault nominates the date of the foundation of the Hôpital Général in France, and of the 'Great Confinement' of madmen, paupers and other 'useless' members of society in 1656 as the beginning of the Classical Age. This great confinement was a 'gesture' of exclusion which was 'just as abrupt as that which isolated the lepers.' (HF:94). The Modern Age begins with a 'sudden new figure – a restructuring, the origin of which was hidden in an imbalance inherent to the Classical experience of madness' (HF:531), and the 'elaboration' of a 'new structure of experience' (HF:481, 547). The date Foucault sets for the beginning of the Modern era is about 1794, when the chains were struck from the inmates of the lunatic asylum, Bicêtre, and the era of psychological medicine and mental illness came into its own. Further, in a later article included in the second edition of *Histoire de la folie*, Foucault claims that this period is at present drawing to a close.[12]

Over the years there has been considerable comment on this periodisation, and in particular on Foucault's notion of the 'Great Confinement'. It is now an idea and a periodisation widely adopted by many historians studying the period or the problem of deviancy in history. The Annales school of historians have found the notion especially useful for their own researches.[13] Other historians, and in particular some English-speaking historians, have wondered if 'there is any firm basis in reality to Foucault's vision of the "age of confinement" ',[14] or have remarked that his periodisation is not 'free of problems'.[15]

Leaving aside these questions of periodisation for the moment, to take up the question of historical change: Foucault makes it clear in the preface to the first edition of *Histoire de la folie*, that he intends to do away with certain traditional historiographical methodologies. So in order to trace that 'gesture to break' (FD:8) between Reason and Unreason, the separation and exclusion of Unreason by Reason, neither the 'teleology of truth', nor the 'rational chain of causes' can be used as an explanation (FD:10). These categories could only make sense *after* the split had taken place, *after* Reason had established itself in its identity, excluding the Other of Unreason. For the same reasons, Foucault concludes that psychology and psychopathology are not useful frames of reference for his study, as psychology only became possible as a result of the 'silencing' and exclusion of madness, constituting as it does a 'monologue of reason *on* madness' (FD:9). Madness did not wait in 'immobile identity', to be finally discovered by psychiatry and 'pass from an obscure existence to the light of truth' (HF:93). Indeed traditional histories of science, psychology and medicine with their notions of 'progress' and the eternity of 'mental illness' are consistently opposed in *Histoire de la folie*.[16] Foucault says, 'What we want to know, is not what value madness has for us, but the movement by which it took its place in the perception of the eighteenth century: the series of ruptures, of discontinuities, of explosions through which it has become what it is for us, in the opaque oblivion of what it was.'[17]

This brings us to the notion of the historical object as it emerges in *Histoire de la folie*. If some writers, in order to explain difficulties over Foucault's classification as a historian, argue that he is dealing with quite different objects from the historian, the difference perhaps goes further than this.[18] Foucault does not simply deal with different objects, he has a different idea of what an object actually is. Of course, it must be emphasised that this difference is not as great as it may once have been, which is due as much to the influence of Foucault's own writings as to those of the Annales historians.

Instead of assuming that madness has always been the same, even if people were unable to recognise its true nature, an assumption which was standard for nineteenth century and popular historians of science, Foucault is more interested in describing how this object was actually constructed in history. As he explains in *L'Archéologie du savoir*:

> The object does not wait in limbo for the order that is going to set it free and allow it to take on a visible and garrulous objectivity. It does not pre-exist itself, held back by some obstacle at the outer edges of the light. It exists according to the positive conditions of a complex group of relations. (AS:61)

A number of critics took these views to be expressive of a certain nihilism or relativism, and a complete denial of the existence of external reality: 'For Foucault there is no reality outside discourse, no madness outside of a particular world view', claims one writer,[19] and others who allied Foucault to the anti-psychiatric movement (supporters and opponents alike) interpreted Foucault's analysis as meaning that madness was entirely the creation of a repressive society, the result of a particular point of view, Hayden White also remarks that Foucault, Lacan, Lévi-Strauss and Barthes 'take seriously Mallarmé's conviction that things exist in order to live in books. For them, the whole of human life is to be treated as a "text", the meaning of what is nothing but what it is'.[20] However, Foucault's position is more subtle than this, for he believes there is a real material basis for madness (such as behaviour or the chemistry of the nervous system). As he notes in *Maladie mentale et psychologie*: 'Every society is conscious of certain aspects in the behaviour and speech of some people which separates them from other people. These people are treated not quite as ordinary people, ill people, criminals or sorcerers' (MMP:90–91). But as Paul Veyne explains further: 'A man must be objectivised as mad in order for the prediscursive referent to appear retrospectively as the material substance *of madness*; because why behaviour and the cells of the nervous system rather than fingerprints?' When Veyne showed his article to Foucault, the latter remarked: 'I have never written personally, that *madness does not exist*, which is something that could be written; because for phenomenology, madness exists, but it is not a thing, whereas we should say on the contrary, that madness does not exist, but for all that, it is not nothing.'[21] These historiographical themes: the discontinuity of the 'object', the rejection of scientific or general historical 'progress', of chains of cause and effect, and the rejection of a humanistic teleology, all remained an integral part of Foucault's approach to history throughout his career. They were all themes that provoked various charges of 'system', anti-history, irrationalism, positivism, nihilism and political conservatism.

Foucault continued to develop his method in his next book, *Naissance de la clinique*. Here he describes the foundation of clinical medicine and the sudden 'mutation' and 'restructuring' of medical knowledge between 1769 and 1825 in France (NC:XIII, 62). Old books and erudition came to be replaced by the doctor's 'gaze' and his examination of the body, and the normal and the pathological became the fundamental organising principles of our view of illness.[22] It was in 1816, when Broussais published his *Examen de la doctrine medicale*, that Foucault considers 'the historical and concrete *a priori* of the modern medical gaze' to have been finally established (NC:197). At the end of the book, Foucault hints at a possible contemporary rupture:

> European culture, in the last years of the eighteenth century, outlined a structure which has not yet been unravelled. We are only just beginning to untangle a few threads, which are still so unknown to us that we immediately see them as marvellously

new or absolutely archaic, whereas for two centuries (not less, yet not much more) they have constituted the obscure but solid backbone of our experience. (NC:203, BC:199)

In an interview conducted some fourteen years after the appearance of *Naissance de la clinique* Foucault speaks of a 'cultural mobilisation' involving medicine which had begun some 'fifteen years' before – that is about the time Foucault wrote his book.[23] Again Foucault's periodisation did not go unchallenged, and the historian of medicine, Henri Ey, argues that 'the clinic was not born on the date that Foucault, using an artificial and contrived socio-ideological analysis, assigns for its entry into the world.'[24]

Just as Foucault rejects in *Histoire de la folie* the traditional frames of reference offered by the history of psychology, here he rejects the picture offered by more orthodox histories of medicine. He condemns 'those slightly mythical accounts' which rewrite the history of medicine in terms of the present, and which see clinical medicine as the advance of scientific discovery overcoming the major obstacles thrown in its path by ignorance, religion, and superstition (NC:54, 138–9). In the Preface, he also criticises a history of ideas which traces long chains of causes and influences, reconstructing 'spirits of the age', or searching for deeper meanings (NC:XIII). Rather, the birth of the clinic can be seen as the appearance of an entirely new relation of words and things, a reorganisation of knowledge: a 'new disposition of the objects of knowledge' (NC:68). It can be examined at that level where words and things are not separated, a level where the grid of ordering what is true and false during a given period, comes into being.[25] Noting the appearance of a 'new structure' (NC:XIV) at the end of the eighteenth century, Foucault comments: 'What counts in the things said by men, is not so much what they may have thought beneath or beyond them, but what systematises them from the outset . . .' (NC:XV). This 'systematisation' of knowledge which he had generally referred to as 'structures of experience' in *Histoire de la folie*, is described variously in *Naissance de la clinique* as 'codes of knowledge', 'the historical and concrete *a priori* of the modern medical gaze', and the 'fundamental dispositions of knowledge'.[26] Hence, in *Histoire de la folie* and *Naissance de la clinique*, Foucault is proposing a highly ordered and structured approach to history, where the emphasis is on spatial arrangements that are re-ordered in time, rather than on the ongoing and disorderly, yet highly determined, linear flow of progress and evolution.[27] This formal and structured arrangement of history is further developed in *Les Mots et les choses.*

The book opens with a quotation from a Chinese encyclopedia imagined by Borges. The startling difference between the improbable classification of animals in this text and our own system of classification prompted Foucault to reflect on the discontinuity between our modern perception of order and way of organising the world, and the views adopted by past ages (MC:7–9). Having noted this difference between the present and the past, Foucault goes on to reflect on the question of how societies organise knowledge into an identity, a coherent orderly system. What principles of order do they adopt so as to render the cosmos intelligible? In a passage from *Les Mots et les choses*, Foucault explains:

> The history of madness could be described as the history of the Other, of what is for a culture both internal and foreign and therefore to be excluded (so as to exorcise the internal danger). But this is done by shutting it away (so as to reduce its otherness). The history of the order of things could be described as the history of the Same, of what is for a culture both dispersed and related, therefore to be distinguished by kinds and collected together into identities. (MC:15, OT:XXIV)

In this book, Foucault is particularly clear in the periodisation he adopts. Hence, we read that 'archaeological' enquiry has revealed two major discontinuities in Western culture, one which ended the Renaissance and ushered in the Classical Age around 1660, and another at the beginning of the nineteenth century marking the threshold of the Modern Age (MC:71). Foucault situates this second break between the years 1795 and 1800, although he nominates 1775 and 1825 as the 'extreme points' of the change (MC:233, 13). Then at the end of the book, throwing all caution to the winds, Foucault makes explicit what he had only cryptically suggested in his previous work, namely that we are currently on the edge, indeed undergoing, another rupture.[28] There have been numerous comments on the periodisation Foucault adopts in *Les Mots et les choses*, some of them to the effect that it is 'scarcely original',[29] others contesting the choices of dates. Raymond Aron also notes the controversy over the fact that

Foucault situated an 'epistemological break' between Adam Smith and Ricardo, and not between Ricardo and Marx.[30] However, by far the most frequent criticism was that these 'ruptures' should not occur at all, and that they destroyed the necessary continuity of history. For some, the appearance of the notions of rupture and discontinuity in the work of Foucault and other contemporary thinkers was no less than a sign of the decadence of the bourgeoisie. The modern thought of rupture 'dreams of terror and the absolute' declares Jacques d'Hondt in apocalyptic tones. He continues:

> Does there exist a social class for whom as far as we can predict, there exists no future and who are in danger of having no descendants? . . . Is not the theory of radical rupture the conceptualisation of the absence of any way out, illusively projected into the past? It would then easily seduce the worried bourgeois youth.[31]

If this was not bad enough, Foucault's introduction of 'systems' of knowledge, or the *episteme*, between these points of rupture, caused further indignation and outrage.

There has been much discussion and confusion over the years about what exactly Foucault means by the episteme. Indeed the word has become so popular that the French dictionary *Le Petit Robert* now offers a definition, with an example drawn from Foucault's work. It defines the episteme as a 'comprehensive body of organised knowledge (conception of the world, sciences, philosophies . . .) characteristic of a social group, an era'. Matters are certainly not helped by Foucault himself, who over the years regularly offered different definitions of the notion, usually in line with his current preoccupations. Even in *Les Mots et les choses* he uses the word in two slightly different ways: firstly to denote the entirety of Western knowledge, complete with discontinuities, from the Renaissance to the present, and secondly to describe different configurations at different periods. Hence he writes of 'two great discontinuities *in* the Western episteme'[32] of a 'general redistribution of the episteme' (MC:356), and of *configurations* of the episteme at the time of the Renaissance and the Classical Age.[33] The second and more widely used meaning (both by Foucault and the critics) is that there are successive *epistemes* rather than different configurations of one *episteme*. Hence there is one episteme during the Renaissance, another during the Classical Age, and a third for the nineteenth century. As Foucault says: 'in a culture at a given moment, there is only ever one episteme, which defines the conditions of possibility of all knowledge, whether it is the one that is manifested in a theory, or the one silently invested in a practice.' (MC:179) For example, this episteme not only renders certain types of discourse such as natural history, the analysis of riches and general grammar both 'possible and necessary' during the Renaissance, but underlies the monetary reforms of 1575, and mercantilist measures at the same epoch (MC:179, 76). In any case, these differences are minor, because whether Foucault is writing of *configurations* of the one episteme or of successive epistemes (although he never uses the word in the plural), there can only be one configuration, or one episteme, at any given period underlying all knowledge. Foucault also sometimes refers to the 'historical *a priori*' which defines the knowledge of a given period. He describes this as 'what in a given age, carves out in experience a field of possible knowledge, defines the mode of being of objects which appear there, arms everyday perception with theoretical powers, and defines the conditions under which one can deliver a discourse on things which is recognised to be true.' (MC:171)

Let us now go on to look a little more closely at the content of these different 'configurations' as they appear in *Les Mots et les choses*. Briefly, according to Foucault, up until the end of the sixteenth century, 'resemblance played a founding role in the knowledge of Western culture' (MC:32, OT:17). In other words, the interpretation of texts and nature was guided during the Renaissance, by a perception of the *resemblances* and similarities between things, whether real or imaginary, empirical or literary. This type of approach was quite different from the organisation of knowledge by sight and demonstration, which was later to be the favoured basis of order (MC:55, 71). Hence, Renaissance thought was a thought of the Same, and the Classical thought that followed it was a thought of identity and difference. As Foucault explains, the 'fundamental network which defined the implicit but inevitable unity of knowledge' during the Classical Age in the seventeenth and eighteenth centuries, and upon which all knowledge rested, was a 'universal science of measure and order' (MC:90, 70, 71). The centre of this knowledge was the classificatory *table* (MC:89). In *Naissance de la clinique*, Foucault also notes that from

1761 to 1798 'the classificatory rule dominated both medical theory and practice: it appeared as the immanent logic of morbid forms, the principle of their interpretation and the semantic rule of their definition . . . . The primary structure offered by classificatory medicine, was the flat space of perpetual simultaneity. Table and picture (*Table et tableau*)' (NC:2, 4). The essential problem for the Classical Age, therefore, was finding names for things which, at the same time, placed them in order, a nomenclature that was at the same time a taxonomy (MC:220). This 'well-made' language, when it was eventually formulated, would designate things perfectly and scientifically, without any residue of error (MC:232). It did not matter whether the language or the system of representation (systems of exchange, systems of plant and animal classification) was arbitrary or natural, although furious debates raged over this issue at the time. The aim was to find a system of representation that was a faithful mirror of the order of the world. Thus, if the mode of organising knowledge during the Renaissance was the interpretation of resemblances, that of the Classical Age was the representation of identities and differences.

But for some mysterious reason, towards the end of the eighteenth century, the Classical dream of order began to fade (MC:222) and a system of knowledge based on the two-dimensional, timeless and uniformly visible order of the table was replaced by a system which toyed with the murky, ambiguous depths of history. A veil of violence, of obscure life-and-death struggles, desire, and the great hidden forces of history was drawn between words and things, obscuring the shape of the real.[34] Foucault becomes positively and macabrely lyrical at this point, giving one of his 'favourite authors', the Marquis de Sade, pride of place, a preference which prompted one critic to comment that 'Foucault's work has a significant place in the current cult of violence for the sake of violence.'[35]

The 'profound rupture' at the end of the eighteenth century was marked by the emergence of the positive sciences, and the appearance of literature and history. It was history that was to form the basis for the 'very tight-knit, very coherent outlines' of the modern episteme, and it is History which has now become the 'unavoidable element of our thought' and the basis of our knowledge and way of thinking.[36] It was no longer a question of elegantly arranged tables but of 'great hidden forces developed from their primitive and inaccessible nucleus, and of origin, causality and history.' (MC:263). But in recent years, argues Foucault, a change has been taking place, and we are seeing faintly on the horizon the return of 'the being of language', a configuration of knowledge in which the 'Man' of the nineteenth-century humanists will have no place.[37]

There were numerous protests about the episteme. Many critics saw it as a 'totality' which excluded history, a 'static system which does not evolve . . . . Order rules, every link is connection, every correlation, law. Nothing ever happens.'[38] Others described it as 'the theory of a system' or as 'a structure, a coherent system', or even as a 'transcendental' notion.[39] Still other commentators noted 'certain problems', such as the problem of why new epistemes occur at all and why past epistemes remain intelligible to subsequent epistemes.[40] English-speaking critics, more familiar with Kuhn's work than critics writing in French, found strong resemblances between the episteme and the paradigm.[41]

But why this succession of different systems which all last approximately one hundred and fifty years? Why does one system replace another, if each system is self-contained and need look no further than itself for explanations of phenomena? 'What event and what law do these mutations obey which mean that suddenly things are no longer perceived, described, enunciated, characterised, classed and known in the same way?' (MC:229). Foucault's answer to this is that he does not really know. It is impossible, he says, to explain why this 'erosion' from outside our systems of thought takes place (MC:64–5), and impossible to define the nature of this 'radical event' which causes an entire change of episteme in 'only a few years'. To discover why thought changed so quickly at the end of the eighteenth century would require an 'almost infinite inquiry involving nothing more or less than the very being of our modernity' (MC:232–3). For the moment, says Foucault, the 'archaeologist' of history can do no more than describe these 'enigmatic' discontinuities.[42] Thus in describing the end of Classical thought, he says that representation was

> paralleled, limited, circumscribed, duped perhaps, in any case, regulated from outside by the enormous upsurge of a freedom, a desire or a will, which was to be considered as the metaphysical underside of consciousness. Something like a will or an energy was to arise in the modern experience forming it perhaps, but indicating, in any case, that the Classical Age was over.[43]

Foucault again emphasised his refusal to 'explain' change in an article in *Esprit*, saying he was more interested in *describing* change than in the impossible task of explaining its fundamental causes.[44] 'After all,' he says, 'mathematical language since Galileo and Newton has not functioned as an explanation of nature but as a description of its processes. I don't see why non-formalised disciplines such as history should not undertake the primary tasks of description as well.'[45] This refusal of historical 'explanation' caused an outcry amongst French critics who not only condemned him for killing history and being a 'poor historian', but also accused him of being a 'desperate positivist'[46] – 'the ultimate insult' as Georges Canguilhem describes it.[47] By 'positivism', most French writers understood an anti-historical scientism, a love of facts divorced from history and humanism. Foucault was very rarely accused of being a positivist in English. In fact, on the contrary, Foucault's work was generally seen to be so theoretical that any remote relation it may once have had to 'facts' was considered to be quite negligible.[48]

Foucault further annoyed his critics by insisting that simultaneous events or structures (synchrony) were just as much a part of history as the linear succession of events through time (diachrony). Indeed, argues Foucault, 'synchronic analysis' which includes both the successive and the simultaneous, is 'much more profoundly historical' than traditional forms of history based on causality.[49] The question asked by causal types of history is, what *causes* a given change? 'Synchronic analysis' on the other hand asks a different question which is, for a change to occur, what other changes must be present at the same time? This view of history, as has often been remarked, favours metaphors of space and geometry, rather than those of evolution and development. This, as Foucault remarks, tends to reinforce a certain impression of 'anti-history' in the minds of some 'fools'.

One might digress at this point to remark that Foucault was never noted for his tolerance towards certain of his critics. His comment about the 'tiny minds' of those 'half-witted "commentators" ' who labelled him a 'structuralist' was famous (OT:xiv) and in 1971 he published an extremely witty if rather unkind article on some of the criticisms of his work. When one of the unfortunate victims of these attacks ventured to defend himself, Foucault merely redoubled his efforts on the next page of the same issue, to the greater if somewhat uneasy amusement of his readers.[50] In later years, Foucault became generally a little more tolerant towards his critics, one exception being Lawrence Stone whose erroneous interpretations of *Histoire de la folie* provoked a careful point-by-point response from Foucault.[51]

Nonetheless, Foucault found himself unable to completely ignore the efforts of various 'fools' in the late 1960s, and from the championship of 'the system' he moved to the championship of systems. He then went to a great deal of trouble to deny that the episteme was a totalising and unified system underlying the knowledge of a particular place and time; it became, instead, the description of systems and differences in the plural. In an article written in reply to a question asked by the readers of *Esprit*, Foucault says firmly that 'the *episteme* is not a sort of *grand underlying theory*, it is a space of *dispersion*, it is an open field of relations, *that can probably be described indefinitely*.' He goes on to add:

> The *episteme* is not a *general stage of reason*. It is a *complex relationship of successive shifts*. As you can see, nothing is more alien to me than the quest for a constraining, supreme and uniform form. I am not trying to detect, by means of various signs, the unifying spirit of a period, the general form of its consciousness; something like a *Weltanschauung*.[52]

He is also at pains to point out that discontinuity is not 'a monotonous and unthinkable vacuum' between events which 'we must hasten to fill . . . with the dreary plenitude of cause or the agile bottle-imp of the spirit *(ludion de l'esprit)*.'[53] He explains in *L'Archéologie du savoir* that discontinuity or 'rupture' is not the 'buttress' of his analyses, 'the limit that it signals from afar . . .'. Rather, 'rupture is the name given to transformations which have an effect on the general system of one or several discursive formations.' (AS:231, AK:176–7). Hence Foucault's final aim, in this revised version of 'discontinuity' is not to point out where the breaks occur but, having once located these 'curious phenomena', to ask what *transformation* made them possible. 'Ultimately, the analysis should not find, then revere, a break indefinitely, it should describe a transformation.'[54]

In *L'Archéologie du savoir*, there is yet another shift in definition of the episteme, and if the episteme had been one of the fundamental notions of the 'archaeological' method in *Les Mots et les choses*, it scarcely rates more than a few pages towards the end of the text.[55] Here it is defined as the group of relations between different sciences at a given period, and not as an attempt to reconstitute the underlying system which regulates all knowledge at a given time. Foucault goes on to add that 'the episteme is not an immobile figure which, appearing one day, might later disappear just as suddenly: it is an indefinitely mobile group of scansions, shifts, and coincidences which establish and dismantle themselves' (AS:250). He describes the episteme as dealing only with the natural, human or social sciences (AS:251–5), whereas in *Les Mots et les choses* the episteme in fact underlies *all* theories and practices of a period. In his earlier book, Foucault also argues that the 'classical *episteme* can be defined in its most general disposition, by the articulated system of a *mathesis*, a *taxonomia* and a *genetic analysis*' (MC:89). But in *L'Archéologie,* he denies that these three axes represent anything beyond the 'interdiscursive configuration' that could be found by comparing the three disciplines of General Grammar, the Analysis of Riches and Natural History. Thus, if other disciplines were compared, a different series of relations would appear. This definition of the episteme offered in *L'Archéologie* is now the standard one adopted by most English-speaking commentators.[56] But what in fact Foucault appears to have done in *L'Archéologie,* is simply to have given another name to the concept of the episteme as it appeared in *Les Mots et les choses*, this new name being the 'historical *a priori*', or the 'archive'.[57] The archive is defined as regulating what can and cannot be 'known' during a certain period: 'It is the general system of the formation of the transformation of statements.'[58] The historical *a priori*, or the archive, is therefore the system which rules the knowledge of a certain period and culture. It gives rise to a number of 'discursive practices', which Foucault defines in the singular as

> a body of anonymous historical rules always determined in the space and time that have defined for a given period and for a given social, economic, geographical or linguistic area, the conditions of operation of the enunciative function. (AS:153–4, AK:117).

To paraphrase this, the 'historical rules' (regularities and patterns) of a discursive practice which could, for example, have produced a text of natural history during the Renaissance, are specific to a given time, space and culture, e.g. Italy during the Renaissance. A modern biological work could not exist during the Renaissance. Not only could it not be written even if the technical knowledge were available, but if a modern text were somehow transported back to the Renaissance it would be totally rejected, as it 'obeys the rules' of a different discursive practice produced by different circumstances. In *L'Archéologie du savoir*, therefore, even if the episteme is scarcely mentioned, it emerges in a more refined form elsewhere in the text.

As for the episteme itself, Foucault was to go on to offer a number of increasingly narrow redefinitions of this notion in the course of his career. In the foreword to the English edition of *Les Mots et les choses*, published in 1970, he only mentions the episteme in relation to the Classical Age, yet almost half *Les Mots et les choses* is in fact devoted to the episteme of the nineteenth century, and the first two chapters deal with the Renaissance episteme. We also notice that Foucault is eager to deny that he had intended 'to draw up the picture of a period', and is at pains to point out that his book 'was to be not an analysis of Classicism in general, nor a search for a *Weltanschauung*, but a strictly "regional" study.' (OT:x) He does admit in a footnote, however, that he occasionally uses terms such as 'thought', or 'Classical science', but, he says, 'they refer practically always to the particular discipline under consideration.'

But in 1974 Foucault changed his mind again, conceding that perhaps he had after all originally conceived of the episteme as a system or a theoretical form, or even as 'something like the paradigm'. This was a mistake, says Foucault, because he really should have been talking about 'that central problem of power' which he had as yet 'still only very poorly isolated'.[59] In his books *Surveiller et punir* and *La Volonté de savoir*, the episteme only appears in passing and is defined as specific only to the sciences (SP:312, VS:189). In 1977 Foucault offered a final definition of the episteme, in terms of his then currently favoured notions of power, knowledge and 'truth'. Noting he was 'still caught in an impasse' when writing *Les Mots et les choses*, he says he would now consider the episteme to be a specific case of the 'apparatus' (*dispositif*), which itself consists of 'strategic' relations of power and knowledge. The episteme only deals with discourse, whereas the apparatus is both discursive and non-discursive. Further, the episteme deals exclusively with scientific or potentially scientific discourse and defines criteria of truth and falsity within science.[60] It is interesting to observe, concerning these last few statements on the episteme and power, that Foucault is no longer making a clear division between his epistemological analyses, concerning the structure and organisation of knowledge, and his ontological theses, concerning what knowledge and society is in itself, its being, its mode of existence. The two levels have merged.

But let us return briefly to *L'Archéologie du savoir*. As we have referred to the contents of this methodological work elsewhere, we need not dwell too long on it here. In this book Foucault is purporting to 'explain' the complex methodology he had practised in his earlier books, although as many commentators point out, he appears to spend more time explaining what he should have been doing, as well as exercising his formidable talent for constructing geometrical methods for analysing ideas and history. Although there have been a number of complaints from some writers that Foucault's method is far too complex to be usable, others have found that it produces novel results. Jean-Claude Bonnet, for example, uses Foucault's method to write about cooking, as it is discussed in a number of eighteenth-century texts, the *Encyclopaedia* in particular. He discusses 'culinary statements' (*énoncés culinaires*), a 'culinary field' and the relationship of 'a new collective subject' to 'alimentary practice'.[61] On the whole, however, such detailed applications are rare and most writers only borrow isolated methodological points or concentrate on theoretical points raised by the book.

L'Archéologie du savoir opens with a discussion about history and discontinuity. Of particular interest are Foucault's view of ideas as historical 'events'[62] and his treatment of documents as 'monuments'.[63] By this Foucault means that instead of using documents to reactivate a collective memory or to point to what people *really* did and said, they should be treated as monuments, traces left by the past, that the historian tries to decipher and organise into intelligible groups in relation to each other, not in relation to some reality we can never quite capture. Foucault insistently made this point throughout his career, that we can never know what *really* happened. As he says to Jacques Léonard in 1978, 'We must demystify the global instance of reality itself as a totality to be reconstituted.'[64]

During the 1970s, Foucault replaced his 'archaeology' with a 'genealogy' and in the definitions he offers of the latter, we are able to see the change from a simple method of ordering documents, to a method which is also a politics and an ontology based on the notion of the universality of power relations. Genealogy, he says, is 'the union of erudite knowledge and local memories which allows us to establish a historical knowledge of struggles and to make use of this knowledge tactically today.'[65] The principle of methodological discontinuity is just as much a part of genealogy as it is of archaeology, and is aimed at highlighting 'local, discontinuous, disqualified, illegitimate' and 'subjugated knowledges'.[66] Reinterpreting 'archaeology' in terms of 'genealogy', Foucault says:

> 'archaeology' would be the appropriate methodology of this analysis of local discursivities, and 'genealogy' would be the tactics whereby on the basis of the descriptions of these local discursivities, the subjected knowledges which were thus released would be brought into play.[67]

Foucault put this genealogical method into practice in *Surveiller et punir* and *La Volonté de savoir*. In these two books Foucault returns to his favourite period, the Classical Age, but this time with slightly different dates of 'rupture'. Hence in *Surveiller et punir*, Foucault fixes 1840, the date of the official opening of the prison of Mettray as the date when the new 'carceral system' was finally formed and the 'disciplinary' society came into its own (SP:300). In *La Volonté de savoir*, although dates are scarcely mentioned, except for some general references to centuries, there is a brief chapter on periodisation. Here Foucault argues that modern attitudes towards sexuality originated in the Middle Ages with the Lateran Council. An important change in attitudes occurred during the Reformation, and later the birth of an 'entirely new technology of sex' was heralded by the publication of *The Psychopathia sexualis* by Heinrich Kaan in 1846 (VS:154). However, in Volumes 2 and 3 of the *History of Sexuality* which appeared in 1984, Foucault changes period entirely and turns his attention to the 'problemisation' of sexuality in Ancient Greek texts of the fourth century BC, and in Greek and Latin texts of the first two centuries AD. In an interview, Foucault explains this change, saying that when he wrote *La Volonté de savoir*, it had been his intention to begin his history in the sixteenth century and continue through to the nineteenth century. In the course of his research, however, he had found himself becoming more and more interested in the question of why sex was perceived as a moral experience in Western Society. To examine this problem he felt obliged to search far back into the beginnings of Western thought and to return to the Ancient Greeks.[68] But at this point, let us leave the historiographical discussion of order, discontinuity and the 'interior limits' in Foucault's work and turn to the 'exterior limits'.

4

In Search of the Limit

If Foucault insists that all is discontinuous, there is a secret continuity in this discontinuity, which is man's confrontation or dialogue with this very discontinuity, his confrontation with the limits, his destiny and the Other. Several times Foucault thought he had discovered that absolute point in history where the Same meets the Other, but each time he changed his mind, finally concluding that all we can do is adopt a *'limit-attitude'* in everything we do or know.[1]

Perhaps the most obvious way of looking at limits in history, is to look at the margins of our society, marginal groups and marginal experiences. As Foucault says: 'It seemed to me interesting to try to understand our society and civilisation in terms of its system of exclusion, of rejection . . . its limits.'[2] One can examine what makes a society, a system of knowledge or a system of beliefs work, by describing what it excludes, what it marginalises. The French historian of prisons, Michelle Perrot, notes the growth of

a history increasingly haunted by the great nocturnal side of society: illness, madness, delinquency, an exogamic part of ourselves, a broken mirror that reflects our image, an experience of the limit (Michel Foucault) where we can read a culture differently, but just as well as in the thick clusters of majority facts.[3]

Foucault begins by examining the present in order to locate where marginal groups or experiences lie. He then looks back through history to the point where this group or experience does not represent a margin or a limit, or at least to a point where it represents a very different kind of limit. Invariably this point lies in the Classical Age, the period when 'Rationalism' began to come into its own. Foucault only departs from this periodisation in his last work, after discovering that the historical parameters of certain categories of our thought went back further than he had expected. The next step is then to examine how the limit or problem gradually took the form it takes in our modern society. In each of his books the problem or limit Foucault examines is one that he thinks is absolutely essential for the understanding of our relation to the Other and hence our modernity. It is from this philosophical point of view that Foucault's subject matter will be considered here, and not from the standpoint of its historical, sociological or political exactitude. The latter kind of analysis has already been undertaken (and indeed is still being undertaken) at great length by a vast array of specialists in a variety of languages and there is no need to attempt to reproduce their findings here, interesting though they are.

But Foucault's reasons for studying the margins of history, those grey problem-areas at the edge of our society, areas which in recent years have become the focus of so much attention, are not simply philosophical or ethical: they are also personal. In an infrequent autobiographical confession, he says somewhat bitterly: 'I was never really integrated into the Communist Party because I was a homosexual . . . . This problem, say, of locking up the mentally ill – did historians bring it up? No, it was necessary for a 'twisted' person to have the bad idea of introducing questions at once personal and political.'[4] Emmanuel Le Roy Ladurie supports Foucault's perception of his marginality in the Communist Party in a description of the 'softer margins' of a cell to which he belonged in the late 1940s and early 1950s. He mentions that Foucault was far less involved than others in the excesses of Stalinism. He adds that the cell treated this nonconformity with indulgence as it knew he was absorbed in his research on madness.[5] Foucault also mentions that he first undertook a 'genealogy' of psychiatry because he had had some experience of the psychiatric hospital (St Anne's in Paris) and had sensed there, 'combats, lines of force, points of confrontation, tensions'.[6] He later admitted that he felt disturbed by his experience working there, as he felt 'very close to, and not very different from, the inmates'.[7] In a different context, Foucault remarks on a sudden awareness of his own methodological 'eccentricity' and 'strangeness' and how far his work 'deviated from the most accepted norms'.[8]

But if Foucault was one of the pioneers of the history of the margins, he was by no means alone in this interest. Indeed, by the end of the 1960s, interest in and studies of marginal groups had become extremely fashionable. The French dictionary *Le Petit*

Robert notes that the French word 'marginal', a person living at the edges of society, came into popular usage around 1968. But what exactly are these margins? Given that there is a 'mainstream' of historical thinking and action, there are certain fringes who exist at the 'limits' of society and do not fully participate in the general activities, behaviour, beliefs or ideas that prevail at the time. It must be understood, however, that these social margins are not entirely synonymous with the limits. Foucault spells this out clearly in an article titled 'Les Déviations religieuses et le savoir médical'. Each society, at any given period, practises certain exclusions, or posits certain limits which invite transgression, thereby creating a 'system of the transgressive'. This system is not entirely defined by the existence of criminals, revolutionaries, mad people, or other abnormal individuals or groups, or even the sum of all these deviant forms.[9] What these elements do indicate is where the limits lie, where the values and the very being of a society are called into question. One must also be careful not to equate the limits with the division drawn between the 'normal and the pathological'. The concept of the normal and the pathological is one that only arose in the eighteenth century, as Georges Canguilhem points out in his classic work.[10] As a consequence, it is more useful to examine why this division took place rather than positing the division itself as a foundation.

Margins themselves can be considered at two distinct levels, as self-contained historical existences or creations, which is the approach Foucault takes in *Surveiller et punir*, or as the markers of the ontological and epistemological boundaries of a culture. Foucault considers both levels in *Histoire de la folie*. As such, the margins have a rather ambiguous significance in the political or moral arena. As elements that have been unjustly excluded and badly treated by the mainstream of society, their deplorable situation needs to be recognised and rectified. Speaking about Foucault and the GIP, Claude Mauriac remarks

> What strikes me in his, in our, activity (including our dealings with migrant workers) is that we believe, or pretend to believe, in the possibility of a just society – no, much more than that – in a human condition delivered finally, (*à la limite*) from suffering, death and evil.[11]

At the same time the margins represent an admirable rebellion against a society that deserves to be overthrown, and their misery is a heroic signpost. Reintegration would destroy the value of their transgressive gesture. But, if on the other hand, one argues that society has always practised exclusions, and will always do so, that no sooner do we reintegrate one group, than another is excluded, then we are provided with a neverending supply of limits and transgressive groups on which to practise our political indignation. As Foucault says in relation to madness: 'Everything we experience today as limits, or strangeness, or unbearable will [one day] be reunited with the serenity of the positive. And what points to this Exterior for us at the moment, might one day point at us.'[12]

Nowhere is Foucault's search for the limit, then for a principle of order, more succinctly evident than in the career of a certain number of literary and artistic figures throughout his work. In each of his books one finds certain writers or artists associated with crucial turning-points or experiences. Hence in *Histoire de la folie*, Cervantes' Don Quixote embodies, in the company of Shakespeare, the last remnants of the Renaissance perception of the 'tragedy of madness', before 'a critical and moral view' of Unreason comes into its own (HF:49–50). Likewise the works of Sade coincide with the end of the Classical Age, as they stretch to the limits and ultimately destroy the Classical conception of madness (HF:551–3). The works of Nietzsche, Artaud, Van Gogh and Hölderlin all signal the bankruptcy of the nineteenth-century conception of mental illness, and indicate a new and altered re-emergence of the 'tragedy of madness' (HF:555–7). In *Naissance de la clinique*, the 'new medical spirit' of Bichat and the works of Sade appear illuminated 'in the same light of day' at the end of the eighteenth century (NC:198, BC:195), and the medical experience and the experience of individuality are related to a lyrical experience expressed in the works of Hölderlin and Nietzsche.[13] In *Les Mots et les choses*, Don Quixote signals the limits of the organisation of knowledge that characterises the Renaissance (MC:61–3), and Sade, by taking classification to its extreme limits, destroys the Classical system of knowledge (MC:222–4, 255). In this book, Nietzsche, Roussel, Artaud and Mallarmé all point this time to the 'being of language'. In *L'Archéologie du savoir*, Nietzsche and Artaud's works are called upon as examples in a chapter on the unities of discourse and Nietzsche is described as a practitioner of an anti-transcendental history.[14] And In *L'Ordre du discours*, Nietzsche, Artaud and Bataille are once again called forward as 'lofty signs' of contestation, but this time they contest the 'will to truth' which imposes prohibitions and seeks to exclude and define madness, and impose a 'true' discourse (OD:22–3). Later Nietzsche is linked with Foucault's ideas on power:

> It was Nietzsche who specified the power relation as the general focus, shall we say, of philosophical discourse . . . Nietzsche is the philosopher of power, but he managed to conceptualise power without confining himself within a political theory to do so.[15]

And finally Sade becomes the master of the secular confession of sex in *La Volonté de savoir* (VS:30–31).

A large part of the following discussion will be devoted to *Histoire de la folie*. There are a number of reasons for this: not only is *Histoire de la folie* Foucault's most extended application of a thought of the limit, but it forms in many ways the blueprint for the rest of his work, introducing many themes that he constantly returns to.[16] Foucault himself, recognising this, remarked in 1982 that 'a researcher, finds perhaps only one or two new things in his lifetime, generally at the beginning.'[17] These recurring themes include the birth of the individual, humanism, Man as both the subject and object of his own knowledge in the modern episteme, a constant anti-historicism, and an interest in describing discontinuities or transformation in history. It is interesting to note that Foucault was far more vigorous in the defence of this book than in the defence of any of his others, indicating perhaps, that it occupied a special place for him amongst his other work.[18]

It is a book which Michel Serres describes as containing a 'secret vision', expressing in its 'geometry'

> the pathetic language of people who undergo the ultimate torture of being cut off, who undergo the disgrace of exile, of quarantine, of ostracism and excommunication. Here is the book of all solitudes. And in the middle of all this suffering, appears the attraction of the limits, the vertigo of proximity, the hope of the renewal of ties, the house at dawn.[19]

Serres is describing a poetic vision of the limits of our society and experience. It is a kind of vision which emerges more clearly perhaps in *Histoire de la folie* than in Foucault's other work. It is an aspect of Foucault's work which is now usually passed over in silence by much contemporary English-language criticism; and generally, in discussions of *Histoire de la folie*, attention is drawn to its analyses of aspects of social and institutional history.[20] In French, however, there appears to have been a revival of interest in recent years in some of the poetic aspects of this book and some of Foucault's other early work.

These theses put forward by Foucault in *Histoire de la folie* are by now well-known. A voluble and free madness was silenced in the Classical Age, both philosophically by Reason, and institutionally by the 'Great Confinement', which locked away a section of the population to create a category of deviants or 'asocials' in society. Then at the end of the eighteenth century and the beginning of the nineteenth century, madmen were 'liberated' from their chains by Tuke and Pinel only in order to be bound by a more sinister and more effective moral enslavement. But the book ends on a note of triumph, declaring the return of the tragedy of madness in literature to reveal the truth of man and his confrontation with his own destiny.

In the preface to the first edition of *Histoire de la folie*, Foucault asks:

> What is this confrontation underlying the language of reason? Where can we be led by an interrogation which does not follow reason in its horizontal course, but seeks to retrace in time that constant verticality which confronts European culture with that which is not, which measures it against the range of its own derangement? (FD:10)

In one form or another, it is this search of 'that constant verticality which confronts European culture', or limit, that underlies all of Foucault's work even if it is only in the negation of that limit. Foucault begins by going back to that point in history where reason and madness were an undifferentiated experience, a point when they did not stand starkly opposite each other in a mutually exclusive confrontation (FD:7). From there, it is a matter of tracing the history of an exclusion and the creation of an object, and of writing: 'A history of *limits* – of those obscure gestures, forgotten as soon as they are accomplished, by means of which a culture rejects something and makes it the Exterior.'[21] It is a matter of describing the appearance of a 'great immobile structure . . . the point where history is immobilised in the tragic which both founds and challenges it' (FD:11).

Foucault's book is a history of man's relation to the Truth and his own truth, through that point of contact with the Other, a madness which today in literature 'hangs over history forever' and 'masters and leads the world's time' (HF:556, M&C:287–8). Madness, in *Histoire de la folie*, is not a 'thing', it is a function or a structure, our point of communication *par excellence* with the Other, that point where history escapes from itself towards the 'unthought' that founds it, and reveals the truth to those prepared to listen. Madness rests on that limit between the Same and the Other, revealing a cryptic glimpse of the truth of both. Although he is far more cautious in *Histoire de la folie*, in an earlier work, *Maladie mentale et psychologie*, Foucault argues this is true for all societies:

> a society expresses itself positively in the mental illness displayed by its members, whether it places them at the centre of its religious life, as is often the case amongst the primitive peoples, or whether it seeks to expatriate them by situating them outside social life, as does our culture.[22]

It is interesting to note, incidentally, that although *Maladie mentale et psychologie* covers similar subject matter to *Histoire de la folie*, there are some differences in approach. For example, in the earlier book, Foucault makes frequent references to non-Western and primitive societies, references that are entirely absent from *Histoire de la folie* (if one excludes the Ancient Greeks). Nonetheless, he does make general references in *Histoire de la folie* to 'fundamental experiences in which a society risks its own values' (HF:192).

Foucault begins his long history of madness with the description of the gradual disappearance of leprosy from the Western world, which left the legacy of a certain form of social exclusion which was first to be inherited by venereal diseases, then two centuries later by madness. The social exclusion of the leper opened another form of spiritual communion, however, and his misery, his share in the passion of Christ, would be rewarded by eternal life in heaven. But even this form of spiritual reintegration would later be denied to the madman. At the end of the Middle

Ages, says Foucault, there was a sudden anxiety about the madman, an anxiety that was embodied in a new symbol: the Ship of Fools. It has been suggested by several critics that Foucault fails to distinguish between literary and real historical figures, granting the Ship of Fools a concrete existence it never actually had.[23] But Foucault argues that the Ship of Fools was by no means purely a literary and artistic invention; it did in fact have a real counterpart. Madmen who had been chased from towns led a wandering existence on boats, their only prison being the threshold of the city; their exclusion from society was therefore a very literal one. Until almost to the end of the fifteenth century, the theme of death had reigned supreme in man's thought about his existence and destiny. But gradually madness had become the living presence of death, the invasion of a previously remote and final nothingness into the everyday experience of existence. If before, it had been an unawareness of death and the end of the world that had been the madness that had threatened man, now it was the existence of madness itself, the living death, the empty head and insane skull-like grimace that presaged the end of the world.[24] Until the end of the seventeenth century, madness was a voice crying in the wilderness, the sign of another world, and of man's mortality, a sign of the end of the world. It pointed to man's limits, his finitude and weakness in the face of death and before God, a salutary, but not always reassuring reminder to men of their place in the cosmos. This 'tragic madness of the world' was most evident in painting during the Renaissance: Bosch, Brueghel, Dürer, Bouts all expressed it in their work (HF:38). It was an experience of madness which revealed the fragility of man and the world (HF:117). For Foucault, this tragic experience represents the focal point (at once real and imaginary) from where men have been able to reflect upon themselves and the cosmos. But one might pause at this point to ask what he means when he describes this experience as 'tragic'. *Le Petit Robert* is helpful here in defining 'tragic' as 'evoking a situation in which man becomes painfully aware of a destiny as a fatality which overshadows his life, his nature or his very condition.'[25] This was the vision of the Renaissance and the Middle Ages, for whom unreason was a spiritual experience, a certain way of experiencing the world as a whole, 'a certain tonality behind all perception.'[26]

It is worth considering here some definitions of 'spirituality', that Foucault proposed at a time when he admitted he was returning to some of the themes he analysed in *Histoire de la folie*. In a lecture delivered in 1982, he defines spirituality as the search of the subject to transform experience and its very being as a subject. He explains that spirituality has possessed three characteristics in the West. Firstly, the subject is obliged to modify itself, become other than itself in order to find the truth, secondly, truth can only be obtained through the conversion of the subject, thirdly, the truth then 'returns' to transfigure the subject. Cartesian rationalism, however, tried to change this relation, arguing that the truth could be reached by the mere accumulation of knowledge: there was no need to work on oneself, to be ascetic in order to be ready to know the truth. For Descartes, says Foucault, *any* subject which could see what was evident could accede to the truth and acquire knowledge of the world. An immoral subject could therefore have access to the truth, something quite unthinkable before Descartes. But, as Foucault argues, knowledge of this type cannot give access of itself to the truth after all, and spirituality has survived.[27] From its very origin, Classical Reason was an ethical choice. A certain deliberate and historical decision was made which identified Truth and Reason. Man's truth came to lie in the exercise of Reason and to choose something *other* than Reason was to succumb to error, illusion, non-being and later alienation. The career of the 'tragedy of madness' is seen very much in these terms in *Histoire de la folie*. It is an experience that the Classical Age did its best to stifle in its efforts to eliminate a certain form of spiritual confrontation. Even by the end of the Renaissance, argues Foucault, madness was beginning to lose its tragic powers, and if its tragedy still appeared in the works of Shakespeare and Cervantes, it was because 'beyond time they renewed a link with a meaning that was disappearing, a meaning whose continuity would no longer be pursued except in the shadows of the night' (HF:49). It was a continuity that was to re-emerge later in literature, in the writings of Nietzsche, Artaud and Nerval, an experience which although it 'received scarcely any other formulation except lyrical', was no less vigorous in 'its power of contestation' (HF:188). Foucault is careful to point out that he is not talking about a 'thing', or an eternal historical object, but about a certain relation of man to himself and to the Other, a relation where man is himself radically in question. Much later in quite a different context, Foucault continued to express his regret at the loss of a certain 'spiritual dimension', present during the

Renaissance. This time it concerned 'a political spirituality' which he believed had re-emerged during the revolution in Iran. 'I can already hear some French people laughing but I know they are wrong', he concluded defensively.[28] Foucault never quite managed to live down this error of political judgement, as a number of the obituaries which appeared in French newspapers indicated. But in fact he is more interested in the spiritual transformation of subjectivity than politics in this interview.[29]

At the beginning of the Classical Age, the possibility of a madness at the heart of reason was excluded by Descartes, who declared that although an individual person might well be mad, *thought*, 'as the exercise of the supremacy of a subject which does its best to perceive the true, cannot be insane.'[30] What Descartes does in fact is banish the possibility of a dialogue with the Other. Truth can only be found within the limits of the Same – reason. Foucault remarks: 'Classical reason does not meet ethics at the end of its truth, in the form of moral laws. Ethics as a choice against unreason is present from the origin of all concerted thought . . . . In the Classical Age, reason is born in the ethical space' (HF:157). Madness was no longer that mysterious figure at the absolute limits of the world and man (HF:53, 453). It certainly remained a sign of the limits, but it was a sign of the limits of a materialistic reason and a bourgeois order (HF:85). Foucault notes an 'extreme rent in the profound life' of the eighteenth century which meant that madness and reason were totally separated from one another. There was no possibility that a contact between these 'two forms of questioning . . . would set off the spark of a fundamental and irremediable question' (HF:190). As a result, reason was no longer tied to madness in a debate involving the 'profound finality' of the destiny of man and his place in the cosmos (HF:198). The language of madness became instead the language of the non-being of error, fantasy and illusion, and the loss of truth (HF:191). It became no more than the 'public shame of reason' and, Foucault continues, we have to wait two centuries until Nietzsche and Dostoievsky for 'Christ to find once again the glory of his madness', and for the scandal of unreason to acquire once again 'a power of demonstration' (HF:171). At the same time, the mad people who had roamed outside the limits of towns and civilisation were enclosed in institutions.

Within a few years of the establishment of the Hôpital Général in 1656, 1 per cent of the population of Paris had been enclosed within its walls (HF:66). What Foucault describes as the 'Great Confinement' was a phenomenon that occurred all over Europe. In a society where sloth was seen as the worst sin, all those unable or unwilling to work, as well as other 'immoral' or 'unreasonable' people were enclosed. 'Unreasonable' people included such people as homosexuals and debauchees, blasphemers and attempted suicides, prodigal sons and finally that most extreme incarnation of 'unreason' – madmen. In being associated with these other forms of unreason, as well as being condemned for their inactivity in this work-orientated society, those who were mad acquired an aura of guilt.

If the Renaissance had seen unreason as part of the world, in the Classical Age it began to be measured as a certain distance from the norm (HF:117). Foucault notes: 'The normal man is a creation and if he must be situated, it is not in a natural space but in a system which identifies the *socius* within the subject of law' (HF:147). What this means, is that if traditionally, the law had argued that a mad person was not responsible for his actions in law, in the Classical Age a practice began of automatically depriving a subject who had been interned, excluded from society, of legal rights. The inverse also applied, and if the law defined a person as being insane, and therefore legally incapable, he had to be interned. In the Middle Ages and the Renaissance, madness threatened the very centre of being, but for Classical man this interiority no longer existed, it was *other* people who were mad. Madness was *other*, different and foreign to the great mass of ordinary men, and as such no longer a threat (HF:199).

But what Foucault describes as the 'absence of madness' was to give birth to something else, the science of mental illness: psychology (HF:198). This change at the end of the eighteenth century was marked by the activities of Pinel and Tuke who liberated madmen from their chains. Foucault's thesis that this constituted anything but a liberation is a well-known one. As he says somewhat incautiously in *Maladie mentale et psychologie*: 'All this psychology would not exist, without the *moralising sadism* in which the "philanthropy" of the nineteenth century enclosed [madness] under the hypocritical species of a "liberation"' (MMP:87). If madness was distinguished from the forms of unreason that surrounded it, and reinstated in its own separate identity, it was not due to philanthropy or the progress of truth, but to all that slow work which took place in the most subterranean structures of experience: not where madness is illness, but where it is tied to the life of men and their history, where they concretely experience their misery and from where the phantasms of unreason come to haunt them. (HF:439)

In the Classical Age, there had been the remains of a dialogue between madness and reason, a dialogue which was to be found in the action that locked madness away (HF:517), and in that moment of freedom when the madman chose to abandon his freedom as a rational being and become the slave of his madness (HF:532). But even this skimpy dialogue and freedom were removed at the beginning of the nineteenth century, and 'reason ceased to be for man an ethic and became a nature' (MMP:103). Madness became the paradoxical truth of man, revealing the limits of his rational nature. But it was a truth acquired only at the cost of the annihilation of madness. For Tuke, internment was aimed at reducing madness to its truth, a truth which was madness minus society and everything unnatural, which meant that the truth of madness was the essential core of man, in other words Nature, Truth and Morality (HF:495). If in the Classical Age, the madman was a stranger in relation to being, the man of nothingness and illusion, the transgressor of the laws of the world, in the nineteenth century he was a stranger to himself, alienated, the transgressor of his own essence (HF:535, 400). Madness was degeneration, the price of progress and unruly passions, the final truth of man. It was also the triumph of the organic reality of man, the madman being totally enslaved by his bodily chemistry.

The madman of the modern age is, therefore, 'other' than himself, but by being 'other' than himself he paradoxically reveals his own nature or truth. The madman thus becomes once again that symbolic figure standing at the limits, the truth of man, and the negation of that truth. 'The man of our days only finds his truth in the enigma of the madman', remarks Foucault, madness being the purest and most extreme form of deviation from the norm of 'human nature' (HF:548). Foucault goes on to say that it was through the madman, that man first became the subject and the object of his own knowledge. Indeed, madness was both pure subjectivity – the experience of madness being so singular as to be inaccessible to others – and pure objectivity – an object of science, the measure of the boundaries of our human nature. Nineteenth-century man substituted the psychological relation with himself for 'his relation to truth, alienating it in that fundamental postulate that he is himself the truth of the truth' (MMP:103).

The process of 'objectivisation' began perhaps with the practice of Cabanis in the 1790s of keeping an 'asylum journal', which recorded the ongoing state of the interned lunatics. As a result, says Foucault, madness acquired a place in time, its past became part of its truth; but at the same time it became an abstract discursive object. It was no longer non-being, it had become the object of knowledge. Just as Foucault was later to talk about the 'creation of the criminal' and of the individual, so we find in *Histoire de la folie* a discussion of the 'creation of the madman' and the role this process played in the creation of the 'individual', as the object of science and social control. But the creation of a 'mental illness', that was nothing more than the buttress of a new anthropologisation of knowledge, its participation in the ascendancy of humanism, still did not succeed in stifling the secret tragedy of madness. It simply reappeared elsewhere, this time in language and literature rather than in 'the figures of the world' where it had reigned supreme during the Renaissance.[31] According to Foucault, madness and dreams expressed the same reality for the thinkers and poets of the early nineteenth century. They both revealed

> a truth of man, which is at once very archaic and very close, very silent and very menacing: a truth which lies beneath all truth, closest to the birth of subjectivity, most widespread at the level of things, a truth which is the most profound retreat of the individuality of man, and the inchoative form of the cosmos. (HF:536)

This secret continuity of the tragedy of madness is to be found in Diderot's *Le Neveu de Rameau*, in the work of Raymond Roussel, Artaud, Nerval and Hölderlin, Van Gogh and Nietzsche, but all too often only at the cost of the madness of the author himself.

Today (or at least in 1961), Foucault argues, we see two different configurations, madness and mental illness, which after becoming confused in the seventeenth century are now 'coming apart before our very eyes, or rather in our language.'[32] But in spite of this return of the tragedy of madness, the writer's madness annihilates his art, even if this madness is its very foundation. Once he crosses the boundary from sanity to madness his writing becomes nothing more than a psychological document, the product of mental illness; conversely, the work of art excludes madness.[33] Language and writing, acts of rational and free creation, cannot be produced from within a madness which is the negation of both reason and freedom, although a work may well present a kind of structural analogy with madness.[34] The work of art can only resemble or produce an *effect* of madness, it is not the language of madness itself. Nonetheless, argues Foucault, culture measures as its highest and most advanced points those works, which at their limits, disappear into madness, tracing 'a contour against the void'.[35] 'Through the madness that suspends it, the work of art opens an emptiness, a pause of silence, a question without a reply, it provokes an irrevocable rupture where the world is obliged to question itself.' (HF:556). So madness triumphs after all in Foucault's account. Western culture, believing that it had managed to neutralise and define madness in the science of psychology, in fact finds itself measured by the extremes of works such as those by Artaud, Nietzsche and Van Gogh. And as it is not sure what madness really is, it cannot even be sure what this measurement means (HF:557).

A number of critics, however, were not overly impressed by this equation of madness with a certain spiritual quest, the point of communication, of dialogue between the Same and the Other. One of the rare English-speaking critics to note that for Foucault madness was 'a fundamental and ultimate category of human existence', complains that Foucault 'heartlessly' forgets that 'madmen are human beings and not metaphors for poetry', a strange remark if one considers that poetry is usually closely concerned with human experience.[36] In a similar vein another critic remarks dryly: 'It is not clear how witches, burnt at the stake, would feel about Foucault's thesis.'[37] A French psychiatrist writing a few years later, is likewise shocked by Foucault's 'poetical' views, but for different reasons. His remarks are worth quoting in full:

Thus we are well advised of the crime that Psychiatry is going to commit by seizing an object that does not belong to it: the marvellous Unreason. We are going to be told that Psychiatry has confiscated poetry!!! Psychiatry is not going to be established, legalised, or mobilised except in the service of and to uphold the pious thought of right-thinking people. It is the fear and trembling of Reason which causes Unreason, the divine Madness to be locked up! Psychiatry . . . [is] like the Police in the service of the Goddess Reason incarnated in the repressive structures of the Law.[38]

At a later date the historian Lawrence Stone and Dr Gerald Weissman of the New York University School of Medicine take the extreme view that

Foucault's pessimistic evaluation of lunatic asylums [was] a factor in the recent discharge of thousands of helpless psychiatric patients onto the pitiless streets of New York . . . these tragic cases are . . . a remote byproduct of Foucault's negative evaluation of the philanthropic dream of Pinel.[39]

But Foucault's enthusiasm for madness as the most extreme limit of our culture throughout history, its moment of truth, the indicator of its being, was to have a rather shortlived career. In an article written in 1962, Foucault had already shifted his position and appeared to have some difficulty in deciding which limit was more important: death, madness or language? Death and language are both to be found as limits in *Histoire de la folie*, but they are subordinated to madness. Certainly 'the fatality of death, the non-written law of the fraternity of men', would appear to be a rather important limit, but on the other hand, madness is that 'emptiness', that 'void', towards which poetry and literature are drawn to find their justification and annihiliation.[40] Yet language certainly seems to possess a 'sovereign structure', as it speaks and emerges from that ontological area that God has vacated. For the moment, however, death seems to win out, and it is the limit that Foucault proposes both in *Raymond Roussel* and *Naissance de la clinique*, although all three 'limits' are present in both books – particularly in *Raymond Roussel*. Indeed, François Wahl reports that Foucault regarded these two works as 'the same book'.[41]

Raymond Roussel will not be discussed in any detail here. As has been remarked before, it is the least-known of Foucault's books and for good reason. Roussel's work remains relatively unknown, in spite of the enthusiasm of a number of *nouveaux romanciers*, probably because it is both extremely cryptic and very tedious. If anything, Foucault's book is even more cryptic, although his style is more elegant than Roussel's. As one critic remarks: 'The amount of factual information would go on a postcard, and even this is not directly offered either as information or as factual basis for an argument, but has to be picked up almost by deduction.'[42] *Raymond Roussel* is the poem of Foucault's own philosophical obsessions about death, language, madness and the Same and the Other: he is describing his own work as much as Roussel's. To list only some of the words and images that constantly recur in its pages: limits, mirrors, repetition, death, the Same, silence, immobility, difference, visibility, absence, void – all images that are found again and again in Foucault's work. This book is a poetical rendition of the obscure drama played out by language and death at the limit of our knowledge. It alludes to the problems of the Same and the Other, form and substance, appearance and reality, the relation of words and things and a language without a subject. Its pages are riddled with tortuously complex plays on words: descriptions and extensions of Roussel's own work. Foucault, in describing Roussel's language, could very well be describing his own work:

> It is not built on the certainty that there is a secret, one only, and one that remains sedately silent. It glitters with a shining uncertainty which is all surface, and covers a kind of central blank: impossible to decide if there is one secret or none, or several and what they are.[43]

This can also be compared with another remark on Roussel which could equally well apply to Foucault's 'archaeological' aims in writing history:

> language is placed flat on things: it skims meticulously over their details, but without perspective or proportion. Everything is seen from afar, but with such a piercing, so supreme and so neutral a gaze, that even the invisible surfaces in one immobile polished light.[44]

The only key to the secret of Roussel's work exists at the threshold of death, but it is a key which at the same time destroys the possibility of ever knowing that secret. The 'key' is a posthumous work, *Comment j'ai écrit certains de mes livres*, which explains the procedures that he had used in writing his book. But in actual fact, if this book reveals the mechanisms with which Roussel constructed his complex plays on words, it does not explain the end-result. Foucault argues that even the physical circumstances of Roussel's death (his body was found before a locked door which was normally left unlocked) reflect the paradoxical relations of death, a secret, and a key in his work.[45]

Death is also a key, a threshold in *Naissance de la clinique*. There are many close similarities in structure between this book and *Histoire de la folie*, but already Foucault's thought has become more complex. As he explains in *Les Mots et les choses*, illness is an experience that can be analysed in terms of both the Same and the Other. Illness is disorder, a dangerous 'otherness' within the human body at the very heart of life, but it is also a natural phenomenon with certain classifiable regularities. According to this interpretation therefore, madness can be classified as the Other, and illness as both the Same and the Other (MC:15, OT:xiv). Foucault, in fact, sums up his book in its often-quoted first sentence: 'In this book it is a question of space, language and death, it is a question of perception' (NC:v). Just as in his previous book, the origins of the human sciences, anthropology, and the rise of the notion of the individual, the truth of man and his world are all inextricably linked to madness, so all these things become inextricably linked to death and its vehicle medicine, in *Naissance de la clinique*. At the end of the eighteenth century, Foucault says, 'death left its old tragic heaven and became the lyrical core of man: his invisible truth, his visible secret' (NC:176). The tragedy of death has now replaced the 'tragedy' of madness, as well as its privileged position at the 'lyrical core of man', and as the 'truth of man' in Foucault's work.[46] Indeed such is Foucault's enthusiasm for medicine that one critic remarks: 'Surely it is one of the few works written in the twentieth century to recognise medicine as central to *all* the human sciences. Its author, a scientific poet to the degree that he sings paean after paean to medicine, has erected this monument to Apollo, the god of medicine.'[47]

However, death does not make its appearance until towards the end of *Naissance de la clinique* when Bichat, breaking with an old form of medical knowledge, based his new science of the functioning of organs and illness on the dissection of corpses, on the introduction of death into life. He showed that rather than illness possessing its own vitalistic essence, of which death was only the possible final term, illness was the appearance of death in life, death becoming a gradual process, as different organs or muscles died during an illness. This introduction of death into knowledge, says Foucault, reactivated a theme which had remained dormant since the Renaissance. As we have seen, Foucault refers to this presence of death in the Renaissance view of the world in *Histoire de la folie*, but it is to link it with madness, a madness which in its 'medicalisation' at the beginning of the nineteenth century was the first instance of the creation of the modern individual. But in *Naissance de la clinique*, it is *death* that is important. Bichat becomes 'the contemporary of the man who introduced abruptly, in the most discursive of languages, eroticism and its inevitable peak, death'. Sade has now become a figure of death, rather than madness, and language no longer the vehicle of madness, becomes the vehicle of that most extreme figure, death. Death was a major theme in the nineteenth century, explains Foucault, summoning up the names of Goya, Géricault, Delacroix and Baudelaire to support his argument. 'The knowledge of life is only given to a cruel, reductive and *already* infernal knowledge which only wants it dead' (NC:175, BC:171). This nineteenth-century perception of death, however, was quite different from the Renaissance perception, which regarded death as the great leveller; for the nineteenth century, on the contrary, death created individuality. An approach to the examination of life and vital functions based on their 'death', meant that death became an analytical tool for creating different individual categories.

Foucault goes on to argue that Western man could only construct himself as an object of science, as an individual, in reference to death, to his own destruction. At this point Foucault pauses to make a slight shift in his view of madness: 'from the experience of Unreason were born all psychologies and the very possibility of psychology, from the placement of death in medical thought was born a science which professes to be the science of the individual' (NC:201). The whole experience of individuality in modern culture now becomes linked to death instead of madness. Death imposes a division and a finitude linking the universality of language to the 'precarious and irreplacable form of the individual' (NC:201). Medicine as a science of the individual who is both the subject and the object of his own knowledge is of paramount importance in the constitution of the human sciences. Although modern medicine reminds man of the limit of death, it also speaks of man's efforts to achieve technical and scientific control over that limit. The medical experience is therefore closely related to a 'lyrical experience' that appears in the works of Hölderlin, Rilke and Nietzsche.

It is surprising that the figures of knowledge and language obey the same profound law and that the irruption of finitude should dominate, in the same way, this relation of man to death, which, in the first case authorises a scientific discourse in a rational form, and in the second, opens up the source of a language which unfolds indefinitely in the emptiness left by the absence of gods? (NC:202, BC:198)

This idea of death is a very abstract one, and goes beyond the simple medical fact in Foucault's work. In an article on language and death published in the same year, he remarks: 'It is quite possible the approach of death . . . hollows in being and the present, that emptiness from which, and towards which, we speak',[48] whereas before, it had been madness that was the void which both founded and annihilated language. Few writers, however, in either French or English, were willing to take up madness and death as the ultimate limits of our culture and its moment of truth, with the same enthusiasm as Foucault. Perhaps they felt that these limits were either too specific, or too negative to be useful. On the other hand, considerably more attention was paid to what was to be his next enthusiasm: language. If quite an extended discussion on language is to be found in both *Histoire de la folie* and *Naissance de la clinique*, it remains simply the contemporary vehicle, mainly in its literary form, for the expression of either the tragedy of madness or the tragedy of death. But before Foucault arrived at language, there were some minor detours en route.

In mid-1963, Foucault ventured an experimental probe into the domain of sexuality as limit, arguing that because of universal prohibitions (incest), sexuality marks the limit of the law, and the transgression of this limit becomes a 'philosophy of eroticism'.[49] Once again this 'philosophy' appears in language, and here Foucault comments very clearly on why he believes language or literature to be so important for contemporary man:

language has ceased being the moment when the infinite is unveiled. It is in its density that we now experience finitude and

being. It is in its obscure dwelling place that we meet the absence
of God and our death, the limits and their transgression.[50]

By this Foucault means that since the 'death of God', there has
been no exterior being, no absolute Other we can call on to
validate our reflection. As a result, we are forced back within the
limits which measure the finite boundaries of our being.[51] As
language approaches the limit of 'death', argues Foucault, it
doubles back on itself in a reflection of mirrors to infinity, striving
to create its own 'meaning' from within itself. As there is nothing
to interpret except itself, once it is no longer able to rely on the
'word of the infinite', a God-given meaning, language is doomed
to infinite self-interpretation, to analyse its own historical meanings, seeking to overcome the limit of death, of the void, by
repeating itself.[52]

   Already we can see the beginnings of a preoccupation with the
'being of language' starting to emerge in Foucault's work. It is a
preoccupation which is developed to its greatest extent in *Les Mots
et les choses*. Hayden White remarks on a similarity of 'plots'
between *Histoire de la folie* and *Les Mots et les choses*. Just as the
former was concerned with the 'disappearance' and 'reappearance'
of madness, *Les Mots et les choses* is about the 'disappearance' and
'reappearance' of its 'hidden protagonist, language'.[53] Although
White does not refer to *Naissance de la clinique* one could likewise
comment on the 'disappearance' and 'reappearance' of death in
this book. What White does not say, however, is that these figures
in fact occupy very similar places in Foucault's analysis. It is not
simply a matter of an analysis of madness, followed by an analysis
of the 'being of language', it is a question of the limits of an entire
culture, that privileged point of communication between the Same
and the Other. Other writers, when they recognise that language
occupies a fundamental position in *Les Mots et les choses*, tend to
extrapolate back to Foucault's previous work, where they can
detect a similar philosophical structure or 'system'. Hence a
French critic writing in 1967 comments: 'Tragic, Same, Other:
different expressions which refer to a single centre, whose real
name is pure language, whose experience is experience of the
outside, thought of the outside.' He goes on to argue that this
encapsulates Foucault's 'deepest intention' in all his books to
date.[54] Where Lemaigre is mistaken, is in equating 'the experience
of the outside' with 'pure language' in *all* of Foucault's books up to

and including *Les Mots et les choses*. In fact, the shift towards this kind of equation only began to occur in 1964, after *Histoire de la folie* and *Naissance de la clinique*, when in 'La folie l'absence d'oeuvre', Foucault remarks that madness is 'excluded language'. If for centuries, madness has been the visible sign of trans-gression, today, 'far from the pathological, from within language . . . an experience is being born which will put our entire system of thought into question.'[55] Madness is no longer *the* limit *par excellence*, it has become simply one limit among many. In a discussion with the new novelists, Foucault explains that at different periods, different limits come more into focus, certain types of behaviour are more 'transgressive' in certain cultures at certain times than at others. Hence, 'the problem Reason–Unreason' assumed a particular importance in the Classical Age.[56] In another article he recommends that the object of critical discourse should not be to reinforce the traditional categories of humanism. Rather it should describe the relation 'of a speaking subject to that singular, difficult, complex and profoundly ambiguous being (because it designates and gives all other beings their being, including itself) which is called language.'[57] But let us now turn to *Les Mots et les choses*.

Until the end of the sixteenth century, he argues in this book, this being which was language was an integral part of the world. Each thing had its own 'signature' put there at the origins of the world, and the task of knowledge was to interpret and read these signatures just as it was to interpret commentaries and the writings of the Ancients. The world formed one enormous book waiting to be deciphered, and if people were unable to read the signs in the world, it was because their vision had been clouded by original sin. Thus words and things formed a continuous whole, as things themselves were a form of language that had to be interpreted. Language therefore existed in its own right as a thing amongst others. With the Classical Age, however, all this changed. Words and things became separated, divided (just as madness had been divided from Reason), and language became 'discourse', arbitrary signs of labels that simply pointed to things. No longer a 'thing' amongst other 'things', language simply came to *represent* things. Just as madness became non-being in *Histoire de la folie* during the Classical Age, and the theme of death is silenced in *Naissance de la clinique*, so language also loses its being in *Les Mots et les choses* during the same period.

Once again, much to the annoyance of some critics, a certain sympathy for the Renaissance, or at least for a certain way of thinking, emerges in the *Les Mots et les choses*. Gérard Mendel undertaking a bizarre but unintentionally entertaining 'socio-psychoanalytical' critique of *Les Mots et les choses*, not only compares it with *Mein Kampf*, but criticises its 'nostalgia' for the Renaissance episteme, for 'a universe of magical thought'. He adds 'We are here at a very regressive level where maternal images reign.'[58] Hayden White also notes Foucault's apparent dislike of 'representation' remarking that

> Foucault proceeds in the manner of the pathologist. He 'reads' a text in the way that a specialist in carcinoma 'reads' an X-ray of tissue. He is seeking a syndrome and looking for evidences of metastatic formations that will indicate a new growth of that disease which consists of the impulse to use language to 'represent' the order of things in the order of words.[59]

However, if language lost its being, the representational knowledge of the Classical episteme had no other access to the 'universal' except through language, and one of the dreams of the eighteenth century was to compile all knowledge into one great Encyclopedia (MC:99–103). Language or rather 'discourse', remained a fundamental key to the truth, and words formed a favoured way of representing order (MC:216). At the end of the Classical Age, however, language ceased to represent things, and words discovered their 'old enigmatic density' (MC:315, OT:304). Because language was so closely tied to representation, this change that transformed general grammar into philology was far more profound than the changes undergone by natural history and the theory of wealth at the same time; it was a change involving 'the very being of representations' (MC:245). Foucault argues that if the birth of philology was a part of that same 'archaeological upheaval' which gave rise to biology and political economy, its birth has not been as well publicised. This is in spite of the fact that the consequences of its foundation have probably been far more widespread in our culture, 'at least at the subterranean levels which underlie and support it' (MC:294). But, as was the case with madness and death, this 're-emergence' of language did not mean a return to the Renaissance. For the Renaissance, the 'beings of words' originated from the Word which had been there since the beginning of time. For the moderns, words are historical objects, whose history one must analyse to find their true meaning, only to discover that language has no meaning but itself.[60] Or as Foucault says in *Naissance de la clinique*, 'We are doomed historically to history, to the patient reconstruction of discourses on discourses, and to the task of hearing what has already been said.'[61] As soon as language becomes the object of knowledge 'it has nothing else to say but itself, nothing else to do but glitter in the brightness of its own being' (MC:313). Language today is torn between commentary – the search to find a secret and hidden meaning – and criticism – the search to ensure that words correspond correctly to things and label them correctly. The human sciences today are trapped in a double obligation, says Foucault, that of finding a hidden meaning and that of formalisation or systematisation.[62] This opposition is in Foucault's view, at least at this stage of his career, the profound dilemma of our modern age. The new 'being of language', the 'enigma of the word, its solid being' re-emerges today in literature (MC:119).

Through literature, the being of language shines once more at the frontiers of Western culture – and at its centre – for it is what has been most foreign to that culture since the sixteenth century; but it has also, since this same century, been at the very centre of what Western culture has overlain. (MC:59, OT:44)

The re-emergence of language spells the death knoll for the Man of the humanists. For as they sought to analyse the interior substance of Man, his nature, all they found were more and more words, more and more history, until eventually, it was words they were examining not a construction called 'Man'. The figure of Man, in Foucault's view, is but an unfortunate aberration doomed to an early death sandwiched between two figures of language. This 'Man', he argues, is a strange 'empirico-transcendental doublet' (MC:330, OT:319). He is both the object of his own knowledge, and the subject, the originator of that knowledge. He is both an empirical entity and its transcendental foundation. We can deal with our finite nature and found it in science, our limits becoming our justification, our positive strength.

The experience which forms at the beginning of the nineteenth century no longer lodges the discovery of finitude within the thought of infinity, but at the very heart of those contents [language, work and life] which are posited by a finite knowledge as the concrete forms of finite existence. (MC:327)

This type of knowledge, by making its own limits its foundations (rather than transgressing them), attempts to eliminate any confrontation with the Other, and neutralises a certain panic before the void. But the dissolution of those limit/foundations into the exteriority of language show that this humanist Man and his scientific achievements is a false security, a mere myth. We are still ultimately faced with the limit, the exterior void. Once again Foucault returns to the examination of a certain relation between man and the Truth, a relation which was almost silenced during the eighteenth, and more particularly, during the nineteenth century. This refusal of the Other or its location within man's own 'nature', which is described in *Histoire de la folie* as a 'psychological sleep' (HF:176), becomes an 'anthropological sleep' in *Les Mots et les choses* (MC:351). In the latter work, Foucault argues that because language reveals the 'truth' of our knowledge and culture, and because it is present in literature, philosophers should turn their attention to literature, but *not* with some theory of meaning in mind (MC:59). In *Histoire de la folie* Foucault had also chastised philosophers for their inattention, but then it was for their failure to recognise madness in their reflection of the world, confusing it entirely with its modern pathological embodiment in mental illness. 'But let us make no mistake about it', Foucault wrote emphatically, 'under their speculative gravity, it is definitely a question of the relation of man to the madman, and of that strange face – so long a stranger – which now takes on the virtues of a mirror' (HF:538).

If madness and death remain limits in *Les Mots et les choses*, it is in reference to the 'being of language'. *Don Quixote* becomes the first modern work, because in this work the Renaissance episteme organised around 'resemblance', fails to correspond to a reality which is based on a form of knowledge based on identity and difference and tables. Until the end of the eighteenth century Foucault argues, the madman was recognised as being 'the one that was Different to the extent that he was unable to know Difference'; everywhere he only sees resemblance. Likewise, at the other end of the spectrum, poets were able to see the similarities between things: the poet 'hears another more profound discourse, which recalls the time when words glittered in the universal resemblance of things' (MC:63). But if the madman annihilated signs in resemblance, the poet listened to the secret wordless 'language' of resemblance and expressed it in signs. Between these two extremes, Foucault argues, a new form of knowledge opened up at the end of the Renaissance, a knowledge based on identities and differences. The being of language was unveiled in our age by the works of such writers as Roussel and Artaud, revealing that 'region where death prowls'. Language shows that man is finite, but in revealing the finitude of man, language – unable to bear this very finitude – overbalances into madness, 'that unformed, mute, meaningless region where language can be liberated' (MC:395).

In *Les Mots et les choses*, noting a current preoccupation with language, Foucault asks:

> Is it a sign of the approaching birth, or, even less than that, of the first glow, low on the horizon, of a day scarcely heralded as yet, but in which we can already guess that thought – the thought which has been speaking for thousands of years without knowing what it is to speak or even that it is speaking – is about to recapture itself in its entirety and be illuminated once again in the lightning flash of being?[63]

But is this preoccupation with language the sign of the end of an old episteme or the appearance of new forms which are incompatible with it? Foucault, recognising perhaps that he is being overly optimistic, admits that he does not know how to reply to these questions or whether he will ever know (MC:318).

By now it will be quite apparent that Foucault had very definitely decided in his work of the 1960s that whatever this secret limit between the Same and the Other is, its presence is revealed today in that 'useless and transgressive fold we call literature'.[64] Although he analyses three different 'things', madness, death and language, he is still describing the same experience, a profound confrontation or dialogue between the Same and the Other at what is, perhaps, ultimately an indescribable or even unknowable level of our history and being.[65]

After *Les Mots et les choses*, however, literature all but disappeared from Foucault's work except in the form of references to literary figures such as Sade and Artaud. It was to re-emerge only once again, in a brief passage where he describes literature as both the product of power and its truth. He says:

> literature forms part of that great system of constraint by which the West compelled the everyday to bring itself into discourse; but it occupies a special place there: bent on seeking everyday life beneath itself, on crossing over the limits, . . . [it takes] upon itself the charge of scandal, of transgression or of rebellion. More than any other form of language, it remains the discourse of 'infamy': it remains its task to say the most unsayable – the worst, the most secret, the most intolerable, the shameless . . . . But we must not forget that this singular position of literature is only an effect of a certain apparatus of power which traverses in the West the economy of discourse and the strategies of the true.[66]

The constancy of a philosophical search to understand our limits, and a historiography that draws attention to those limits, even if the content of those limits changes, points to more than just a theoretical 'tool box'. Foucault's works up to 1966 represent a very definite view of the world, but rather than a philosophy based on an unchanging central focal point, it is a philosophy based on a changing boundary, a changing relation between the Same and the Other, mysteriously apparent in the events of history. Hence Foucault's philosophy is of necessity also a history. It does not matter that Foucault is unable to discover which limit is the 'right one'. Indeed as he realises later, it is impossible to do so. It is the awareness of limits, of a dialogue, the possibility of a history which is not merely a sterile repetition of the Same, which is the important point that emerges from Foucault's work.

5

The Limits Forgotten

After *Les Mots et les choses*, the outer limits begin to disappear from Foucault's work, and after about 1970, the notions of 'power' and 'politics' come to occupy an important place in his work. A tremendous amount has been written about this phase of Foucault's work and it has now become quite a familiar ground. For this reason it is not essential to concentrate too closely on the detail of Foucault's theories here. In addition, this work will be approached from quite a different angle from that which is usually taken, in keeping with our theme of the 'history of the limits'.

One might begin by remarking, that for all the intrinsic interest and usefulness of Foucault's work on power, discipline and regimes of truth, it falls back into the political myth which he had exposed so convincingly in *Les Mots et les choses*. He argues in this book that because modern thought has transformed the limits of Man and his knowledge into transcendental foundations, it becomes both knowledge and transformation of its object of reflection. Hence, modern thought is already a morality, already an ethics: it is not a reflection on an exterior Other, but a totally self-referential and self-transforming system. Man has in fact located the 'Other' of himself, that undiscoverable 'something' he searches to know within himself. What need is there, then, for philosophy to declare its political or ethical allegiance when it is in itself an ethics or a politics or a thought of the self-realisation of Man? From its very origin modern thought deliberately chooses to locate the truth within the finite boundaries of Man's reason. Speaking of the awareness of thought as 'a perilous act', Foucault remarks:

> Sade, Nietzsche, Artaud and Bataille knew it for all those who wanted not to know it; but it is also certain that Hegel, Marx and Freud knew it. Can one say that all those, who in their profound stupidity affirm that there is no philosophy without political choice, that all thought is 'progressive' or 'reactionary', do not

know it? Their foolishness is to believe that all thought 'expresses' the ideology of a class, their involuntary profundity is that they point to the modern mode of being of thought. (MC:339)

But having criticised the limitations of modern knowledge so well, Foucault does not go beyond them. Of his subsequent work, Jean Baudrillard remarks in 1977, that Foucault remains within the system of power he criticises, and that his writing is the mirror-image of the spirals of disciplinary and molecular power he condemns. 'Foucault stops at the threshold of a present revolution of the system which he never wanted to cross . . . one remains within the discourse of politics – "one never escapes it" says Foucault – whereas it should really be a matter of grasping the radical indefinition of politics, its inexistence . . .'.[1] This sudden withdrawal and inability to take his own thought to its logical conclusions, was remarked upon also by Maurice Clavel, in relation to *Les Mots et les choses*. Foucault in a letter to Clavel said that he would have liked to have 'traced the outline' of humanism and structuralism, but 'the task appeared so immense, it required such an uprooting, that I didn't carry it through to the end, I didn't formulate it as I should have, and at the last moment I closed my eyes.'[2]

Not only is there a difference of approach, but there is a marked difference between the style, imagery and tone of the work Foucault produced during the 1960s and that of the 1970s. After 1970, he appears to find thinking and writing rather dreary and burdensome and a certain enthusiasm vanishes from his work, leaving in its place, what Jacques Léonard describes as a 'veiled anger against the . . . normalising society'[3] and Richard Rorty as 'more and more sophisticated expressions of resentment'.[4] And as Clavel remarks, 'in spite of the quality, the intelligence of *Surveiller et punir*, he appears in a way to be writing 'to keep himself busy'. Clavel also argues that Foucault had said everything for once and for all in *Les Mots et les choses*, which is perhaps rather an overstatement of an intuition that Foucault had lost a kind of enthusiasm 'which unified his thought, his action, his being . . .'[5] This change of tone is more than simply just an impression one gains from Foucault's increasingly rapid changes of mind about what the essential key to thought is today, or a certain insistence on the 'fictive' nature of his writings. One also finds him commenting directly on the difficulty of thinking and writing. In an article written in 1970, in which he invites us to liberate difference and to engage in 'a thought of the multiple', he remarks: 'Thinking does not console or make you happy. Thinking crawls along apathetically like a perversion . . .'[6] and he says to Fons Elders in 1974:

> I do not say things because I think them; I say them rather with the aim of self-destruction, so that I will not have to think any more, so that I can be certain that from now on, they will lead a life outside me, or die the death, in which I will not have to recognise myself.[7]

In an interview in 1975, he also remarks that he does not like writing: 'It is a very difficult activity to master. Writing only interests me in so far as it can be incorporated into the reality of a combat . . . . I would like my books to be sorts of scalpels, Molotov cocktails or minefields and that they would explode after use like fireworks.'[8]

In any case, it would appear that Foucault did not find a vision of the world in which the Same and the Other were totally coextensive a particularly easy one to think through. This can also be seen in the fact that for much of this period, Foucault spent his time insisting that he was doing the precise opposite of what he was actually doing. While recommending that his readers should use history to show that people have not always thought the same way they do now, that there is no such thing as historical necessity, and that ideas are historical events, in *Surveiller et punir*, *La Volonté de savoir* and a number of articles, he paints a picture of a world totally determined down to its finest particles by the inescapable workings of an anonymous and insubstantial 'power'. It was not until after 1981 that Foucault was able to resolve this fundamental contradiction in his work, with the introduction of the freedom of the Other.

Foucault's interest in the simple 'there is', or in an order which does not communicate with the disorder of the void, dates back to 1966, when he says to Raymond Bellour: 'My object is not language but the archive, that is, the accumulated existence of discourses.' He goes on to explain that he is 'haunted by the existence of discourses, by the fact that words took place . . . [and] left traces behind them.'[9] In *L'Archéologie du savoir* he proposes a systematic method of describing this great mass of discourse (AS:183), and in his insistence on a principle of discontinuity, notes that instead of simply existing at the limits of our history, the Other pervades the very fabric of history at the most everyday level of the event. Archaeology, he says, is intended as 'a description of what has already been said at the level of its existence'.[10] It is a 'theory-free' description, if by theory is meant 'the deduction from a certain number of axioms, of an abstract model applicable to an indefinite number of empirical descriptions' (AS:149). Rather than 'founding a theory', Foucault claims he is doing no more than 'establishing a possibility';[11] if theory is unity, then archaeology is multiplicity.[12] Foucault does express some passing regrets that he had as yet been unable to formulate a 'theory', but the possibility of a type of thought which could undermine 'totalities' and unifying theories, and do away with 'transcendental' categories, was one that returned with increasing insistence and frequency in his work during the 1970s. This would appear remarkably like the aims espoused by positivist and empiricist types of thought, if it were not for one thing: the undermining of that paradoxically transcendental category upon which this type of thought is based, namely the 'fact'. Following Nietzsche, Foucault insists that there is no such thing as a 'fact', that there are only interpretations of other interpretations. 'If interpretation can never end', he says,

> it is quite simply because there is nothing to interpret. There is absolutely nothing primary to interpret, because fundamentally, everything is already interpretation, each sign is in itself not the thing which is offered to interpretation, but the interpretation of other signs.[13]

Any perception of 'reality' we have is already an intellectual construction. This 'surprising mixture . . . [of] positivism and nihilism' as Vincent Descombes describes it, led some of Foucault's critics, and Foucault himself at a certain period, to describe his histories as 'novels' or 'fictions'.[14]

In *L'Archéologie du savoir*, the existence of discourse replaces the being of language, just as the latter had replaced death, and death had replaced madness. Revising his views on madness, Foucault claims that in *Histoire de la folie*, he had been trying to reconstitute madness, going on to say that this was *not* what he should have done:

> We are not trying to reconstitute what madness itself might have been, in the form in which it first presented itself to some primitive, fundamental, vague, barely articulated experience, and in the form in which it was subsequently organised (translated, deformed, travestied, repressed perhaps) by discourses, and the oblique, often twisted game of their operations.

He adds in a footnote that 'This is written against an explicit theme of my book *Madness and Civilisation*, and one that recurs particularly in the preface' (AS:64, AK:47). In this passage we notice a number of interesting shifts: first of all, in *Histoire de la folie*, Foucault, rather than attempting to define what madness was, had been far more concerned with the existence of a certain experience of the limit, which he argued, was found in its most pure form in madness. Secondly, 'discourses' (even repressive ones) as a concept or even as a word, scarcely rate a mention in *Histoire de la folie*. However, a large number of critics, particularly in English, have taken this description of *Histoire de la folie* at face value, and we find quite a number of criticisms of this book, couched in either the terms Foucault uses in the passage above, or those of an interview conducted in 1977.[15] In this interview the 'discursive' reinterpretation was replaced by one in terms of power: 'At the point of junction of *Histoire de la folie* and *Les Mots et les choses*, there was, under two very different aspects, this central problem of power which I had as yet only very poorly isolated.'[16] He also remarks that he wrote *Histoire de la folie* on the horizon of questions which could all be summed up in two words, 'knowledge and power'.[17] His discussion in the same interview of the Marxists' lack of interest in topics such as madness, has also led some English-speaking critics to take it for granted that 'Foucault's work from *Madness and Civilisation* onwards was motivated by a wish to address a series of intellectual–political questions which had been either neglected or badly discussed by the Marxist-dominated intellectual left'.[18] This, however, was far from being the case, as we have suggested in previous chapters. In the same interview, Foucault also describes and rejects a methodology of history based on the ordering of discourse; this being, of course, a rejection of his own archaeological approach. In a passage reminiscent of *L'Archéologie du savoir* he remarks: 'the problem is both to distinguish events, differentiate the networks and levels to which they belong, and to reconstitute the threads which bind them, make them give rise to one another.' He goes on to say, however: 'relations of power, not relations of sense . . . . [History] should be able to be analysed down to the slightest detail, but according to the intelligibility of struggles, of strategies and tactics.'[19]

In recent years, however, there has been an interesting trend amongst English-language critics towards 'reinstating' *L'Archéologie du savoir*, as discussion becomes more widespread concerning major difficulties with Foucault's genealogies of power. Jeffrey Minson remarks, for example, 'For myself, the whole (theoretical) question of power in Foucault has become an unprofitable one . . . the *Archaeology* is an exemplary . . . book; loyalty to its precepts would have precluded many of the excesses of *Discipline and Punish* and *The History of Sexuality*.'[20] Others such as Colin Gordon suggest that certain aspects of this book, contrary to popular belief, form the 'essential ground' for the further concepts Foucault was to introduce.[21] But Foucault's attempt to be a 'happy positivist' (AS:164, AK:125, OD:72), even if his 'facts' were all fictions, met with a shortlived success indeed, as a host of critics rushed forward to point out the inherent difficulties with this approach.[22] By the time he came to write *L'Ordre du discours*, he had abandoned the vision of a systematic description of the discursive 'artefacts' left by the past, for one in which 'discourses' became the dangerous and precious objects of political struggle. In every society, Foucault says, the production of discourse is carefully controlled and regulated in an effort to reduce its nonconformity, its propensity to escape from a manageable system. As in his earlier books, he proposes the existence of a certain division in our history, but it is no longer situated at that limit where our discourses and knowledge fade into silence and ignorance. It is a division which is internal to the operation of discourse and knowledge, a principle which *orders* the production of discourses in a society.

Starting with the Ancient Greeks, Foucault describes the means by which a constraining system of exclusion operates in our discourse, noting three major procedures of exclusion. The first is prohibition: the areas of sexuality and politics becoming the areas where the rules of prohibition and exclusion are most concentrated; the second is the opposition between reason and madness. As Foucault so often does, in a most curious fashion, he treats his previous ideas as the work of somebody else in order to refute or modify them: 'I will be told that . . . the word of the madman is no longer on the other side of the division; that it is no longer null and void; that on the contrary it puts us on our guard . . . . But so much attention does not prove that the old division is no longer operative' (OD:14). The third and most important principle, and the one that governs the first two is the 'will to truth'. Foucault also takes the opportunity to reinterpret some of *L'Archéologie du savoir*. The unities of discourse (the work, the author, the discipline) are no longer simply the remnants of a metaphysics based on continuity, a metaphysics that should be done away with; they become sinister forms of restriction and constraint imposed upon discourse (OD:38). But on the other hand the solution offered to this problem is similar, and Foucault proposes a way of countering this ordering of discourse by using notions such as those of the 'event' and the 'series' and the other related ideas of 'regularity, chance, discontinuity, dependence, transformation' (OD:58–9).

It is not a question either of the succession of moments of time, or of the multiplicity of various thinking subjects. It is a question of *caesurae* which break the moment and disperse the subject into a plurality of possible positions and functions . . . . One must conceive of relations between these discontinuous series, which are not of the order of succession (or simultaneity) in one (or several) consciousnesses.[23]

At about the same time that discourses became the objects of political struggle in Foucault's work, the 'unconscious' grid of order that underlay their production, governing the division of truth and falsity for a given period, underwent a politicisation.[24] This 'unconscious' was gradually transformed into what Foucault was to describe later as 'an absolutely conscious organised, considered strategy which can be clearly read in a mass of unknown documents which constitute the effective discourse of a political action . . . . A logic of the unconscious must . . . be replaced by a logic of the strategy.'[25] But whether conscious or unconscious, the same level is still being addressed: that grid between words and things which systematically orders the world into a particular form of intelligible existence for a given society or period: in other words a historical *a priori*. During the 1960s in Foucault's work, the order of the Same and an exterior Other confronted each other at the limits, and change at this level occurred as the result of that dialogue. Once the exterior limits vanish, however, internal relations become more important and it becomes a question of power, of who controls this level and by what means. In 1970, Foucault put it this way (again in an unacknowledged rejection of his own earlier ideas): 'new problems have appeared: no longer what are the limits of knowledge (or its foundations), but who are those who know? How is knowledge appropriated and distributed?'[26] Thus, as soon as the limits began to retreat in Foucault's work, politics began to advance, discreetly at first, then quite stridently in a self abnegating crypto-Maoism during the early 1970s. In the interview with Madeleine Chapsal in 1966, where he proclaims his discovery of the 'there is', and the System, he remarks, much to the surprise of the interviewer, that the opposition of the thinkers of the System to existentialism and humanism is a 'political' one.[27] *L'Archéologie du savoir* also mentions 'politics' in its last few pages as many critics note with grave approval.[28]

But politics did not really become a major issue in Foucault's work until after about 1970. In the early 1970s, Foucault, who was involved in a number of political activities with the Maoists, proposed revolution on several occasions, defining revolutionary action 'as the simultaneous agitation of consciousness and institutions'; which implies, he says, that we should attack the relationships of power in institutions and in knowledge.[29] He recommends that prisoners should rebel collectively against 'the system of training' to which they are subject.[30] He also remarks more moderately in a discussion with Chomsky, that 'the real political task is to criticise the workings of institutions'.[31] In 1972, we find him proposing that the 'non-proletarianised pleb' (which included marginal groups such as the mentally ill, delinquents and prisoners) should join in the 'revolutionary battle' against 'capitalism' and the 'bourgeoisie' under the leadership of the proletariat. 'Because what capitalism is basically afraid of . . . [is] the lads who go out into the streets with their knives and guns, ready for direct and violent action.'[32] However, after some of Foucault's non-Maoist friends expressed reservations about the violence of his views in 1972, he eventually toned them down.[33]

Elsewhere we find him referring to 'a regime of the dictatorship of class', or 'class struggles'.[34]

At this point, with the appearance of a certain type of revolutionary rhetoric, it is worth pausing to consider the much-discussed issue of Foucault's relation to Marxism. The variety of opinion on Foucault's relation to Marxism has been immense and impassioned, and two entire books, not to mention a large number of articles have been devoted to this subject.[35] The few remarks that Foucault made on the subject of Marx or Marxism have been endlessly repeated and discussed from every possible angle. So much so, in fact, that Foucault was heard to say furiously to an unfortunate enquirer in 1975: 'Stop asking me about Marx! I never want to hear about the gentleman again. Talk to those whose profession it is, who are paid to talk about him! As for me, I am totally finished with Marx!'[36] It is interesting to note that whereas most French critics tend to agree that Foucault is not a Marxist, a number of English-speaking critics seem to operate under the assumption that all French intellectuals entertain some necessary, even if tortured, link with this body of thought. And if English-speaking critics have been more interested in the relation of Foucault's later work to Marxism, in France the most lively discussion on this topic occurred mainly after the appearance of *Les Mots et les choses*.

When this book appeared, not only were a number of Marxist writers in France annoyed that Foucault had cavalierly ignored the dialectic and 'history', they were shocked by his deliberately provocative statement that Marxism had not represented a break in Western knowledge and constituted a mere storm in a children's paddling pool.[37] Even the non-Marxist Raymond Aron, although generally delighted at Foucault's challenge to the Sartrian and Althusserian Marxist 'Holy Families', suggested Foucault might have taken his 'Nietzschean' rhetoric a bit too far: 'Ripples on the surface of a children's paddling pool those tens and tens of millions of deaths?' he asks dramatically.[38] What was more, it was claimed that Foucault's studious effort to ignore Marxism condemned him to sterile description and an incomplete view of the world. Dominique Lecourt remarks, for example, that what is missing in *L'Archéologie du savoir*, is the 'class point of view', and that only by introducing class into theory and practice, would Foucault be able to pass from 'ideology' to 'science'.[39] Some Marxists tried to make the best of the situation and suggested that

Foucault's ideas could, in fact, make a very useful contribution to Marxist thought. Jacques Milhau in the *Cahiers du communisme* describes Foucault as occupying 'a place in the forefront of non-Marxist philosophy', and considers that his 'archaeology' would be most useful for Marxists.[40]

On the other hand, remarks in English on Foucault's relation to Marxism tend to be more complex. Some writers argue that Foucault is either an anti-Marxist, or simply a non-Marxist, and others that even if he is not exactly a Marxist, he is Marxist in spirit (or at least *almost* Marxist). Still others claim that Foucault is more Marxist than Marx. For example, in a desperate effort to claim Foucault as a true follower of Marx, it is stated in one work: 'If Foucault can be called a Marxist, this can be done only in the most general and idealist manner . . . . he avoids Marxist rhetoric, always employing Marx's own means of analysis, focusing on empirical facts.'[41] Another critic remarks that one of the most important differences between Foucault's thought and Marxist theory, is the fact that Foucault avoids 'global theorising' and 'totalising analysis and is generally critical of systematicity'.[42] Mark Poster also repeats the now familiar argument that Foucault is more materialist than Marx (because of his emphasis on 'bodies'), saying that he has accomplished a 'similar task to that of Marx, but without much of the accompanying metaphysical baggage'.[43] For these critics, Foucault is a model philosopher who miraculously escapes from the weaknesses and the totalising dogmatism of the 'system', incarnating only its best points. Hence, he is not only more 'materialist' than Marx, he is also a return to a purer pre-Marxist (empirical) Marx. He also avoids the 'metaphysics' and 'system' associated with Marx and his followers, maintaining a constant critique of 'totalities' and great truths – in other words – a sensible empiricism. Unfortunately even if this were, in fact, an accurate description of Foucault's intentions, a pure empirical Marxism without the 'system' or the philosophy would be logically impossible. For, as François Châtelet quite correctly points out, it is impossible to separate a method from its philosophical bases.[44]

But what is most interesting about this discussion over Foucault's relation to Marxism, perhaps, is the writers' apparent need to make Foucault's work fit into some pre-existing system of explanation. As Jean-François Revel remarks incisively:

The need to be grouped under an authority, so that challenging a theory, preferring one book to another, becomes not only a matter of intelligence or taste, but a *serious action*, to which is attached a nuance of righteousness or guilt, is a situation which leads numerous readers to infringe on the magic of one authority only on condition that they are sheltered behind another authority.[45]

This kind of activity is by no means restricted to the Marxist commentators. During the late 1960s the widespread repetition and unquestioning acceptance of Sartre's comments on Foucault was a case in point. In more recent years the German philosopher Jürgen Habermas has come to occupy a similar position of authority in relation to the interpretation of Foucault's work.

The fact of the matter is that Foucault is simply not interested in defining his work in relation to Marx. He does not see himself as 'completing' the Marxist project with a much needed theory of 'superstructures'. Neither is he embarking on a single-minded anti-Marxist crusade, as some of the 'new philosophers' would have it, or otherwise providing an alternative or replacement for Marxism. Certainly, the early political writings in which he adopts a kind of Maoist/Marxist rhetoric are not amongst his most original efforts and led a number of writers in France to wonder how these writings and his militant activities in support of the marginals and the oppressed were connected with his more serious work. When asked by Maurice Clavel, a particularly enthusiastic exponent of Foucault's ideas on the death of man, why he engaged in his various political activities, he replied 'In the name of the excluded and the imprisoned, through humanism.' 'Therefore for a vaster, universal, finally a real humanism!' added Clavel, but did not manage to elicit a response from Foucault.[46]

Out of Foucault's political activities in the early 1970s came the book *Surveiller et punir*. In this book Foucault describes the birth of the modern prison system between 1760 and 1840. He traces the disappearance of torture and public executions as a legal means of punishment in the penal system and the development of a different regime which no longer punished the body but sought to control the 'soul'. The objective of this new system was to 'cure', correct and train, rather than to punish. Foucault quotes Mabley writing in 1789, 'let punishment . . . strike the soul rather than the body' (SP:22). But even if physical punishments such as imprisonment, isolation and hard labour remained current, their object was no longer the same, for the body had become the means of access to the 'soul', of depriving an individual of certain 'rights' or 'possessions', such as his liberty. 'Punishment passed from an art of unbearable sensations to an economy of suspended rights' as Foucault puts it (SP:16). The torturer and the executioner were replaced by a 'whole army of technicians': prison guards, doctors, psychiatrists, psychologists, teachers and chaplains (SP:26). But one must not make the mistake, says Foucault, of thinking that the suppression of torture in the penal system was the proof of a growing humanitarianism. The old methods were simply no longer an effective means of controlling a certain element of the population in a rapidly changing society (SP:80, 90). This is, of course, a similar argument to the one Foucault uses in *Histoire de la folie* concerning the birth of the science of psychiatry, and the more 'humane' treatment of madmen.

It is at this point that Foucault introduces his famous (some would say notorious) notion of power: 'That thing which is so enigmatic, both visible and invisible, present and hidden, invested everywhere, which is called power.'[47] It is indeed enigmatic, for Foucault never explains why he thinks it is so important. It would seem that he has simply adopted a variation of Nietzsche's notion of a 'will to power' underlying all pretensions to morality. But, as Jeffrey Minson correctly points out, Nietzsche in revealing the 'immoral bases' of morality, saying that 'morality' is nothing but the workings of a rapacious and naturalistic 'will to power', is only setting up one 'essentialist moral argument' against another.[48] Power was a notion, either on its own or in its variant form 'power–knowledge', that many writers came to see as being the 'unity of Foucault's work',[49] a 'fundamental theme' of his history and genealogy as well as a 'fundamental question concerning our present'.[50] Indeed so popular was the idea that, as Robert Maggiori remarks, 'the power–knowledge relationship became the pivot of what one could call the current mode of thought.'[51] In English-speaking countries, the notion of 'power' continues to thrive and acquire new dimensions and applications, especially in sociology and as a form of intellectual politics. In France, however, the question of power has virtually dropped out of sight, to be replaced by an interest in ethics and subjectivity.

Foucault describes the birth of the prison in terms of a change in 'tactics of power', from a discontinuous 'macropower' exercised by the sovereign to a 'microphysics of power' (SP:31), which now permeates all levels of social relations, focusing on the 'body', producing 'individuals' who are 'useful' and 'productive'.[52] Rather than being simply the victim of power, therefore, the individual is in fact created by power, as a means of facilitating the control of power over bodies.[53] Much has been said about Foucault's ideas of the creation of the modern individual, and recently some critics have begun to use the ideas Foucault expressed on the subject in *Naissance de la clinique* to complement his power-centred analyses in *Surveiller et punir*. It is a process that interested Foucault right throughout his career but, contrary to what now seems to be a widespread belief, he did not always see the rise of the individual in terms of 'power'. In *Histoire de la folie*, it was the result of the alienation of madness and the creation of a science based on the silencing of the language of the Other. In *Naissance de la clinique*, it was the sinister entry of death into knowledge which was the basis on which the individual could be created. In *Les Mots et les choses*, 'man in his positivity (a living, working and speaking being)' (MC:364) was the end-product of an epistemic configuration which posited as an empirico-transcendental foundation, a humanist Man.

In the 'new regime of truth' (SP:27) that was established at the end of the eighteenth century, the criminal was no longer simply the symbolic enemy of the king, he was the enemy of the entire social body, a monstrous aberration, abnormal, no longer quite human. Punishment was no longer the vengeance of the sovereign, but the defence of an entire society (SP:92–3). But in the figure of the delinquent, the occupant of prisons, this monster could become the object of disciplinary power and knowledge. 'In its functioning, the power to punish is not essentially different from that of healing or educating', comments Foucault (SP:310). The prisoner thus became the model for a 'knowledge of individuals' which was to spread beyond the prison to the whole of society (SP:128–9). In 'retraining' the prisoner as a useful member of society, power was exercised over him in the form of 'discipline'. This 'microphysics of power' which discipline represented (SP:141) regulated the actions and behaviour of the body down to the most minute detail. Discipline was embodied in 'a politics of coercions which act on the body and form a calculated manipulation of its elements, gestures, behaviour. The human body enters into a machinery of power, which scrutinises it, takes it apart, then puts it back together again' (SP:139). If relations of power have always been with us, in Foucault's view, their microscopic, 'multiple' and 'multiform' incarnation in 'discipline' is a modern development.[54] It is a power which insinuates itself into 'the very texture of individuals, . . . introducing itself into their gestures, their attitudes, their discourse, their experience, their daily life.'[55] Disciplinary power can be exercised through institutions, states, the police or families, permeating the whole of society down to the most 'infinitesimal' level (SP:218, 215).

This disciplinary 'technology' of power, says Foucault, first manifested itself in the operation and organisation of such institutions as schoolrooms, hospitals and army barracks. This organisation was initially, at the end of the eighteenth century, undertaken in terms of the 'table', which in *Surveiller et punir* becomes a 'technique of power and a procedure of knowledge' (SPL:150), almost an intentional conspiracy imposed on things and people, rather than simply the (unconscious) mode of being of knowledge it had been in Foucault's previous books. Jacques Léonard remarks of *Surveiller et punir*:

> there is a *knowing machination*, but it is obstinately *impersonal or abstract*. Structuralists and existentialists are equally disappointed. What is a strategy without generals? Battle of who against whom? Of the bourgeoisie against the people? Of Satan against the Archangel?[56]

Disciplinary procedures also led to an evolutionary, linear view of time, orientated towards progress and a fixed end. In *Les Mots et les choses*, this appearance of 'historical' time had been linked to a fundamental separation of words and things, a shift away from a language which represented things in the two-dimensional space of the table.

Disciplinary power was also to be enforced by continual surveillance, of which Jeremy Bentham's Panopticon is the model. 'There is no need for weapons, physical violence or material constraints, only a gaze. A gaze which watches attentively and which each person feeling its weight, ends up by interiorising to the point of watching himself.'[57] If this surveillance is exercised on the individual, it is dependent for its effective operation on every individual watching every other individual. Alongside 'surveillance', 'normalisation' also became 'one of the great instruments of power' at the end of the Classical Age (SP:186). One of the objectives of disciplinary power was to ensure that every individual conformed to a certain 'norm' or idea of normality, to become uniform, therefore manageable for the purposes of power. The judges of normality are everywhere in this system: in schools, prisons, hospitals. All the individualising mechanisms of our civilisation, Foucault says, have come to be concentrated on the people at the margins of society, and when the sane, normal and law-abiding adult is individualised, it is always in reference to those secret elements of madness, disease, criminality and child-ishness he bears within him (SP:195). Again, this echoes certain themes in *Histoire de la folie* where the madman becomes the alienated truth of man in the nineteenth century.

However, not content with this long list of controlling 'strat-egies' (discipline, surveillance and normalisation), Foucault goes on to suggest that the 'examination' where power and knowledge intersect to form a 'normalising surveillance which allows qualifi-cation, classification and punishment' (SP:186–7), is at the centre of disciplinary procedures which form the individual. Foucault almost reaches a point of overkill at this stage. 'Discipline' is everywhere, it explains everything: the rise of the bourgeoisie and capitalism. The 'police inquiry' forms a model for the procedures of empirical science, and the birth of the human sciences is to be found in the 'unglorious archives' of the rise of disciplinary power. As he says

> The archaeology of the human sciences has to be established through studying the mechanisms of power which have in-vested human bodies, acts and forms of behaviour. And this investigation enables us to rediscover one of the conditions of the emergence of the human sciences: the great nineteenth-century effort in discipline and normalisation.[58]

This, of course, is quite a different explanation from the ones offered in his previous books, in which he had located the birth of the human sciences in the silencing of madness, in the study of death in medicine, and in an anthropologisation of knowledge. Society becomes an extension of the prison, that 'concentrated and austere figure of disciplines' (SP:259).

By the time he came to write *La Volonté de savoir*, however, Foucault had lost interest in discipline, although not in power, which, if anything, had become even more all-pervasive. In this book, Foucault argues that far from repressing sex, modern

Western civilisation has done nothing but produce endless 'talk' on this topic. Western society, he says, has perfected the work of creating 'subjects' (in both senses of the word) who aid the task of power by confessing all. Sexuality according to Foucault, occupies a very important place in what he terms the 'science of the confession', as it has become the ultimate secret which must be revealed. If the 'truth' about sex is known, then we will know 'who we are', we will know our own truth.[59] Over the centuries, as a result of this conjunction of confession and sexuality, he says, 'the project of a science of the subject began to gravitate around the question of sex', not because of some natural property of sex itself, but because of the workings of power.[60] But why, Foucault asks, has sex acquired such capacities for containing the truth? Why not some other object or experience? This is a question to which he fails to provide any convincing answers in *La Volonté de savoir*. Indeed, later in Volumes 2 and 3 of *Histoire de la sexualité*, he abandons the idea that sexuality is *the* privileged area of experience. It is simply one of many domains in which 'techniques of the self' have been applied and are still being applied.

The main focal point of discussion in relation to *La Volonté de savoir*, however, was Foucault's revised theories of power. 'Discipline' is ousted from its central spot and becomes one of the two forms of 'biopower'. The second form of biopower is the control of population, acting through such disciplines as demography, studies of resources and population, and economics. Biological life, he goes on to argue, became the object of knowledge, control and power in the nineteenth century. 'The political significance of the problem of sex', Foucault concludes, 'is due to the fact that sex is located at the point of intersection between the discipline of the body and the control of the population.'[61] Not content to reinterpret discipline in terms of biopower, he also reinterprets the 'normalising society' which, no longer the result of disciplinary power, becomes the result of a 'technology of power centred on life' (VS:190).

Almost as soon as these ideas appeared Foucault left them aside, and in the same year as the publication of *La Volonté de savoir*, we find him declaring that 'the task of an intellectual today [is] quite simply the work of truth', or in other words unmasking the 'truth' which is created by power for its own ends.[62] One also notes his complaints in 1977, concerning his characterisation as 'the melancholic historian of prohibitions and repressive power', when in reality his problem had always been 'the effects of power and the production of "truth" '.[63] By 1978, his 'problem' had become 'knowing how men govern themselves and others through the production of truth'.[64] By truth, Foucault means here, the way in which the truth and falsity of propositions are defined in a given society. The will to forge new relations between 'government' and 'truth' is defined by Foucault as a 'political spirituality'.[65]

In both *Surveiller et punir* and *La Volonté de savoir*, and in a number of other writings, Foucault criticised traditional and essentialist views of power, and was careful to emphasise that power was not a 'thing' but a relation: 'Power is not an institution and it is not a structure, it is not a certain strength with which some are endowed; it is the name that is lent to a complex strategic situation in a given society.'[66] It is interesting to note certain similarities between this definition and some of the definitions in *L'Archéologie du savoir*. There he emphasises that the 'formation of objects', the 'statement', and the 'discursive practice' are neither things, structures, nor the property of individual psyches, but are functions or relations.[67] In *La Volonté de savoir* Foucault also argues that complaints that we can never escape power, and that there is no 'absolute exterior' in relation to power, 'misunderstand the strictly relational character of power relations'; then, after having made this rather tautological statement, he suddenly and mysteriously proposes a 'multiplicity of points of resistance', which, it might be noted, are inextricably linked to the operations of power.[68] Elsewhere Foucault discusses resistance to power in terms of a 'plebness' which exists in bodies and souls, in individuals, in the proletariat and the bourgeoisie. Although it is not outside power, it exists as the 'limit' or 'underside' of power constantly seeking to escape it. Foucault emphasises, however, that this 'plebness' does not ever escape the order of power.[69]

But this theory of a totally coextensive and predetermined relation of the Same and the Other, does nothing to solve Foucault's problem. As Jean Baudrillard so correctly points out, even if power is not a 'thing', it becomes in spite of everything, a 'final principle' of intelligibility and reality in Foucault's work:[70]

Power is an irreversible principle of organisation, it manufactures the real, always more of the real. Quadrature, nomenclature, dictatorship without redress, nowhere is it rendered void, nowhere does it twist back on itself and become entangled with death. In this sense, even if it is without finality or a last judgement, it becomes itself a *final principle* – it is the last term, the irreducible texture, the last fable that is told, what structures the indeterminate equation of the world.[71]

Cornelius Castoriadis also makes a similar point when he observes that for Foucault 'this mysterious entity' power, forms 'an impersonal instance of absolute rationality' in history.[72]

In other words, Foucault's power-centred analyses form a *system*, an all-explaining vision from which nothing escapes. A cohort of hopeful revolutionaries have condemned Foucault's views as 'pessimistic', arguing that the oppressed are doomed to eternal defeat by the inexorable system. Heinz Steinert comments, for example:

> From reading these accounts one gets a feeling of inevitability; one is confronted with a monstrous social machine that grinds along relentlessly and very intelligently at the top, making no mistakes, anticipating all possible opposition, which it does not crush, but rather draws in, involving it in its own destruction.[73]

Other critics find that *Surveiller et punir* induces a 'deep despair' in the absence of any 'utopian alternative',[74] or that 'a paranoid tone' permeates the whole of *La Volonté de savoir*,[75] or that 'there appears no way that human agency can transform this "permanent, repetitious, inert and self-reproducing" power'.[76] Jacques Léonard remarks to Foucault that *Surveiller et punir* produced a somewhat sterilising and anaesthetising effect on penitentiary educators in the sense that his 'logic had an implacability which they were unable to escape'.[77] Castoriadis is particularly critical of Foucault's ideas on resistance and the 'pleb'. 'Resist if it amuses you – but without a strategy, because then you will no longer be pleb, but power.'[78]

At the same time, however, that Foucault was constructing these systems of power, he was conducting a vigorous campaign against all forms of totality, favouring all that was 'local', 'specific' and 'fragmented', all that was against received 'truths'. Two of the standard references for the multitude of critics who have eagerly rallied to this doctrine of the destruction of doctrines, are a discussion between Gilles Deleuze and Foucault published in

1972, and an interview titled 'Truth and Power' which originally appeared in Italian in 1977 and then appeared in French the same year. Foucault begins by declaring that the days of the nineteenth-century 'universal intellectual', the 'bearer of universal values' who spoke in the name of the oppressed, are over. In the place of this universal intellectual, we now find, according to Foucault, the 'specific intellectual' who is involved in 'specialised' and 'local struggles', the specialist (such as a doctor or a nuclear scientist) rather than the generalist. The specific intellectual does not speak in the name of all and has no 'grand theory' which will point in the direction of 'truth' and solve problems.[79] 'The role of the intellectual', continues Foucault in a popular passage, 'is no longer to place himself "a little in front or a little to the side" so as to be able to express the unspoken truth of all', rather it is to struggle against localised forms of power of which he is himself 'both the object and the instrument'.[80] This new intellectual, says Foucault, has a 'three-fold specificity': this relates to his class position, to his position as an intellectual or researcher, and to the 'politics of truth' in his own society. His 'specific struggles' in his own field can affect the way 'true' statements are produced in a society by mechanisms of power.[81] Foucault also notes that the figure of the 'great writer' has disappeared to be replaced by that of the 'absolute expert', dealing with 'local' scientific truth. He describes the now superseded universal intellectual as having three functions: to pronounce on the destiny of mankind, to speak for man in general, and to say where the good is – what it is and what has to be done.[82] He argues that he is not himself a universal intellectual, because he does not have a vision of what the ideal society should be like and he has never spoken in anybody's name, even for prisoners or madmen. He has simply exposed the workings of the system and left it up to others to draw the logical conclusions and take action. Foucault believes that telling the truth about something poses much more of a problem than laying down a new set of laws on how things *should* be done.

At the same time Foucault develops his discussion on 'theory'. Again, his ideas on a 'plurality of theoretical work', as opposed to 'totalising philosophy', began to form in the late 1960s, when he declared that a certain type of 'contemporary philosophy' as practised by Sartre and Merleau-Ponty was null and void today.[83] Later, in his discussion with Deleuze, Foucault defines theory as a practice but a 'local and regional' and 'non-totalising' practice.[84]

Gilles Deleuze agrees with this assessment and goes on to describe theory as a 'tool-box', tools to be used at will for any useful purpose. Foucault later took up this idea himself and offered the following definitions.

Theory as a tool-box means:

> that it is a question of constructing not a system but an instrument: a *logique* appropriate to power relations and to the struggles taking place around them.

> that this research can only be done step by step, on the basis of a reflection (necessarily historical in certain of its dimensions) on given situations.[85]

This is the kind of research that Foucault considers himself to be undertaking, commenting further:

> All my books, *Histoire de la folie* or *Surveiller et punir* are, if you like, little tool-boxes. If people want to open them, use a sentence, an idea, an analysis as a screwdriver or a spanner in order to short-circuit, disqualify and break systems of power, including if need be, those which have given rise to my own books, well, so much the better![86]

Foucault's notion of 'theory as a tool-box', as a mode of politico-intellectual activism, attracted an enormous amount of attention in the 1970s and early 1980s. The theme of a fragmented philosophy, the championship of 'local' forms of knowledge which 'by their mere liberation have split the already crumbling ground of total-ising discourses linked to institutions exercising centralised power',[87] became immensely popular. As Dominique Grisoni remarks in 1976, using the jargon of the time: 'The philosophical-body exists. Temporarily. In its most "realistic" form, that is such-as-it-really-is-in-itself, segmented, exploded, differentiated, bloated, bearer of all subversions, rich with all possibilities.'[88]

The theme of theoretical 'tool-boxes' became equally wide-spread in English and quite a number of writers describe either Foucault's books, their own book, or both, as 'tool-boxes'.[89] But this overwhelming interest in tool-boxes in English is not simply because a number of these writers wish to adopt a certain political stance concerning the role of the intellectual, as might appear at first glance. It is also a matter of that well-known and well-worn cliché of Anglo-Saxon thought: empiricism. As one writer says, for the Anglo-Saxons, 'no theory is better than a poor one, while [for the French], a poor theory is better than none at all.'[90] For all their scorn of 'traditional' Anglo-Saxon intellectual practice, the English-speaking supporters of the 'tool-box' method are, in many cases, only supporting a new, and perhaps more insidious, version of the empiricist dream of a theory- and ideology-free approach to the real. These ardent advocates of Foucault's lack of system paradoxically build his thought into an all-explaining structure that can be applied to any situation and thus open our eyes to its stark and sordid reality. 'Foucault has persistently and dexterously avoided the canonical roles of revolutionary guru, great-and-good writer or "master thinker" ', enthuses Colin Gordon.[91] The remark that Foucault's aim is to 'attack great systems, grand theories and vital truths and to give free play to difference, to local and specific knowledge and to rupture, contingency and discontinuity' is also quite a standard one in its various permutations.[92] But it is Edward Said who best encapsulates, perhaps unwittingly, the English-language discussion on the subject of Foucault's much-fêted struggles against theory:

> Not for him is the noisy appeal to a cult of doctrine or of apocalypse or of dogma: he is persistently interested in the responsibilities and the offices of this method, as well as in the untidiness and the swarming profuseness of detail . . . . The impersonal modesty of Foucault's writing co-exists (paradoxically) with an unmistakable tone of voice that can deliver both insight and learning; he gives the impression nonetheless of having experienced first-hand every one of the books he has read.[93]

Foucault becomes an empiricist's dream. Not only does he immerse himself in an overwhelming mass of detail devoid of annoying and interfering subjective viewpoints or ideologies, but he is also closer than anyone to the objective truth of these details, having experienced the 'facts' for himself. Such a theoretician is to be admired indeed.

More recently some critics have begun to argue that Foucault does not go far enough in this direction. In a critique of Foucault's genealogical method, Jeffrey Minson, taxing Foucault with a certain historicism, says that genealogy 'ought to be able to set up the possibility of constructing intelligible trains of events and transformations which are conceived as expressions neither of their past nor of their future'.[94] In other words, we should consult only the succession of true facts existing in an eternal present, viewed from a god-like point outside history. This, of course, is the very kind of history that Foucault had gone to such lengths to undermine.

But, as we shall see in the following chapter, enthusiasm for the 'tool-box' approach has started to wane, and the criticism that this approach is a political mistake which dooms Foucault's thought to helpless moral and political pessimism has begun to acquire increasing acceptance. For Foucault, however, the rejection of universal 'systems' and philosophies was to remain of major significance and he devoted a good deal of time and space in his last work to working out an approach which did not fall into the contradictions of the schema he had proposed during the 1970s. Indeed after 1981, quite suddenly the vision of a society rigidly bound together by the subtle and anonymous webs of discipline and power vanished from his work. The grey and meticulously constructed prison walls of genealogy crumbled and the limit/ horizons glittering in the distance became once again visible. Another decade had ended and a long weary struggle had reached its term.

6

The Return of the Limits

At a conference held in California in 1981, followers of Foucault's work were more than a little surprised to learn that Foucault's real intention was not to analyse 'power' but 'to create a history of the different modes by which, in our culture, the human being is made "subject" '.[1] What was more, he repeated these claims the following January in his course at the Collège de France, a course uncharacteristically titled *The Hermeneutic of the Subject*. Admittedly, Foucault did concede rather grudgingly that he had been 'quite involved with the question of power',[2] but it looked suspiciously likely that this involvement was drawing to an end. For those (particularly in America) who had invested so much time and interest in the notion of power, this sudden change of tack on Foucault's part was somewhat alarming. Indeed, by the time the second and third volumes of *Histoire de la Sexualité* appeared, it had become apparent that Foucault's work had undergone yet another of its famous mutations, even if as before, not all critics could agree on its importance.

Nonetheless, even those who denied that Foucault's work had in fact undergone a significant change had to admit *something* had happened. Most obvious, perhaps, is the change of historical period, from the 'Classical Age', the eighteenth century, to the Ancient Greek and Roman period. The much maligned 'subject' also makes a reappearance and there is a quite remarkable change of style. As Gilles Barbedette and André Scala remark at the beginning of an interview with Foucault in 1984: 'What is striking when reading your last two books, is a clear, pure and smooth style of writing, very different from what we have been used to.'[3] Maurice Blanchot also describes these books as 'calm, peaceful, without the burning passion of his other texts'.[4] Indeed, the clear and simple style of Volumes 2 and 3 of *Histoire de la Sexualité* and his later articles and interviews bears little in common with either the enthusiastic, if sometimes obscure poetry of the 1960s or the 'grey and meticulous' jargon of the 1970s.

But this new clarity is in fact highly deceptive, as it tends to create the illusion that what is being said is easy, uncontroversial and straightforward. That this is far from being the case can be seen from the wide variety of views and interpretations surrounding this work. Thus, if some critics are content to analyse Foucault's last writings in terms of his work on power, or at least make very little distinction between his writings on power and his writings on the subject, others take up these last writings on their own terms. But in general, the most noteworthy feature of criticism since Foucault's death has been the clearer-than-ever polarisation into two opposing schools of thought: one which views our world and its reality as an ongoing and ever-changing interplay of differences and one which seeks to define the unifying principle or 'foundation' of that reality.

These two schools of thought were plainly in evidence at the international conference held on Foucault's work in Paris in 1988. But, if one notes a return to the classical accusations of former times, that the 'abyss' of 'total critique' can only lead to relativism, irrationalism and cynical nihilism not to mention a 'political quietism' and 'conservatism', one very important change has taken place.[5] In the 1960s, these anathemas were hurled by the intellectual establishment against an embattled radical avant-garde who were themselves to gain ascendancy during the 1970s, but in the 1980s this situation has undergone a complete reversal. These criticisms have now come to be packaged as startlingly new: the discovery and righteous condemnation of the inevitable consequences of the 'cynical antics of the deconstructionists', who are now being exhorted to seek their niche in the museum of discarded ideas.[6]

Foucault is credited with no less a feat than distilling the 'Elixir of Pure Negation',[7] and berated for adopting an unrepentant and highly irresponsible 'anarchic Nietzscheanism'.[8] 'The political utility' of Foucault's 'permanent diagnosis of the ruses of power is unclear', says one critic, complaining that Foucault's stance against *all* 'totalising alliances of knowledge and power, is difficult to define as situated and responsible'.[9] Nor does Foucault 'offer us [any] grounds for encouraging resistance or struggles', as his rejection of 'human nature and human subjectivity' removes any such grounds, leaving us to struggle for the sake of struggle.[10] There is no way of persuading people 'to give up some of their power for the greater good'.[11] Iain Wright likewise condemns the ideas of Foucault and his followers, describing as a 'counsel of despair' what he sees as their message to abandon 'dreams of progress . . ., meaning in history . . ., the rational pursuit of utopias'. Wright's own solution is radical: a return to 'old-fashioned "humanism" ' and 'rationalism'.[12] Richard Rorty, in a similar vein, wishes that Foucault *'would* speculate. His obviously sincere attempt to make philosophical thinking be of some use, do some good, help people, is not going to get anywhere until he condescends to do a bit of dreaming about the future.'[13]

In the final analysis, what many of these commentators are in fact criticising, is Foucault's failure to be convinced that a universal rational rule or some form of underlying rationality is sufficient grounds to guarantee the adequacy of any particular system of morals, value or truth. Foucault, in declaring his irritation with 'metaphysical' inquiries into 'the foundations of power in a society or the self-institution of a society', goes altogether too far.[14] If we remove the possibility of rational foundations, on what basis can we operate? How can we guarantee the truth of our systems of value and knowledge, how can we escape the dread trap of historical relativism? For thinkers such as Habermas, the solution is simple: the only 'way out' of these dilemmas, which loom so alarmingly in the contemporary consciousness, is to 'go back';[15] in other words, to posit a 'substantive foundation', a 'resistant structure, namely the structure of a rationality which is immanent in everyday communicative practices'.[16] But for Foucault this 'solution' is simply no solution. As Paul Veyne points out 'Foucault admits to being incapable of justifying his own preferences: he cannot invoke human nature, reason, functionalism, essence or adequation to an object.'[17] It is scarcely surprising that such a position which deprives the philosopher of a god-like legislative power and which undermines the reassuring faith in the absolute and certain value of Reason, is unpopular.[18] But for Foucault, this uncertainty is merely a sign of our finitude, holding out the constant invitation to freely transgress the limits wherever possible.

If, as we have seen, Foucault's rejection of certain 'metaphysical' types of inquiries was, in fact, more rhetorical than actual during the 1970s, after 1981 he manages to solve the problem by reintroducing the limits. Once again, the Same and the Other become distinct and free terms, and again two separate analyses emerge in Foucault's work, one relating to how the Same orders itself and the second to how that order communicates at the limits with the Other. In more specific terms, Foucault looks at how human beings order themselves and are ordered into historical entities known as subjects, and how those subjects exercise their freedom by working on the limits of that order. This order and this work on the limits is at the same time both individual and collective. The subject is, at its very origin, a historical and social entity. It does not pre-exist history or relations with other subjects as does the Cartesian subject. As this point, a clear continuity with certain early themes in Foucault's work becomes apparent, but this time, instead of analysing the interaction of the Same and the Other as it appears at the general level of collective social experience, Foucault narrows his focus to the individual. He also goes to some lengths to acknowledge both the similarities as well as the considerable differences between his past and present work, outdoing himself in his habitual self-reassessments and statements of current position.

These remarks vary: first of all, there are the kind of remarks that became familiar to his readers during the 1970s, namely that he had *always* been dealing with one particular problem and with no other; in this case, the subject. So, in reply to one rather bemused interviewer, he boldly asserts that he is 'far from being a theoretician of power' and that 'power, as an autonomous question' does not interest him. Instead he is 'working on the history . . . of the way reflexivity of self upon self is established.'[19] These remarks occur at a point when Foucault was only just beginning to work through his new ideas. Later, he went on to refine his approach, developing the idea that a 'field of experience' is composed of three 'fundamental' axes, areas or problems, namely truth, power and individual conduct. Or to put it another way, one can examine history with a view to understanding how we constitute ourselves as subjects who know, who act on others and who are moral agents.[20] Needless to say, of course, Foucault's own *oeuvre* constitutes the examination *par excellence* of these three axes. They are all to be found, for example ('albeit in a somewhat confused fashion'), in *Histoire de la folie*. The 'truth axis' is then analysed in *Naissance de la clinique* and *Les Mots et les choses*, and 'power' in *Surveiller et punir*. Finally, the 'ethical axis' appears in Volumes 2 and 3 of the *Histoire de la sexualité*.[21] In *L'Usage des plaisirs* Foucault puts it this way:

Through what mechanisms of truth does man conceive of his own being when he perceives himself as mad, when he looks at himself as ill, when he reflects as a living, speaking and working being, when he judges and punishes himself as a criminal? Through what mechanisms of truth has the human being recognised himself as a man of desire? (UP:13)

In a final interview, Foucault explains that the problem with his earlier books was that he had largely ignored the question of 'individual conduct', an effort which had required the deployment of a variety of 'slightly rhetorical methods'. If there were a number of things which had definitely been implicit in the earlier work, the exclusion of 'one of the three fundamental domains of experience', meant that they could not be properly dealt with. Thus in his last work, Foucault sees himself as finally attempting to come to terms with some of the issues he had avoided earlier on. He makes this clear in the introduction to *L'Usage des plaisirs*, where he draws attention to the efforts and risks involved in trying to 'change one's way of seeing, in modifying the horizon of what one knows' (UP:17). In the end these changes brought him full circle and he was able to see far more clearly what he had been doing all along without being entirely aware of it. Why write books, he concludes, if they simply stockpile information and have no effect on the author himself? Rather than being a self-righteous exercise in laying down the law for others, philosophy should be an 'ascescis', an attempt to work on the limits of oneself in thought, to see how far it is possible to think differently.[22]

The transition from 'power' to the 'subject', and the reintroduction of the limits into Foucault's work can be clearly observed in a most interesting article appended to a book by Dreyfus and Rabinow. The article appears in two sections. The first section, titled 'Why Study Power? The Question of the Subject', is noticeably inferior in style, organisation and conceptual clarity to the second section, titled 'How is Power Exercised?'. Here, a certain confrontation emerges between the notions of the subject and power; between Foucault's old and new ideas. So, although the first section opens with various pronouncements in favour of the subject, it is still power that wins out: 'it is a form of power which makes individuals subjects' (in both senses of the word) writes Foucault.[23] The subject, in this version, is created by the exterior and anonymous mechanisms of power which impose a 'law of truth' on the individual, forcing him and others to recognise in him a particular type of subject. The struggle against these forms of individuality is a desperate one indeed. This is, of course, still very much the type of analysis typical of Foucault's work during the 1970s.

But one very important change emerges. If all of Foucault's previous work had been one long effort to link the experience of the limits and order to one particular historical form, here he renounces this search. So, in order to examine 'the way a human being turns him – or herself into a subject', he explains that he has 'chosen the domain of sexuality – how men have learned to recognise themselves as subjects of "sexuality"'.[24] In other words, sexuality is not the only, or even the most important, historical area of human experience in relation to the formation of the subject or the self. Rather, it is simply the area that Foucault has chosen to interest himself in, for a variety of reasons, some of them no doubt personal as a number of critics have suggested. In La Volonté de savoir, sex had been endowed by the workings of power with a privileged capacity for containing the truth, but it loses this exceptional position by Volumes 2 and 3. Indeed, when Foucault was asked in 1983 whether he still thought that the understanding of sexuality was central to an understanding of who we are, he declared that he was 'much more interested in problems about techniques of the self and things like that than sex . . . sex is boring', adding that the Greeks and early Christians had in fact been far more interested in food, than in sex.[25] Once the critical investigation of limits and of order is no longer bound to a particular historical content, every area of historical experience becomes equally important, even if different experiences are more 'problematic' at different times in history. As Foucault went on to remark in 1983, 'nothing is fundamental . . . there are only reciprocal relations.'[26]

But it is not until the second half of 'The Subject and Power', that the major change in Foucault's thought becomes really clear. Here he not only reworks his ideas on power, but in doing so, reintroduces the limits and departs from the increasingly sterile huis clos of a frozen and predetermined confrontation between power and its mirror underside resistance. As before, he emphasises that power is not a 'thing', but this time, he says it can only be exercised over free subjects who are themselves capable of acting. By 'free subjects', Foucault means 'individual or collective subjects who are faced with a field of possibilities in which several ways of behaving, several reactions and diverse comportments must be realised'.[27] Power is not merely a relation between these free subjects, 'it is a way in which certain actions modify others'.[28] But because of the freedom of the acting subjects, no matter what violence or seduction those 'structure[s] of actions' which make up power may choose to exercise, the object of power can ultimately escape and refuse the relationship of power, even if only through death. Or as Foucault puts it poetically:

> The exercise of power may produce as much acceptance as may be wished for: it can pile up the dead and shelter itself behind whatever threats it can imagine. In itself the exercise of power is not violence: nor is it a consent which implicitly is renewable.[29]

Once the freedom and the 'specific nature' of the subject are abolished by violence or physical constraint it is no longer a matter of a power relationship. Indeed, each term in a power relationship 'constitutes for the other a kind of permanent limit, a point of possible reversal'.[30] This is very different from the sombre views of *La Volonté de savoir*, where Foucault argues that there is no 'absolute exterior' in relation to power, and where the reign of power, of the Same, of Order, knows no limits. Of course, Foucault still believes that there is no such thing as a society without power relations, but this time in place of the impersonal and abstract mechanisms of power, bearing down in all their invincible inevitability, a far less apocalyptic and far more personal vision emerges. As long as people continue to live and act, Foucault says, they will try to 'structure the possible field of action of others'.[31] Foucault also implicitly criticises some of his earlier ideas, pointing out the dangers of analysing power relations by simply focusing on the study of institutions. This type of analysis tends to foster the assumption that institutions are at the origin of relations of power, and that the specific mechanisms they employ to perpetuate their own existence are the same mechanisms which operate in other areas of human experience. This is not in fact the case: society is not an institution, something Foucault had certainly come very close to saying before.

After 'The Subject and Power' Foucault, much to the chagrin of many of his supporters, virtually abandoned the question of power, except to fit it into an overall description of his past work. In general, after 1982 Foucault addresses himself to three tasks. The first of these is the examination of the question of 'individual conduct', and the analysis of how ethical systems actually function. Ethics is defined by Foucault as 'the kind of relationship you ought to have with yourself, *rapport à soi* . . . and which determines how the individual is supposed to constitute himself as a moral subject of his own actions'.[32] Secondly, Foucault undertakes the task of working out arguments to support his own personal ethical stance. Finally, he looks at some concrete historical practices in the area of ethics, notably at how 'sexual behaviour was problematised, becoming an object of concern, an element for reflection, material for stylisation' (UP:30) in Greek texts of 400 BC and Greek and Latin texts of the first two centuries AD. At the same time, he introduces some comparisons with the way later Christians defined themselves as the moral subjects of a 'sexuality'. If these three areas are all in fact closely linked in Foucault's work, the following discussion will concentrate mainly on the first two, which have been the subject of most debate in the critical literature. Foucault's detailed examination of the prescriptions concerning sexual practice in Antiquity tend on the whole to raise mainly questions of empirical historical interpretation, and as such, will not be dealt with here.

Morality, Foucault says, is a notoriously ambiguous notion and can be defined in a variety of ways. For example, morality can be seen as a code, that is, 'a collection of values and rules of action which are proposed to individuals and groups through the intermediary of various prescriptive mechanisms such as the family, educational institutions, Churches, etc.' (UP:32). But 'morality' can also be defined as the way in which individuals behave, and how far they conform or do not conform to the 'prescriptive systems' of their society. If there is a certain permanency (although not total immutability) about certain moral principles, what *does* change quite noticeably, is how and why individuals put these rules and precepts into practice. It is precisely these changes that Foucault is interested in analysing, rather than in writing a history of how moral codes have changed or a history of people's moral (or immoral) behaviour.

He begins by distinguishing between two types of societies or systems: those 'orientated towards codes' and those 'orientated towards ethics'. In the first system, the code or the system of rules acquires a great importance, and the individual, on pain of punishment, is exhorted to conform to the code as it is handed down by recognised authorities. At the other end of the spectrum, systems 'orientated towards ethics' place less emphasis on the letter of the law and correspondingly more on very personal 'practices of the self' aimed at transforming the individual's own mode of being. Foucault describes the morality of the Ancient Greeks as falling into the latter category. He is careful to emphasise, however, that contrary to a popular contemporary cliché, the subsequent Christian tradition of morality cannot be entirely encompassed within the repressive structure of the Law. There have in fact been numerous Christian moralities of both types and between these we find 'sometimes juxtapositions, sometimes rivalries and conflicts, sometimes composition' (UP:37). A moral action, Foucault says, is not simply an act which conforms to the rules, it is the way in which an individual seeks to transform himself into a certain type of subject.

In *L'Usage des plaisirs*, as in all his other work, Foucault begins by locating certain patterns of intelligibility in the empirical material he is considering. From there, he proposes a series of 'methodological rules' which he uses to order his own analysis. As Henri Joly quite correctly remarks, even if Foucault introduces new themes and problems such as the 'subject' and 'ethics' into his final work, his methodology remains the same: 'It is the same history which continues and the same methodological network that is deployed. History of "practices" and "discourses" . . . but not a history of representations or a sociology of behaviours.'[33] Thus, Foucault describes the relation to self as having four aspects. The first of these concerns what he describes as the 'determination of ethical substance' (UP:33), or in other words, the definition of which part of the individual's self or behaviour should be addressed in carrying out a particular ethical practice. For example, the practice of fidelity might simply be a purely external matter of ruling one's acts, or it might also be the mastery of one's inner desires and the resistance to temptation. Or again, acts themselves might be unimportant, the emphasis being on the quality of one's feelings for one's partner. Acts, desires and feelings thus become at different periods of history the areas which are to be worked on in relation to a certain type of moral behaviour. The second aspect of the relation to oneself – the mode of subjectivation' (UP:34) – concerns the way in which

people are invited or persuaded to recognise their moral obli
gations. For instance, people might be persuaded to act morally by
divine law revealed in texts, or by a natural law or a rational
(Kantian and universal) rule. Or, on the other hand, rather than
acting morally in order to conform to divine or rational law, people
might act morally so as to conform to an ideal of beauty, of an
'aesthetics of existence'. The third aspect involves the 'elaboration'
and 'ethical work' performed upon the self, or the ascetic practices
by means of which individuals change themselves so as to become
ethical subjects (UP:34). These practices include a variety of
mental and spiritual exercises as well as physical techniques such
as the regulation of diet and exercise. The final aspect of the
relation to self is a teleological one. What sort of being does the
individual wish to become in adhering to a moral code and acting
morally? Hence, the aim might be to gain eternal life or it could be
to become detached from the agitations and passions of this world
or alternately it might be to acquire mastery over oneself.[34]

One problem with this schema is that the second aspect de
scribed by Foucault – the mode of subjectivation – could equally
well be included under the 'teleological' category. If people act in
conformity with divine or rational law, it is not simply because
they are seeking to conform to the 'necessity' of things or that they
might fear some kind of punishment, it is also because they are
seeking to become God-like or fully rational (therefore true)
human beings. Likewise to set up the ideal of beauty as an
incentive for moral action (as do the Ancient Greeks in Foucault's
account) is to exhort people to become beings who are 'beautiful',
who lead a 'beautiful existence'. In other words, the 'mode of
subjectivation' and the teleology of moral action are indissolubly
linked. The aims that Foucault lists under 'teleology' are, in fact,
but subsets of far wider aims.

Nonetheless, Foucault's methodological analysis of the four
aspects of the historical relation to self is a most useful and
interesting one. Rather than setting out to discover which values
are the 'right ones' and should therefore be adopted by all right
thinking people, Foucault prefers to concentrate on how ethical
systems function in their historical context, leaving the reader or
the 'moral subject' to make his or her own decisions about the
rightness, wrongness or effectiveness of any particular ethical
system or course of action. Again and again, Foucault insists that
the task of philosophy is not to reinforce or create systems of

belief, but to understand the workings and limits of such systems. It must be pointed out quite emphatically, however, that Foucault's own position is by no means neutral. He makes his own ethical position very clear indeed, but at the same time, he does not present his position as a necessary truth which the reader is obliged to accept.[35] This is precisely the state of affairs which Foucault had tried so unsuccessfully to bring about in his work during the 1970s: a thought of the limits which made its own limits clearly visible.

Foucault begins by restating his longstanding opposition to a certain 'mode of subjectivation' embodied in a philosophical tradition that goes back to Descartes and Kant, and which starting from the rational subject of knowledge asks, 'what is universally true for all men in all ages?' For Foucault, the assumption that there is such a universal and rational subject of knowledge is a metaphysical one – a matter of belief. He prefers to make the more modest, and perhaps for some, less reassuring, claim that human beings are historical beings and the way they form their experience and subjectivity is through concrete historical practice. There is no 'true' subject or self which can be discovered by stripping away social, psychological, historical and other determinations which are purported to veil its pure and true identity. The way we see ourselves, perceive and construct experience, the way in which we organise and work on our consciousness of self, on our subjectivity, are all part of provisional processes that human beings have developed over time and in which each subject freely participates.[36] It would be pointless, indeed impossible, to shut ourselves away in splendid Cartesian isolation to discover that pure essential subjectivity which exists before history and before our relations with others. As Pierre Macherey explains in a paper given at the 1988 conference on Foucault, if the subject is unique and singular, 'it is a singularity which only appears and is distinguished against a background of belonging, tying the subject not only to other subjects with whom he communicates, but to the global process which constitutes him by normalising him and from which he draws his own being.'[37]

'Criticism', concludes Foucault, 'is no longer going to be practised in the search for formal structures with universal value, but rather as a historical investigation into the events that have led us to constitute ourselves and to recognise ourselves as subjects of what we are doing, thinking, saying.'[38] Thus, instead of seeking to locate and define formal and evident truths, the question becomes 'What is the work which I must effect upon myself so as to be capable and worthy of acceding to the truth?'[39] This question, of course, has a long history in various spiritual and pre-Cartesian traditions. The search for universal values or moralities acceptable to everybody, 'in the sense that everyone must submit', appears to Foucault to be 'catastrophic' as well as historically inapposite.[40] In a society marked by its fragmentation and its scepticism regarding older legal and religious systems, it is unlikely that all groups and individuals would be willing to believe, or even agree to act as if they believed, in one unique set of values no matter how 'abstract' or 'general'. Indeed, the examination of history shows that no such 'consensus' has ever actually existed. It has never been more than a philosopher's dream.[41] The 'non-universal' point of view has perhaps been more readily adopted by historians and social scientists dealing with the minutiae of mundane human activity than by some philosophers. Thus, Philippe Ariès, writing in 1977, remarks in a statement which is most true of Foucault's later work:

> The empiricism of historians has allowed this philosopher, who has truly remained a philosopher, to escape from the univocal character of systems (and perhaps from philosophies?) and to grasp the extraordinary diversity of human strategies, the profound meaning of that irreducible diversity.[42]

Pierre Bourdieu, likewise unenthused by a 'prophetic' school of philosophy which from the Olympian heights of ontological abstraction looks down on the vulgar world of ordinary thought and activity, suggests that instead of asking questions about the existence of 'universal interests', one would do better to ask 'who has interests invested in the universal?' or 'what are the social conditions which must be fulfilled in order that certain agents become interested in the universal?'[43] If Bourdieu applies these questions to the workings of educational institutions and the professional activity of intellectuals, Foucault adopts a very similar approach in his examination of the history of thought.

If the 'truth' is not something one can hope to acquire without a serious work of self-transformation, there is no possibility of any theory, institution, political system, law, object, system of rationality, philosophy or any other external mechanism ever being able to do the work for us and handing us the truth or freedom on a platter. It is certainly true that all these things can help, but the very same objects and theories can equally well be used to serve the causes of error and oppression. No matter how marvellous a theory or an ideology, there is no guarantee that it will not be misused. For instance, 'humanism' has been used to support a number of totalitarian regimes in the twentieth century. Likewise, certain architectural projects originally intended to promote the freedom of workers have been used to produce the reverse effect. Conversely, no matter how tyrannical a system such as a concentration camp may be, there are always possibilities for resistance. The only way freedom can exist and be guaranteed is through its practice. Foucault remarks, 'If one were to find a place, and perhaps there are some, where liberty is effectively exercised, one would find that this is not owing to the order of objects, but . . . to the practice of liberty.'[44] In other words, freedom is not a goal we work towards or an object we struggle to possess, it is the capacity for choosing one of several possibilities of action.

Likewise, 'reason' and 'rationality' cannot save us. 'One should not forget', Foucault remarks, 'it was on the basis of the flamboyant rationality of social Darwinism that racism was formulated, becoming one of the most enduring and powerful ingredients of Nazism.'[45] This does not mean we should not use our reason to criticise other 'rational' practices: on the contrary. What it does mean, is that there is no such thing as 'a kind of founding act whereby reason in its essence was discovered or established and from which it was subsequently diverted by such and such an event.'[46] The Enlightenment is a historical event, not something we should be 'for or against'. So instead of trying at all costs to locate an 'essential kernel of rationality' in those events, it might be more useful, Foucault says, to undertake a precise series of historical enquiries, to examine the functioning of a plurality of rationalities and think about 'what is not or is no longer indispensable for the constitution of ourselves as autonomous subjects.'[47] Once again, it is a question of the limits of the present rather than of permanent foundations. On several occasions Foucault underlines this refusal to submit to what he describes as the 'blackmail of the Enlightenment', the view that 'either you accept rationality or you fall prey to the irrational'. There are in fact many rationalities, all of them the product of very concrete historical practices.[48] In short, there is no general formula which will save us the work, give us a comfortable certainty and do away with our anxiety before the limits. But if this is the case, how should we go about defining our own relation to the truth? Again, for Foucault, it is a matter of referring to history, of situating ourselves within historical experience.

Philosophers, particularly since Hegel and Nietzsche, Foucault says, have had an unfortunate tendency to dramatise the present, heralding it as the high point in history, the apocalyptic dawning of a new age, the age of the 'end of philosophy'. This is a view which Foucault wishes to criticise all the more strongly for once having held it himself, notably in *Les Mots et les choses*. Instead, we should be much more modest and start from the view that 'the time we live in is not *the* unique or fundamental or irruptive point in history where everything is completed and begun again'. In fact we live in 'a time like any other, or rather, a time which is never quite like any other'.[49] This 'modesty' about our present has a double advantage: first of all, it means we need no longer occupy the triumphant and superior position which condemns all the effort of past ages to irrevocable error and blindness. On the other hand, we need not stand in awe of the past or look back nostalgically to a mythical golden age.[50] Instead, every period in history has its own very specific problems whose solutions are also quite specific to that time. But for all their specificity, these problems and solutions can be of considerable use to us in our attempts to think through our present relation to truth and how we form ourselves in relation to truth. As Foucault remarks:

> Among the cultural inventions of mankind there is a treasury of devices, techniques, ideas, procedures, and so on, that cannot exactly be reactivated, but at least constitute, or help to constitute, a certain point of view which can be very useful as a tool for analysing what's going on now – and to change it.[51]

It is precisely in this spirit that Foucault undertakes the examination of the Ancient Greeks, noting certain similarities between our own concerns and those of the Greeks, but at the same time emphasising that we cannot apply the solutions of another age to our own. No period in history can be held up as an example to another.[52]

Thus if we can certainly make a limited use of some of the ideas proposed by the Ancient Greeks, the Greeks cannot form a model for today. Indeed, Foucault finds the Greek 'ethics of pleasure' with its emphasis on virility and the exclusion of the Other 'quite disgusting',[53] and his last two volumes on sexuality go a long way towards demonstrating how distant the Greeks are from us, and how repressive and male-centred were their sexual mores and ethics. These two volumes also undermine the popular myth that the pre-Christian Greeks enjoyed a sexual freedom that the later Christian era was to do away with.[54] It would be quite absurd, indeed impossible, remarks Foucault, to attempt to found a modern morality based purely on Antique morality, ignoring the whole of intervening history.[55]

But the study of others' 'truths' is all very well, it might be objected, how do we decide which are the 'right ones', or what the right use of those ideas should be? There is no easy solution to this. Spiritual traditions, Foucault says, maintain that a subject desiring to know the truth must undertake a work of ascetic preparation or a 'modification of activity'; the truth then 'returns' and transforms the subject who is then better able to continue his search for truth, and better able to discriminate between the true and the false.[56] As with freedom, the search for truth is its own guarantee. Like freedom, truth is not guaranteed by external objects but depends upon the practices of individuals who are seeking precisely to form their subjectivity in relation to truth. This is far from being an easy task and Foucault notes that 'a demanding, prudent "experimental" attitude is necessary; at every moment, step by step, one must confront what one is thinking and saying with what one is doing, with what one is.'[57] His own practical and personal solution to the problem of how subjectivity should be formed in relation to the truth, the 'mode of subjectivation' which he suggests as a possible guide for contemporary action is the idea of an 'aesthetics' or 'stylistics' of existence, an idea he borrows from the Greeks. Foucault explains that 'the arts of existence' in Antiquity were voluntary practices by means of which people fixed their rules of conduct and sought to modify their mode of being, giving their lives a certain aesthetic and stylistic form. These 'arts of existence' and 'techniques of self' lost some of their importance with the historical development of a highly codified and juridical form of Christianity. Nonetheless, they did resurface briefly during the Renaissance and also later during the nineteenth century with such figures as Baudelaire.

This idea of an 'aesthetics of existence', of turning one's life into a work of art and forming it according to a notion of style has been the source of considerable difficulties for many of Foucault's critics. For the most part, these problems have been occasioned by differing interpretations of what is meant by 'aesthetics' and 'style'. For many commentators to speak of aesthetics is to invoke judgements of taste which are 'beyond good and evil'.[58] James Bernauer, commenting on the critical reception of Foucault's last work remarks: 'Typical of [American criticism] was the charge that Foucault had elevated the quest for beauty in life over all other intellectual and moral virtues . . . . Foucault's "aesthetics of existence", . . . has been taken as a sign of his allegiance to a Greek morality or to an a-moral aestheticism.'[59] Likewise to speak of 'style' for many critics is to invoke the notion of distinction, the search for an aesthetic and rare refinement which distinguishes its practitioner from the common and vulgar masses of people without style or taste.[60] Thus, the project of an 'aesthetics of existence' can only be indulged in by a privileged elite, who are not obliged to confront the harsh material and political realities of life, an elite who 'can employ all their energy in perfecting the refinement of their life style'.[61]Making one's life into a 'work of art' can be nothing more than a purely private undertaking, with little or no effect on existing mechanisms of power, a self indulgent exercise which distances itself entirely from the difficult confrontation with problems occurring in our societies. 'Politics' and the noble goals of 'social reform' and 'social liberation' are totally bypassed by the 'stylistics of existence'.[62] Richard Rorty, for example, offers a bizarre analysis of Foucault's 'private' search for 'self autonomy', a search which he claims, is quite independent from his 'conduct towards other human beings'. Rorty adds that Foucault – a 'romantic intellectual' – wanted to help people, while at the same time 'inventing a self which had nothing much (indeed, as little as possible) to do with theirs'. But on occasions, Foucault made the terrible mistake of thinking that other people besides himself also had 'a moral duty to achieve the same inner autonomy as he himself [had] achieved'. Such a projection of a 'search for autonomy out into public space', as Rorty puts it, could only have the most dire social and political consequences.[63]

But as Pierre Hadot and Paul Veyne point out, Foucault's concept of the 'aesthetics of existence' entails neither an amoral aestheticism nor the notion of distinction. Hadot, even if he is not entirely in agreement with Foucault's analyses, notes that for the Greeks, the notion of 'beauty' used in relation to people, implied moral value, even if the word had lost such connotations for the moderns.[64] Similarly, Veyne comments that for the Greeks 'an artist was first of all an artisan and the work of art, a labour'.[65] For Foucault, to make one's life a work of art is to lead a life that in its perfection and brilliance is an 'example' and an inspiration to others.[66] It is to make of one's life an object of knowledge, to create a certain form of *order*, but an order whose limits must be constantly challenged. It is by no means simply an exercise reserved for a decadent few who wish to alleviate the deadly *ennui* of their existence. It is something that requires a good deal of thought, work and practice by every individual in relation to a variety of historical 'mechanisms of truth' and to his or her own historical situation in the present, no matter how lowly or marginalised that situation might be. The modification of the self (a self which does not exist prior to society or history) produces a modification of one's activity in relation to others, and hence a modification in power relations, even if only at the micro-level to begin with. Thus Foucault's position certainly does not lead to the refusal of political or social action. As he explains in relation to the 'question of Poland', if he is convinced that very little can be done 'in strictly political terms' by supporters outside the country, it is quite essential 'for ethical reasons' not to accept what is happening there. This ethical attitude is also a political one: 'it does not consist in saying merely, "I protest", but in making of that attitude a political phenomenon that is as substantial as possible, and one which those who govern, here or there, will sooner or later be obliged to take into account.'[67]

As the individual is an integral part, indeed the product of his own society and history, the examination of that society and history can help him to understand what he is and where it is possible to change. Conversely, the understanding of the way he is ordered and orders himself is essential if he is to try to produce effective change at an inter-individual or societal level.[68] Of course, Foucault is doing no more than restating a position which has a very long history in reflection, but as Paul Veyne remarks on several occasions, people appear to have an incurable tendency to forget their limits and to want absolute certainty at any price, hence reminders can do no harm. 'The originality of Foucault amongst the great thinkers of this century', he says, 'has been that he does not convert our finitude into the foundation for new certainties'.[69]

At this point, we might ask once again the question which forms the title of this book: is Michel Foucault a historian or a philosopher? The answer to this question, as has been suggested here on a number of occasions, is that Foucault is a philosopher who writes history, transforming it into philosophy.[70] In adopting this historical point of view, the philosopher abandons all his well ordered certainties, but it is an abandonment that Foucault was more than willing to defend, right until the very last:

> I would like to say that as for those for whom going to a lot of trouble, beginning and beginning again, trying, being wrong, starting again from scratch, yet still managing to find a way of hesitating with each step, that as for those, in short, for whom working amidst reservations and anxiety, is equal to giving up, well, it is obvious that we are not on the same wavelength. (UP:13)

Such hesitation is not cause for a nihilistic despair as some have claimed, rather it offers the constant hope that the power of the Same can always be resisted, that it is not invincible. Foucault's work not only invites us to think for ourselves as 'free beings' beyond our historical limits, wherever possible, it also warns us not to accept any system without thinking about it very carefully first. Unfortunately his own work, particularly when it was at its most systematic and most oppressive during the 1970s, is in danger of itself becoming yet another constraining system. This is a tendency which should be resisted at all costs, because as Foucault himself shows, there are many ways of interpreting – and facilitating – the free dialogue at the limits between the Same and the Other, and they are certainly not all encompassed in Foucault's books. As one phase of his work demonstrates all too clearly, once that freedom is forgotten, the tyranny of the System and the Same, returns in force.

Notes

Preface

1. d'Hondt 1971, p.253. d'Hondt rejects the new alternative out of hand as a form of bourgeois mystification.
2. Foucault, 'Polemics, Politics and Problemizations', in Rabinow 1984, pp.383–3.
3. The term 'Anglo-Saxon' includes all English-language writings. For practical reasons, we will not distinguish between the products of England, America or other English-language countries. Such differences as do exist are not of overwhelming significance for the purposes of the present analysis.

1 A New Generation of Thinkers

1. Foucault, 'Entretien avec Madeleine Chapsal', 1966, p.15; see also 'Foucault répond à Sartre', 1968, p.22.
2. Revel 1971, p.13.
3. Furet 1967, p.10.
4. Ibid, p.4.
5. See Le Roy Ladurie 1982, p.95 and Daix 1976, chapter titled: 'Un symbole: le cas Nizan', pp.86–97.
6. de Beauvoir 1963, p.17.
7. Le Roy Ladurie 1982, p.45.
8. Merleau-Ponty 1961, p.10.
9. Althusser 1966, p.12.
10. Le Roy Ladurie 1982, p.150.
11. Lefort 1979, p.8.
12. Le Roy Ladurie 1982, pp.83, 109–10.
13. Sartre 1965, pp.151–2.
14. See for example Lefort, 'Kravchenko et le problème de L'URRS', *Les Temps Modernes*, no.29 (February 1948), republished in 1979. Lefort remarks in the preface to this book that his article criticising the Stalinist regime was received 'with suspicion or indignation' by the Left (p.8).
15. Le Roy Ladurie 1982, p.45.
16. Castoriadis 1981, p.286.
17. Le Roy Ladurie 1982, p.171.
18. In particular, Frantz Fanon's hymn to violence: *Les Damnés de la terre* 1961 with its equally inflammatory preface by Jean-Paul Sartre, created a considerable stir. See also Furet 1967, pp.4–5.
19. Althusser 1966, p.21; cf Akoun 1978, p.17.

20. Furet 1967, p.6.
21. Domenach 1966, p.26; cf. Domenach 1967, pp.772, 774, 775; Domenach 1981, pp.19–20. Domenach is referring to Foucault's interview with Madeleine Chapsal in 1966, pp.14–15.
22. Foucault is perhaps being a little extreme here, as he has in fact, spent a good deal of time and paper discussing the last two problems in one form or another.
23. See Foucault, 'Vérité et pouvoir', 1977, pp.16–17; 'Sur la sellette' 1975, p.3; 1984, p.4; Friedrich and Burton 1981, p.94.
24. Ariès 1980, p.145; See also Ariès 'La Singulière Histoire', 1978, p.88.
25. Serres, August 1962, pp.683–96, September 1962, pp.63–81; Barthes 1961, pp.915–22; Blanchot 1961, pp.676–86. (Foucault was particularly pleased about this review); Fernand Braudel, note to Mandrou 1962, pp.771–2.
26. Howard 1961, pp.653–4. See also Sheridan 1981 for an account of the reception of *Histoire de la folie* based on Foucault's own comments. In addition, the book was awarded the prestigious medal of the Centre National de la Recherche Scientifique.
27. Lindon 1981, p.23.
28. Foucault, 'Polemics, Politics and Problemizations', in Rabinow 1984, p.385.
29. These discussions were published in *Evolution, psychiatrique: cahiers de psychopathologie générale* 36, no.2 (1971), *La conception idéologique de 'L'histoire de la folie' de Michel Foucault: Journées annuelles de 'L'évolution psychiatrique' 6 et 7 décembre 1969*.
30. Baruk 1976, pp.72, 67; see also Baruk 1974, p.8 and 1978, pp.29–32.
31. Foucault, 'Non au sexe roi', 1977, p.113.
32. Clark 1983, p.xxvii; and Sheridan 1981, p.37.
33. Wright and Treacher 1982. For comments on the usefulness and the problems of Foucault's analyses for the history of medicine see also Ey 1981, pp.10, 210–13.
34. 'Old New Novelist' 1963, p.511.
35. Robbe-Grillet 1963, p.1029.
36. Caws 1971, p.34.
37. Howe 1974, p.118.
38. Gordon 1983, p.761.
39. Lévi-Strauss 1964, p.20.
40. Althusser 1976, p.57; cf. section titled 'Marxisme et humanisme' 1966, pp.225–58.
41. Barthes, 'The Death of the Author' in 1977, p.143. This article was originally published as 'La Mort de l'auteur' in *Mantéia* V, 1968.
42. de Certeau 1967, p.344; Godard 1967, p.21.
43. Clark 1983, pp.504–6.
44. Sartre 1966, p.4. Foucault replied to some of these criticisms in 'Foucault répond à Sartre', 1968, pp.20–22. In *L'Archéologie du savoir*, in a footnote about '*tableaux*' (p.19) a word which can be translated into English as tables, tableaux or paintings (amongst other things), Foucault remarks: 'Is it necessary to point out to the last dawdlers, that a "*tableau*" (probably in every sense of the word) is formally a

"series of series"? In any case, it is not a little fixed image which is placed in front of a lantern to the great disappointment of children, who at their age, of course, prefer the vivacity of cinema.' This footnote is not included in the English translation. Perhaps the translator thought in 1972, that the allusion to Sartre's criticism was too obscure for the English reader.

45. Foucault, 'Foucault répond à Sartre', 1968, p.21.
46. Kahn 1967, p.41.
47. For valuable comments on this French practice of 'reading' see Lemert 1981, pp.3–32.
48. Revel 1971, p.417.
49. Bourdieu 1979, p.597. Bourdieu further outraged certain journalists and intellectuals by declaring that *Lé Nouvel Observateur*, that well-known weekly arbiter of the latest intellectual fashion in Paris, was the 'Club Mediterranée of culture'.
50. For other scathing attacks on the way intellectual life functions in France see: Hamon and Rotman 1981; Débray 1979. For a more 'theoretical', although no less critical approach see the work of Bourdieu and Passeron 1977 and Bourdieu, 1984.
51. Domenach 1981, p.20.
52. Revel 1971, pp.44–5.
53. For an interesting analysis of the relationship between the celebrity status of an intellectual and the number of his or her appearances in *Le Nouvel Observateur* see Hamon and Rotman 1981, pp.236–42.
54. Concerning these types of declarations, Jacques Bouveresse remarks acutely: 'a philosopher who says "philosophy today is . . ." should consider that he is perhaps simply giving a "persuasive definition", and that it is always a little suspect to present as a historical necessity what might simply be a personal option, in itself perfectly legitimate and defensible.' Bouveresse 1978, p.118.
55. Michael Clark remarks that most of this book was written before the end of 1967 (that is before May 1968), Clark 1983, p.xxxiii.
56. Revel 1971, p.44. Maurice Blanchot (1986, p.26) also remarks that Foucault adopts the techniques of 'negative theology' in *L'Archéologie*.
57. See Mauriac 1976, pp.509–11. For his fascinating accounts of the day-to-day events and conversations involving Foucault and other intellectuals from 1971 to 1975, see the section in his book titled 'La Goutte d'Or'; see also Nemo 1972, p.40; Kravetz 1975, p.13. Also on the GIP see Patton 1979, pp.109–10.
58. For a copy of the script of this film, a number of stills as well as some comments by the director René Allio and press reactions, see *L'Avant-Scène: Cinéma*, 1 March 1977. Most of the issue is devoted to the film.
59. Lefort 1984, p.6; see also Scholes 1979, p.E1.
60. See Clavel 1975, pp.137, 141 and most of the articles and books he wrote after this date (see Bibliography for a selection). Foucault notes not unkindly 'the verbal inflation of our friend Clavel' in Mauriac 1976, p.552.
61. Foucault, 'Notre ami Maurice Clavel' 1979, p.88.

62. See for example Glucksmann 1977; Lévy 1977.
63. Foucault, 'La grande colère des faits', 1977, pp.84–6.
64. Proust 1968, p.24. Huppert 1974, p.191.
65. Benamou and Pudlowski 1983, p.x; see also: Hamon and Rotman 1981, p.292; and Maggiori 1984, p.5. Foucault was certainly aware of these remarks and defended himself, drawing attention to his numerous publications in the press. 'Structuralism and Post-Structuralism', 1983, p.209.

2 The Same, the Other and the Limit

1. Sheridan 1981, p.2.
2. Bourdieu 1987, p.171.
3. 'Is his discourse prophetic, cynical, chimerical, or simply academic?' asks one radical English-speaking critic ironically. Racevskis 1983, p.116.
4. Howe 1974, p.118.
5. Lévi-Strauss 1958, pp.10–11.
6. Rousseau 1975, p.793. D'Amico 1973, p.101. Barham 1979, p.111; Cranston 1968, p.39.
7. Domenach 1981, p.48.
8. For a brief historical account of the reasons for this French philosophical journalism see Foucault, 'Le Piège de Vincennes', 1970, pp.33–5.
9. Russell 1968, p.10.
10. Rousseau 1972–73, p.256, cf.196. Jean-Paul Brodeur comments: 'As one would expect, he has been reproached for being too great a writer to be a true philosopher.' 1977, p.562.
11. For a most interesting discussion on this difference between the two traditions, see Hottois, 1978, pp.373–6.
12. This is not to say that certain scientific propositions are not true. They are true in the sense that they can form a coherent system of explanation and provide an effective basis for technology, but the question of whether they describe the true 'essence of things' is quite a different one. Georges Canguilhem and Foucault have written at length on this subject, see Canguilhem 1978; see also Veyne 1978, pp.234–5.
13. Bouveresse 1978, pp.121, 122.
14. See the various comments of the 'new historians', on 'popular' history versus 'specialist history', and the exposure of history in the media, as well as the dryness of 'positivist university history'. Bellour 1977, pp.10, 23. For an excellent analysis of this division and its institutional locations and stakes see Bourdieu, *Homo Academicus*, 1984, pp.26, 45, 140–67.
15. Bouveresse 1978, pp.101, 97.
16. See Lipovetsky 1983 and 1987. Finkielkraut 1987.
17. Farias 1987. Incidentally, Foucault in 1983 briefly addressed the issue of Heidegger and Nazism noting, 'there is a very tenuous "analytic" link between a philosophical conception and the con-

crete political attitude of someone who is appealing to it . . . . The key to the personal poetic attitude of the philosopher is not to be sought in his ideas . . . but rather in his philosophy-as-life, in his philosophical life, his ethos.' 'Politics and Ethics', in Rabinow 1984, p.374.

18. Veyron 1983; see also in this same issue of *Lire*, François Châtelet's excellent article, pp.32–3.

19. Gérard Lefort (1984, p.6) speaking of the 1970s, describes them as 'years of stormy insurgence against the education system in general and the intellectual elite in particular.'

20. Distributed as a tract at a meeting of the CNT (Conféderation Nationale du Travail) and the FAI (Fédération Abolitioniste Internationale) to support the struggle of the Spanish people against Francoism, held at the Mutualité on 20 April 1969. Cited in Mendel 1969, p.191; cf. 'A conversation with M. Foucault', 1971, pp.194–6.

21. Revel 1975, p.10.

22. Bellour 1977, pp.20–23.

23. Ariès, 'L'Histoire des mentalités' 1978, pp.411, 412; 1980, p.144; 'La Singulière Histoire', 1978, p.88. See also Veyne, 1978, pp.203–4, 231, 242; Bellour 1977, p.21. Veyne declares that after reading Foucault he changed his practice of history. Foucault in his turn acknowledges his debt to Paul Veyne and the latter's influence on his last two books. UP:14.

24. Braudel, 'Preface' to Stoianovich 1976, pp.16–17; for other comments in a similar vein see Revel 1975, pp.11–12; Solé 1972, p.473; Le Goff 1978, p.15; Quétel 1981, p.17; Misrahi 1959, pp.99, 105–6.

25. Bouveresse 1978, pp.118–20.

26. Kemp 1984, p.103.

27. Dews 1981, p.21.

28. Wuthnow 1984, p.136; see also the remarks of Poster 1984, pp.73–4. Colin Gordon (1986, p.933) also draws attention to this myth and remarks, 'Comparing it to the English situation, one can say that the relative richness of the relations between the historical and philosophical registers in French thought has been one of the factors that has most favoured Foucault's work and its reception in France.'

29. Ariès, L'Histoire des mentalités', 1978, p.412. Ariès' own work on death, childhood and population has contributed to this trend. See also Veyne, 1984, p.11.

30. Bellour 1977, p.17.

31. Burke 1973, p.329. 'There is no other truth than that of successive historical productions', remarks Paul Veyne, in Bellour 1977, p.21.

32. Bellour 1977, p.16.

33. Furet (1967, pp.11–12) expresses his surprise that (in France at least) the 'dissolution of ideological certainties and the "meaning" of history has not led to a reinstatement of Anglo-Saxon style empirical research and information. Not that this type of research and information has not been developing . . . but it all remains more than ever subordinated . . . to the elaboration of a general theory.'

34. Handlin 1979, p.409; see also the lengthy discussion on history as

'fiction' or the 'theatrical' reconstruction of the past and its relation to 'reality' in Bellour 1977, pp.19–21 and White 1978.

35.   On the Same and the Other and the 'horizon of finitude' or the 'finitude of the horizon' (limits) and history, see also Derrida, 'Violence et métaphysique', 1967, esp. pp.165–74.

36.   Althusser 1965, p.144. It is now of course fashionable to treat any reference to Althusser with the highest suspicion, an understandable attitude in the face of some of the more extravagant excesses of his followers during the 1960s and 1970s, not to mention his own confusing recantations and autocritiques. Cf. Althusser 1976. But if one leaves aside his (some would say Stalinist) devotion to the cause of Marxism, a number of very clear and useful observations relating to empiricism, historicism, humanism and the aims of philosophy, emerge in his writings.

37.   François Wahl made this point in an excellent paper delivered at the Foucault Conference in Paris in 1988.

38.   Foucault, 'Theatrum philosophicum', 1970, p.899.

39.   MC:351–4; cf. Foucault, 'Préface à la transgression', 1963, p.758.

40.   Aron 1948, p.10.

41.   Foucault, 'La Pensée du dehors', 1966, p.528. For an excellent analysis of Foucault's 'archaeology' as a 'theory of frontiers, a marginalism', see Michel Serres, 1968, p.195. Bourdieu (1984, p.10) also remarks 'Foucault's work is a long exploration of transgression, of the crossing of the social limit.'

42.   Foucault, 'What is Enlightenment?', in Rabinow 1984, p.45.

43.   Foucault, 'Préface à la transgression', 1963, pp.755, 757; cf. 'What is Enlightenment?', in Rabinow 1984, p.47.

44.   Foucault, 'What is Enlightenment?', in Rabinow 1984, p.46.

45.   Foucault, 'Hommage à Jean Hyppolite', 1969, p.132.

46.   Foucault, 'Débat sur la poésie', 1964, p.76.

47.   See de Certeau 1974, pp.32–3. For a further discussion of the dual historical and ahistorical characteristics of events, see Bertrand 1975, pp.162–73.

48.   See Foucault, 'Un cours inédit', 1984, p.35.

49.   For a similar point concerning Foucault's methodology, Colin Gordon recalls 'that the historicisation of the Kantian problem is a pre-eminently Nietzschean theme.' 'Afterword', in PK:236. Cf also Rajchman, *The Freedom of Philosophy*, 1985, pp.103–4.

50.   Foucault, 'On the Genealogy of Ethics', in Rabinow 1984, p.351.

51.   On history as an anti-metaphysical solution see Foucault, 'Nietzsche, la généalogie, l'histoire', 1971, pp.150, 159; cf. 'Space, Knowledge, Power', in Rabinow 1984, p.250. It must be emphasised that this does not mean that a 'history of the limits' is not devoid of its own kind of metaphysics.

52.   Foucault 'Le Retour de la morale', 1984, p.40. It may be noted, however, that when asked at different stages of his career about 'influences', Foucault gave a variety of different answers.

53.   Popper 1957, p.3. For several definitions, see Iggers, 1973,

pp.456–65. In recent years the term has often been used to denote any kind of interest shown in history by 'philosophers'.

54. Hegel 1975, p.29.
55. Popper 1957, p.50.
56. Hegel 1975, p.54.
57. Ariès 1954, p.40. This remarkable volume written at the end of the war takes up themes in historiography (discontinuity, the history of the present, the history of difference, reactions to anti-humanism) that were not to become widely discussed until much later.
58. Cf. Hegel 1975 pp.44–5; Popper 1957, p.33. See also Althusser's most useful discussion of Hegel's conception of the nature of historical time. He points out that for Hegel 'historical time does nothing but reflect the essence of the social totality of which it is the existence.' Althusser 1966, p.39. For other useful remarks on Hegel's idea of history see Cassirer 1961, pp.29–30. Gadamer 1968, pp.452–3.
59. Althusser 1966, p.73; cf. AS:22.
60. AS:32; cf. Foucault, 'Deuxième entretien', 1971, p.193; 'Linguistique et sciences sociales', 1969, p.254.
61. Foucault, 'Foucault répond à Sartre', 1968, pp.21–2.
62. AS:31, cf. p.44; cf. Foucault, 'Réponse à une question', 1968, p.854.
63. Foucault, 'Foucault répond à Sartre', 1968, p.21.
64. Léonard 1980, p.26.
65. See AS:31–43, chapter titled 'Les Unités du discours' for a detailed analysis and rejection of these categories. See also Foucault, 'Réponse à une question', 1968, pp.851–2; and 'La Situation de Cuvier', 1970, p.88.
66. Burguière 1971, p.ii. For a discussion of some of these criticisms see Iggers 1975, pp.68–72.
67. Foucault, 'Deuxième entretien', 1971, p.205.
68. Foucault, 'A conversation with M. Foucault', 1971, p.192; cf. 'Deuxième entretien', 1971, pp.189–91; the introduction to AS and pp.225–7, 265; 'Réponse à une question', 1968, pp.857, 860; 'Foucault répond à Sartre', 1968, pp.21–2.
69. Veyne 1984, p.11.
70. Stone 1982, p.29.
71. See Le Goff 1978, pp.210–41. For further treatment of the 'new history' and remarks on Foucault's contribution see Coutau-Begarie 1983, and Bourdé and Martin, 1983.
72. Foucault, 'What is Enlightenment?', in Rabinow 1984, p.47.
73. Veyne 1978, p.216.
74. See Foucault, 'La Poussière et le nuage', 1980, p.44; 'Structuralism and Post-Structuralism', 1983, p.206. Or as Foucault puts it in 'Theatrum philosophicum', 1970, p.906: 'In its fracture, in its repetition, the present is a throw of the dice', cf. p.895. In 1970, Foucault seems to have developed quite an enthusiasm for describing history as the result of 'a throw of the dice': cf. 'Croître et multiplier', 1970, p.13 and 'Préface à Brisset', 1970, p.x.
75. July 1984, p.3.

76. Foucault, 'Le Retour de la morale', 1984, p.38. In reference to these rhetorical methods, Fons Elders (1974, p.288) adding his own rhetorical exaggeration, considers that Foucault's 'style conjures up images of a general of the Ming dynasty or a Count Dracula. He likes to reject any expression of emotion.'
77. Foucault, 'La Folie l'absence de l'oeuvre', in HF 1972, p.578.
78. Kemp 1984, p.85.
79. Foucault, 'On the Genealogy of Ethics', in Rabinow 1984, p.351.
80. Jean-Marie Domenach (1966, p.77) observes the 'outline of a cosmic dialogue' in Foucault's work.
81. See for example Minson 1985, p.114.
82. Foucault, 'Vérité et pouvoir', 1977, p.19, trans. as 'Truth and Power', in Morris and Patton 1979, p.34.
83. Said 1978, p.708. Gordon (1977, p.15) locates a development from the rules of discourse to a discursive 'police' in *L'Ordre du discours*.
84. Foucault, 'Interview with Lucette Finas', in Morris and Patton 1979, p.67.
85. Foucault, 'Power and Norm', in Morris and Patton 1979, pp.88–9.
86. Foucault, 'Des supplices aux cellules', 1975, p.16. Jean Baudrillard comments: 'The very perfection of this analytical chronical of power is worrying' and describes Foucault's writing as 'too beautiful to be true', 1977, p.12.
87. Foucault, 'What is Enlightenment?', in Rabinow 1984, p.47.
88. Ibid, p.50.
89. Bellour 1977, p.17.

3 Discontinuity and Order

1. Etienne Balibar (1978, p.222) uses this expression in describing the episteme and Althusser's 'problematic'.
2. Clifford 1980, p.213; see also a comment by Racevskis 1983, p.131: 'His work is predicated on an evasive tactic that produces identity only to dismantle it.'
3. Poster 1984, pp.73, 72.
4. Clavel 1975, p.142.
5 Bouveresse 1978, p.103.
6. Benamou and Pudlowski 1983, p.xi.
7. Ewald 1978, p.46. Incidentally Roger-Pol Droit (1984, p.10) uses the same sentence ('Elusive and fleeing') to describe Foucault.
8. Droit 1984, p.10.
9. Foucault, 'Truth and Power', in Morris and Patton 1979, p.31; 'Débat avec Michel Foucault', 1980, p.43.
10. Sheridan 1981, p.71; cf. Rousseau 1972–73, pp.238–56. Rousseau condemns Foucault's 'inflated rhetoric' in terms of outrage hardly less inflated.
11. Foucault, 'Deuxième entretien', 1971, pp.191, 194; cf. 'La situation de Cuvier', 1970, p.86.
12. Foucault, 'La Folie l'absence de l'oeuvre', in HF (1972), pp.575, 581. This article was originally published in 1964.

13. See a representative collection of articles translated from French: Forster and Ranum 1978. Roger Chartier, writing in the *Annales* (1973, p.578), comments on the 'already classical framework' of confinement proposed in *Histoire de la folie*. See also Knibiehler 1976, p.840; Schmitt 1976, p.23; Tricart 1977, pp.688–9.
14. Stone 1982, p.28; see also Merquior 1985, pp.26–9. Merquior provides a useful summary of Anglo-Saxon and German criticisms of Foucault's notion of the Great Confinement and his periodisation.
15. Midelfort 1980, pp.257–8.
16. See HF:131–3, 138–9, 150–51, 231–2, 446.
17. HF:415, cf. pp.94, 118.
18. Roth 1981, p.37.
19. Pace 1978, p.294.
20. White 1973, p.53.
21. Veyne 1978, p.229.
22. See Foucault, 'Les Déviations religieuses', 1968, p.19.
23. Foucault, 'Une Mobilisation culturelle', 1977, p.49.
24. Ey 1981, p.211.
25. NC:vii–viii; cf. 'Critique de *La Revolution astronomique*' 1961, p.1124 and 'Critique de *Hölderlin et la question du père*', 1962, p.127.
26. NC:89, xi, 197, 202. For similar notions, this time relating to the possibility of finding 'isomorphisms' (similarities of structure) between the texts of a given period, see Foucault, 'Distance, aspect, origine', 1963, pp.932–3.
27. Jean-Paul Sartre (1966, p.90), irritated by this structured arrangement of history in Foucault's work, counters: 'history is not order. It is disorder.'
28. MC:396–8. Cf. 'Entretien avec Madeleine Chapsal', 1966, pp.14–15.
29. de Certeau 1967, p.353. Etienne Verley (1973, p.151) comments that Foucault uses 'the traditional periodisations of the history of ideas'.
30. Aron 1970, p.340.
31. d'Hondt 1971, pp.255, 260; cf. Milhau 1968, p.67.
32. My emphasis: MC:13, cf. pp.219, 337, 379, 390.
33. MC:47, 55, 183, 219.
34. MC:222–4, cf. pp.263–4.
35. Cranston 1968, p.35. In 1966 Foucault declared 'the writers we like the most . . . are Sade and Nietzsche'. 'Interview with Madeleine Chapsal', 1966, p.15.
36. MC:395, 231, OT:384, 219.
37. MC:396–8, cf. p.339. For other comments on this contemporary rupture and the possible dawn of a new episteme see Foucault, 'Entretien avec Madeleine Chapsal', 1966, pp.14–15; 'Foucault répond à Sartre', 1968, p.20; 'Deuxième entretien', 1971, p.206; 'L'Homme, est-il mort?', 1966, pp.8–9; 'La Naissance d'un monde', 1969, p.viii; 'Préface à la transgression', 1963, p.761 and 'Non au sexe roi', 1977, p.124.
38. Le Bon 1967, pp.1303–4.
39. Dufrenne 1968, p.32. Burgelin 1967, pp.844, 855.
40. Proust 1968, pp.8–9.

41.　See for example, White 1973, p.27; Caws 1971, p.34; Brodeur 1977, p.557. For a more detailed comparison of the episteme and the paradigm see Leary 1976, p.292.

42.　MC:64–5, cf. pp.232–3. In an interview with Raymond Bellour, Foucault again emphasises the 'most enigmatic' character of these 'very rapid' changes. 'Deuxième entretien' 1971, p.193. One critic remarks that Foucault's description of 'enigmatic' for these changes must 'surely [be] the understatement of the year'. 'Contented Positivist', 1970, p.698.

43.　MC:222, OT:209; cf. HF:401. Foucault remarks here: 'During the eighteenth century something moved as regards madness . . . . In the homogenous space of unreason, something was slowly working very obscurely, in a hardly formulated manner, and of which only the surface effects can be perceived. A profound upsurge allowed madness to reappear, to isolate and define itself.'

44.　Foucault, 'Réponse à une question', 1968, p.855.

45.　Foucault, 'Deuxième entretien' 1971, p.194.

46.　Le Bon 1967, pp.1311, 1299.

47.　Canguilhem 1967, p.603; cf. Bourdieu's comments on the practice of 'labelling' as an academic form of insult, 1987, p.169.

48.　See for example Rothman 1971, p.xviii; Kurzweil 1977, p.297, Wuthnow, pp.141, 177.

49.　Foucault, 'Linguistique et sciences sociales', 1969, p.254. Cf. AS:220, and 'Deuxième entretien', 1971, p.191. Pierre Daix, defending Foucault against Sartre's accusations of anti-history, makes a similar point. 1967, p.10.

50.　Foucault, 'Monstrosities in Criticism', 1971, pp.57–60. 'Steiner responds to Foucault', *Diacritics* 1 (Winter 1971), p.59.

51.　Stone and Foucault 1983, pp.41–3. For an interesting discussion on Foucault's style of polemics see Auzias, 1986, pp.39–40, 82–4.

52.　Foucault, 'Réponse à une question', pp.853–4. Also on systems see pp.851, 857, 861.

53.　Ibid, p.858.

54.　Foucault, 'La Situation de Cuvier', 1970, p.86.

55.　Dominique Lecourt also comments on this 'very remarkable absence' of the episteme, 1972, p.100.

56.　See for example, Sheridan 1981, p.105 and Philp 1979, p.91.

57.　AS:206–11. Roth also draws attention to the apparent equivalence of the notions of episteme, archive, and historical *a priori*. 1981, p.36.

58.　AS:171, cf. p.170; the chapter entitled 'The historical *a priori* and the archive', pp.166–73 and 'Réponse à une question', pp.859–60.

59.　Foucault, 'Truth and Power', in Morris and Patton, 1979, p.32.

60.　Foucault, 'The Confession of the Flesh', in PK:196–7.

61.　Bonnet 1976, pp.891, 911.

62.　'Foucault's central effort is to consider thought taking place *primarily as events*', remarks Edward Said 1975, p.291. For discussions by Foucault of the 'event' see 'Débat avec Michel Foucault', 1980, pp.43–5. Here Foucault coins the word 'eventialisation' to describe what he is doing.

63. AS:14–15; see also Foucault, 'Réponse à une question', 1968, p.860 and 'Deuxième entretien', 1971, p.191; Jacques Le Goff recommends this idea of the *document/monument* to other historians 1978, p.238.
64. Foucault, 'Débat avec Michel Foucault', 1980, p.34.
65. Foucault, 'Two Lectures', in PK:83.
66. Ibid, pp.81, 85.
67. Ibid, p.85.
68. Foucault, 'Le Retour de la morale', 1984, p.41; cf. UP:11–12, 16.

4 In Search of the Limit

1. Foucault, 'What is Enlightenment?', in Rabinow 1984, p.45.
2. Foucault, 'A conversation with M. Foucault', 1971, p.193. Forster and Ranum (1978, p.2) comment: 'the standard procedure for sneaking the study of marginal groups into history has been to assert that knowledge about them sheds light on the aspirations, fears and conditions of the mainstream of dominant groups of society . . . . The moral and social values of a society, . . . are clarified by the study of those who reject those values and are cast out of society.'
3. Perrot 1975, p.67. Le Roy Ladurie (1978, p.62) also notes the importance of the poor and the rejected for the contemporary historian. See also Midelfort 1980, p.247 and de Certeau, 1974, pp.27–8.
4. Friedrich and Burton 1981, p.94.
5. Le Roy Ladurie 1982, p.46.
6. Foucault, 'Questions à Michel Foucault sur la géographie', 1976, p.72.
7. Friedrich and Burton 1981, p.92.
8. Foucault, 'Réponse à une question', 1968, p.851.
9. Foucault, 'Les Déviations religieuses', 1968, p.19.
10. Canguilhem 1951.
11. Mauriac 1976, p.324. In the present context, Mauriac's commonplace locution *à la limite* takes on unexpected and complex resonances.
12. Foucault, 'La Folie, l'absence d'oeuvre' (1964), in HF (1972), p.575.
13. NC:202, BC:197–8. The reference to Nietzsche does not appear in the second edition of *Naissance de la clinique*.
14. AS:23–4, 35–6. See also 'Nietzsche, la généalogie, l'histoire', 1971, pp.145–72.
15. Foucault, 'Entretien sur la prison: le livre et sa méthode', 1975, p.33.
16. This is a point that has now been made by several commentators: See Wuthnow 1984, pp.141, 144; Dreyfus and Rabinow 1982, p.9.
17. Poirot-Delpech 1984, p.10.
18. See for example: 'Mon corps, ce papier, ce feu' (1964) in HF (1972); 'Monstrosities in Criticism', 1971, pp.57–60; 'Foucault Responds/2', 1971, p.60; Foucault and Stone, 1983, pp.41–3.
19. Serres 1962, p.696. He goes on to remark with unstinted enthusiasm: 'This language is the geometry of negativities. It can be used at leisure to explain the Greek and the Classical meaning of the

other, its logical, existential, ontological, moral, epistemological and religious meaning. It can be used to express under one denomination, Platonic otherness, Marxist alienation, medical alienation and existentialist foreignness.' 1962, p.72.

20. Paul Veyne (1986, p.936) makes a similar point saying that 'the transcendental level has been rather forgotten by many readers . . . his aim was to show that every gesture without exception performed by the state or not never fills the universalism of a reason and always leaves emptiness outside.'

21. Blanchot 1969, p.289.

22. MMP:75, cf. pp.91, 95.

23. Pelorson 1970, p.90. See Foucault's refutation of this criticism in 'Monstrosities in Criticism', 1971, pp.58–9; see also Midelfort 1980, p.253.

24. HF:26–7; cf. MMP:91–2.

25. The Nietzschean resonances of this word need not concern us here. Far too much has been said already on Foucault's relation to Nietzsche, much of it quite irrelevant. It is quite possible to read Foucault's work without constantly having to refer to Nietzsche for explanation, as some critics appear to do. In any case, a comparison of both bodies of work quickly reveals their very marked differences and disagreements, as well as any similarities.

26. HF:117. Foucault describes madness and unreason as 'spiritual experiences', but hastens to add 'but the word spiritual is not right'. 'Débat sur le roman', 1964, 12–54.

27. Foucault, 'On the Genealogy of Ethics', in Rabinow, pp.371–2. See also Lectures delivered on 5 and 6 January 1982 at the Collège de France as part of a course titled *L'Hermeneutique de soi*. Foucault also points out that if Descartes' work represents a break, in writing *Meditations* he still remains part of a tradition of spiritual exercises aimed at modifying the subject. See also 'Mon corps, ce papier, ce feu' in HF 1972, pp.593–4 where he remarks 'In the meditation the subject is continually altered by its own movement . . . meditation implies a mobile subject which can be modified by the very effect of the discursive events which are produced'. Pierre Hadot (1987, p.232) was perhaps unaware of these qualifying remarks when he disagrees with Foucault for making Descartes responsible for a rupture which he argues took place in the Middle Ages.

28. Foucault, 'A quoi rêvent les iraniens?', 1978, pp.48–9; cf. 'L'Esprit d'un monde sans esprit', 1979, pp.227–9.

29. One of the very few critics who has supported this interpretation of Foucault's intervention is Christian Jambet 1988.

30. HF:58. For an extended and much referred to criticism of Foucault's analysis of Descartes and madness, see Jacques Derrida 1963, pp.460–94.

31. Cf. Foucault, 'Critique de *La Révolution astronomique*;, 1961, p.1124.

32. Foucault, 'La Folie, l'absence d'oeuvre', in HF 1972, p.577.

33. HF:557. See also ibid, pp.575–82; 'Critique de *Hölderlin*' 1962, pp.125–7 and 'Le Non du père', 1962, pp.200, 208.

34. Rousseau, texte présenté par Michel Foucault, 1962, p.xxiv.
35. In an interview given in the same year as *Histoire de la folie* was published, Foucault declares that he had been influenced by Maurice Blanchot and Raymond Roussel and that what 'interested and guided him was a certain form of the presence of madness in literature'. 'La folie n'existe que dans une société', 1961, p.9.
36. Marcus 1966, p.8.
37. Mazlish 1980, p.111.
38. Ey 1971, p.255; see also in the same issue Daumézon, pp.227–41. Likewise Henri Baruk (1978, p.30) accuses Foucault of 'attacking and putting psychiatric hospitals in the pillory'.
39. Stone 1983, p.42.
40. Foucault, 'Le Non du père', 1962, pp.204, 208.
41. François Wahl made this remark after a paper delivered at the conference on Foucault held in Paris in 1988. At the same conference Denis Hollier also described these works as 'twin books'.
42. 'Old New Novelist', 1963, p.511.
43. Foucault, *Raymond Roussel*, 1963, p.19.
44. Foucault, 'Pourquoi réédite-t-on l'oeuvre de Raymond Roussel?', 1964, p.9.
45. Foucault, *Raymond Roussel* 1963, pp.10–12, 86.
46. Of this statement one English-speaking critic remarks, 'Foucault, who leaps shamelessly overboard at times like these, may be history's most hyperrational romantic.' Howe 1974, p.119.
47. Rousseau 1975, p.793.
48. Foucault, 'Le Langage à l'infini', 1963, p.44. See also Foucault's remark on 'the visible emptiness of the origin from where words come to us'. 'Distance, aspect, origine', 1963, p.945.
49. Foucault, 'Préface à la transgression', 1963, pp.751–69; see also the Preface to Bataille, 1970, p.5 and a remark in VS:145: 'If one grants that the threshold of every culture is the forbidden incest, then sexuality since the beginning of time is to be found under the sign of law and right' (that is, according to the ideas of modern Western society).
50. Foucault 'Préface à la transgression', 1963, pp.767–8; cf. an article written in 1962, in which Foucault discusses an idea that each period has its own 'erotic science' which operates at the Limit. 'Un si cruel savoir', p.601. Incidentally sexuality occupies quite a different place in this article from the position it occupies in the three volumes of *Histoire de la sexualité*. In the latter it is a matter of quite different limits, of quite a different relation of the Same and the Other.
51. Foucault uses the term the 'death of God' to refer to what he describes as the 'constant space of our experience', rather than to refer to a 'historical death' of God or to make a statement about his inexistence. 'Préface à la transgression', 1963, p.753.
52. Foucault, 'Le Langage à l'infini', 1963, pp.45–6, 53.
53. White 1973, p.29.
54. Lemaigre 1967, p.451. On the other hand, Pierre Bourdieu (1984,

p.10) sees a progression: 'The social critique of reason leads to the social critique of language, that major limit of human thought.'
55. Foucault, 'La Folie, l'absence d'oeuvre', 1972, pp.578, 582.
56. Foucault, 'Débat sur la poésie', 1964, p.76.
57. Foucault, 'Le Mallarmé de Jean-Pierre Richard', 1964, p.1004.
58. Mendel 1969, p.333.
59. White 1973, p.31.
60. On modern 'commentary' which tries to translate a non-existent primary word, which turns out to be language itself, see also NC:xii–xiii; cf. 'La Prose d'Actéon', 1964, p.459.
61. NC:xii, BC:xvi. See also, 'Le Mallarmé de Jean-Pierre Richard', 1964, p.1002.
62. Foucault, 'Entretien: Michel Foucault', 1971, p.140; cf. MC:94–5.
63. MC:317, OT:306. Lemaigre (1967, p.452, 459) remarks that Foucault 'discovers . . . the being of language at the heart of the thought of the outside, at the common focus of multiple experiences revealed by so much poetry, mysticism, philosophy'.
64. Foucault, 'La Folie l'absence d'oeuvre', 1972, p.581.
65. Foucault refers to 'episodes in this profound history of the *Same*'. MC:398.
66. Foucault, 'Interview with Lucette Finas', in *Michel Foucault*, eds Morris and Patton 1979, p.91.

5 The Limits Forgotten

1. Baudrillard 1977, pp.20, 79. Baudrillard's criticisms of the notions of power have provided some useful ideas for the present analysis.
2. Clavel 1975, pp.133–8, 139.
3. Léonard 1980, p.19.
4. Rorty 1981, p.6.
5. Mauriac 1976, pp.518–19; Clavel 1975, p.142. For a refutation of Clavel's criticism that he is just 'keeping himself busy', see Ewald 1978, p.46. Ewald does not refer to Clavel by name.
6. Foucault, 'Theatrum philosophicum', 1970, pp.899, 908.
7. Fons Elders 1974, pp.288–9. This can be compared with Foucault's well-known remarks in *L'Archéologie du savoir* about writing so as 'to no longer have a face' and in *L'Ordre du discours*, where he says that he would prefer not to have to begin speaking, to be instead 'the point of its possible disappearance'. OD:7–8. However, these statements are far more 'philosophical' in tenor, and refer to Foucault's idea of a subject dispersed and fragmented by language.
8. Foucault, 'Entretien', 1975, p.3; cf. OD:73 where Foucault remarks that Georges Dumézil encouraged him to write 'at an age when I still believed that writing was a pleasure'.
9. Foucault, 'Entretien avec Raymond Bellour', 1971, p.201; see also 'Entretien avec Madeleine Chapsal', 1966, p.15.
10. AS:173. Archaeology 'liberate[s] a coherent area of description'. AS:150.

11. AS:150; MC:64–5, 229–30.
12. AS:150, 209, 269. Deleuze (1972, p.29) considers that L'*Archéologie du savoir* 'represents the most decisive step in a theory-practice of multiplicities'. See also his remarks to Foucault about his work, and his political activities alongside prisoners. Foucault and Deleuze, 'Les Intellectuels et le pouvoir', 1972, pp.3–5.
13. Foucault, 'Nietzsche, Freud, Marx', 1967, p.189. This is, of course, a restatement of the views on the modern 'being of language' that were expressed in *Les Mots et les choses*.
14. Descombes 1979, pp.138–9. See Foucault, 'Interview with Lucette Finas', in Morris and Patton, 1979, p.74. 'As for the problem of fiction, to me this is a very important problem; I am fully aware that I have never written anything other than fictions. For all that, I would not want to say that they are outside truth. It seems possible to me to make fiction work within truth, to induce truth-effects within a fictional discourse, and in some way to make the discourse of truth arouse, "fabricate" something which does not as yet exist, thus "fiction" something.'
15. See for example Colin Gordon, who adopts the definition offered in L'*Archéologie*. 'Afterword', in PK:235–6. Robert Wuthnow et al. (1984, p.144) adopt the definition in terms of power.
16. Foucault, 'Vérité et pouvoir', 1977, p.18; 'Truth and Power', in Morris and Patton, 1979, p.32. See also 'Sorcellerie et folie', 1976, p.18. Here Foucault declares that 'madness is no less an effect of power than is non-madness'.
17. Foucault, 'Vérité et pouvoir', p.16; 'Truth and Power', p.28. In another interview given in the same year Foucault describes 'two great technologies of power: one which was weaving sexuality and one which was dividing off madness'. 'Interview with Lucette Finas', in Morris and Patton 1979, p.68.
18. Minson 1985, p.12.
19. Foucault, 'Vérité et pouvoir', p.19; 'Truth and Power', p.33; cf. 'Body/Power' in PK:62 and 'Questions à Michel Foucault sur la géographie', 1976, p.73.
20. Minson 1985, pp.114, 116.
21. Gordon, 'Afterword', in PK:244.
22. François Châtelet comments in 1966 (p.20) that archaeology remains purely descriptive, suggesting that Foucault try the genealogy of Nietzsche, which of course he did, some years later.
23. OD:60; cf. Foucault, 'Theatrum philosophicum', 1970, p.895.
24. 'What I would like to do . . . is to reveal a *positive unconscious* of knowledge: a level that eludes the consciousness of the scientist and yet is part of scientific discourse', Foucault remarks. OT:xi; see also Foucault's remark on p.xiv: 'What conditions did Linnaeus (or Petty or Arnauld) have to fulfil, not to make his discourse coherent and true in general, but to give it, at the time when it was written and accepted, value and practical application as scientific discourse?'
25. Foucault, 'Des supplices aux cellules', 1975, p.16.

26. Foucault, 'Le Piège de Vincennes', 1970, p.35.
27. Foucault, 'Entretien avec Madeleine Chapsal', 1966, p.15.
28. AS:273; Alan Sheridan (1981, p.110) remarks for example that *L'Archéologie* ends on a 'prophetically political note'.
29. Foucault, 'Revolutionary Action "Until Now" ', in Bouchard 1977, p.228. This interview was originally published in French in 1971.
30. Foucault, 'Michel Foucault on Attica', 1974, p.157. Much later, Foucault declared it was the duty of prisoners to try to escape, since the prison could turn them into 'dangerous' characters. 'Attention: danger', 1978, p.9.
31. Foucault and Chomsky, 'Human Nature', 1974, p.171.
32. Foucault, 'On Popular Justice' in PK:26, originally published in French 1972; cf. 'Table ronde', 1972, p.698.
33. See Mauriac, 1976, pp.373–4.
34. Foucault and Chomsky, 'Human Nature', 1974, p.170; Foucault et le GIS (Groupe Information Santé), 'Médecine et lutte de classes', 1972, pp.67–73.
35. See for example Smart 1983; Poster 1984. The discussion still continues. Etienne Balibar, an ex-collaborator of Althusser, presented a paper at the conference on Foucault's work in Paris in 1988. Ex(?) Marxist Pierre Macherey also presented a paper, and other well-known (ex?) Marxists (Jacques Rancière and Jeannette Colombel) were present in the audience.
36. Mauriac 1975, cited in Roy 1976, p.53.
37. MC:274. See Le Bon 1967, p.1319; Revault d'Allonnes 1967, p.41.
38. Aron 1970, p.341.
39. Lecourt 1972, p.133.
40. Milhau 1968, pp.52, 60–61; Garaudy (1969, p.244) also suggests that *Les Mots et les choses* can be useful for Marxism. See also Lecourt 1972.
41. Wuthnow 1984, pp.136, 153. Another critic claims on the contrary, that Foucault is a 'disciple of Marx the rhetorician'. Robinson 1978, p.30.
42. Smart 1983, pp.41, 74.
43. Poster 1984, pp.86–7; cf. Sheridan 1981, p.159. For other comments on Foucault's 'Marxist affinities' see Lemert and Gillan 1977, p.313; Philp 1979, p.111; Hillyard 1979, p.64.
44. François Châtelet (1979, p.186) criticises those 'who stake their honour on specifying "that they are not philosophers" and that they are only retaining the method from Marxism, as if a method could be separated from its ontological and epistemological assumptions.'
45. Revel 1971, p.418.
46. Clavel 1975, pp.140–41; cf. Domenach 1984, p.9. There are numerous remarks about Foucault's dedication to helping the powerless. Serge Livrozet (1984, p.8) comments: 'For all the manifestations of the rights of Man, whether they were immigrants, handicapped, prisoners or taxed with madness, Michel Foucault integrated, as if in spite of himself, into the system, always displayed a categorical intellectual refusal of all forms of exclusion.' Foucault's lawyer

Georges Kiejman also comments 'It is less well known what a modest, obstinate and exemplary defender he was of those who have no rights.' 1984, p.9.
47. Foucault and Deleuze, 'Les Intellectuels et le pouvoir', 1972, p.7.
48. Minson 1985, pp.71–2. For a similar point see Cousins and Hussain 1984, p.264.
49. Jambet 1973, p.17. Jambet (1988) has since become more interested in how Foucault's last writings can be used to study Iranian Muslim spirituality.
50. Gordon, 'Preface' in PK:viii. More unusually, Cousins and Hussain consider that Foucault's emphasis on power is 'inflated' and 'unwarranted'. 1984, pp.201, 227.
51. Maggiori 1984, p.5.
52. Cf. Foucault, 'Questions à Michel Foucault sur la géographie', 1976, p.81.
53. Foucault, 'Two Lectures', in PK:98.
54. Foucault, 'Powers and Strategies', in Morris and Patton 1979, p.55.
55. Foucault, 'Entretien sur la prison' 1975, p.28; cf. 'Power and Norm', in Morris and Patton, 1979, p.60.
56. Léonard 1980, p.15.
57. Foucault, 'L'Oeil du pouvoir', 1977, p.19.
58. Foucault, 'Body/Power' (1975), in PK:62.
59. VS:93; cf. Foucault, 'Non au sexe roi', 1977, p.93.
60. VS:94; cf. Foucault, 'L'occident et la vérité du sexe', 1976, p.24.
61. Foucault, 'Truth and Power', in Morris and Patton 1979, p.41.
62. Foucault, 'Preface to L'Affaire Mirval', 1976, p.x; cf. 'Questions à Michel Foucault sur la géographie', 1976, pp.72, 74.
63. Foucault, 'Non au sexe roi', 1977, p.105.
64. Foucault, 'Débat avec Michel Foucault', 1980, p.47, Foucault redefines his 'problem' or his 'project' at least three or four times in this same interview. See also pp.51, 55.
65. Ibid, p.51. As was pointed out in Chapter 4, this notion also appears in 'A quoi rêvent les iraniens?', 1978, pp.48–9.
66. VS:123; cf. also 'The Confession of the Flesh', in PK:198, 'In reality, power means relations, a more-or-less organised, hierarchical, coordinated cluster of relations.' 'Power and Norm', in Morris and Patton 1979, pp.59–60 and SP:31.
67. AS:93, 115, 153. Incidentally Pamela Major-Poetzl compares archaeology with 'field theory' or quantum physics on the basis of this shift from things to relations. 1983, pp.5, 21.
68. VS:125–6; cf. 'Power and Strategies', in Morris and Patton 1979, p.55.
69. Foucault, 'Power and Strategies', in Morris and Patton, 1979, p.52.
70. See SP:196. 'One must stop always describing power in negative terms: it "excludes", it "represses", it "quells", it "censures", it "abstracts", it "masks", it "hides". In fact, power produces; it produces the real. It produces areas of objects, and rituals of truth.'
71. Baudrillard 1977, p.55.
72. Castoriadis 1981, p.288; Dominique Wolton also remarks 'Speaking

about a plural and omnipresent power does not in the final analysis transgress the idea of the unity of power.' 1977, p.46.

73. Steinert 1984, p.95. He also adds, 'The seemingly closed inevitability of the system is the product of a certain kind of analysis', p.96.
74. Poster 1984, p.150.
75. Storr 1979, p.20.
76. Plummer 1980, pp.313–14; cf. a similar remark by Clifford 1980, p.213. 'Foucault's recent writings leave one with the impression of a brilliant bleakness, savagely pessimistic if, in some ultimate sense, true.' For other English-language remarks on Foucault's failure to take 'resistance' into account see: Lucas 1975, p.1090; Giddens 1981, p.173; Rothman 1978, p.26.
77. Léonard 1980, p.51.
78. Castoriadis 1981, p.287.
79. Foucault, 'Vérité et pouvoir', 1977, p.22; 'Truth and Power', in Morris and Patton, 1979, p.46; Foucault and Deleuze, 'Les Intellectuels et le pouvoir', 1972, p.4.
80. Foucault and Deleuze, 'Les Intellectuels et le pouvoir', 1972, p.4. See also 'The political function of the intellectual', 1977, p.12. This article originally appeared in French in 1976.
81. Foucault, 'Vérité et pouvoir', 1977, pp.25–6; 'Truth and Power', in Morris and Patton 1979, pp.46–7. 'The essential political problem for the intellectual, is not criticising the possible ideological contents of science or making sure that his scientific practice is accompanied by the correct ideology, but knowing that it is possible to establish a new politics of truth. The problem is not one of changing people's "consciousness" or what is in their heads, but changing the political, economic and institutional order of the production of truth.'
82. Foucault, 'Vérité et pouvoir', 1977, p.24; 'Truth and Power', in Morris and Patton 1979, p.43.
83. Foucault, 'Foucault répond à Sartre' 1968, pp.20–21.
84. Foucault and Deleuze, 'Les Intellectuels et le pouvoir', 1972, p.4.
85. Foucault, 'Power and Strategies', in Morris and Patton 1979, p.57; cf. 'Body/Power', in PK:62: 'What the intellectual can do is provide instruments of analysis, and at present, this is the historian's essential role.'
86. Foucault, 'Des supplices aux cellules', 1975, p.16. Cf. also 'Sur la sellette', 1975, p.3. In this interview he portrays himself rather dramatically as a 'seller of instruments, a provider of recipes, a register of symptoms, a cartographer, a surveyor of plans, a manufacturer of arms.' See also 'Questions à Michel Foucault sur la géographie', 1976, p.73 and 'Débat avec Michel Foucault', 1980, p.41.
87. Nemo 1976, p.7.
88. Dominique Grisoni 1976, pp.17–18. This collection includes an interview with Foucault and an article about him. The language that Grisoni uses, a type of apocalyptic philosophico-journalistic style, characterises much discussion in France during the 1970s. It is a style that a number of recent English-speaking supporters of

Foucault have adopted, to the greater confusion of their readers, though writers such as Grisoni have long left such language behind.

89. See for example Alexander 1978, p.20; Clark 1983; Cousins and Hussain 1984; Sheridan 1981, p.1.
90. Jorion 1984, pp.495–6; cf. Hayman 1976, p.74.
91. Gordon, 'Preface', 1981, pp.vii–viii; cf. 'Afterword', 1981, pp.233, 246, 255; Davis 1975, p.238; Racevskis, *The Freedom of Philosophy* 1985, p.126.
92. Philp 1984, p.12; cf. Poster 1984, pp.73, 90, 131, 159; Ignatieff 1984, p.1071; Cousins and Hussain 1984, pp.9, 10.
93. Said 1975, pp.293–4.
94. Minson 1985, p.108.

6 The Return of the Limits

1. Speech made at a conference titled 'Knowledge, Power, History', organised by the Centre for the Humanities at the University of Southern California, 31 October 1981. Cited in Racevskis 1983, pp.15, 215; cf. UP:12 where he says 'it was a matter of looking for the forms and modalities of the relationship to self by means of which the individual forms and recognises himself as a subject.'
2. Foucault, 'The Subject and Power', 1982, p.209.
3. Foucault, 'Le Retour de la morale', 1984, p.37.
4. Blanchot 1986, pp.62–3; cf. John Rajchman who notes the 'serene and scholarly' and 'low-keyed' style of these volumes. 'Ethics After Foucault', 1985.
5. See Habermas 1981, p.13; 'The Entwinement', 1982, pp.13, 29, 22; 1985, pp.82–3. See also Wright 1986, p.16. For examples of these kind of criticisms during the 1960s see Colombel 1967, p.13; Revault d'Allonnes 1967, p.14; Domenach 1966, p.26; 1967, pp.772–5. Mendel 1969, p.328. Mendel also describes Foucault's book as a 'psychotic' and irrational negation of reality; pp.289, 361.
6. Habermas 1985, p.83.
7. Merquior 1985, p.159. Cf. pp.155–6.
8. Rorty 1988.
9. Clifford 1980, pp.213–14.
10. Philp 1984, p.13; cf. similar remarks by Poster 1984, p.25.
11. Lodge 1984, p.487.
12. Wright 1986, p.16.
13. Rorty 1981, p.6.
14. Foucault, 'Space, Knowledge, Power', in Rabinow 1984, p.247; cf. p.250 where he remarks that he does not share Habermas' problem, which is 'after all, to make a transcendental mode of thought spring forth against any historicism'. See also 'The Subject and Power', 1982, p.218 where Foucault remarks 'When Habermas distinguishes between domination, communication, and finalised activity, I do not think that he sees in them three separate domains, but rather three "transcendentals".'

15. Habermas, 'The Entwinement', 1982, p.29; cf. pp.22, 28.
16. Habermas 1985, pp.78, 80, 84; cf. 'The Entwinement' 1982 p.30; 'A Reply' 1982, pp.226–7. It is not our intention here to embark on yet another comparison of the ideas of Foucault and Habermas, an exercise which has become a minor industry in itself in recent years. One of the best and most detailed treatments to date of Habermas' criticisms of Foucault was presented by Dominique Janicaud at the Paris conference in 1988. In his paper he looks closely at Chapters 10 and 11 of Habermas' book *Der philosophische Diskurs der Moderne* (Frankfurt: Suhrkamp, 1985). See also Rochlitz 1988, Wuthnow 1984, Rajchman, *Michel Foucault: The Freedom of Philosophy*, 1985, Dreyfus and Rabinow 1986.
17. Veyne 1986, p.977, 936. In this short article, Veyne provides a masterful summary of Foucault's final ideas and his thought of the limits.
18. John Rajchman (1985) observes that for Foucault 'there can be no "philosophical" answer to the question "what is the correct kind of morality".'
19. Foucault 'Structuralism and Post-Structuralism', 1983, pp.207–8; cf. 'The Subject and Power', pp.208–9.
20. Foucault, 'Polemics, Politics and Problemizations', in Rabinow 1984, p.387; 'On the Genealogy of Ethics', in Rabinow 1984, p.351; 'Le retour de la morale', 1984, p.38; UP:10.
21. Foucault 'On the Genealogy of Ethics', in Rabinow 1984, p.352. For variations on this analysis see 'Polemics, Politics and Problemizations', in Rabinow 1984, pp.387–8; 'What is Enlightenment?', in Rabinow 1984, pp.48–9. And for somewhat less enlightening if not obscure discussions see 'The Subject and Power', 1982, p.208 and an early version of the Preface to *L'Usage des plaisirs* in Rabinow 1984, pp.336–8.
22. UP:17, 14–15. See also 'Preface to The History of Sexuality', in Rabinow 1984, p.339.
23. Foucault, 'The Subject and Power', 1982, p.212.
24. Ibid, p.208. My emphasis; cf. UP:39.
25. Foucault, 'On the Genealogy of Ethics', in Rabinow 1984, pp.340–41; cf. UP:44, 55, 166. For a similar point see Auzias 1986, p.234.
26. Foucault, 'Space, Knowledge and Power', in Rabinow 1984, p.247.
27. Foucault, 'The Subject and Power', 1982, p.219.
28. Ibid, p.221.
29. Ibid, p.220.
30. Ibid, pp.221, 225.
31. Ibid, p.222.
32. Foucault, 'On the Genealogy of Ethics', in Rabinow 1984, p.353; cf. UP:33.
33. Joly 1986, p.100; cf. pp.102–3.
34. See also Foucault's discussion of these categories in 'On the Genealogy of Ethics', in Rabinow 1984, pp.357–9.
35. As Paul Veyne (1986, p.938) remarks: 'People cannot prevent themselves from valorising, any more than they can prevent them-

selves from breathing or fighting for their values. Foucault therefore tries to impose one of his preferences updated from the Greeks, a preference which appears to be relevant today; he does not claim to be right, but he hopes to address present issues.'

36. Foucault, 'Le retour de la morale', p.41; UP:10–11.
37. Macherey 1988.
38. Foucault, 'What is Enlightenment?', in Rabinow 1984, pp.45–6.
39. Foucault, 'On the Genealogy of Ethics', in Rabinow 1984, p.371.
40. Foucault, 'Le retour de la morale', p.41. 'On the Genealogy of Ethics', in Rabinow 1984, p.343.
41. One recalls that Habermas discusses 'consensus' in the following terms: 'Processes of reaching understanding are aimed at a consensus that depends on the intersubjective recognition of validity claims; and these claims can be reciprocally raised and fundamentally criticised by participants in communication.' 1984, p.136. Cf. 'A Reply' 1982, p.227, 1985, p.94. Foucault, on the other hand, remains highly sceptical about the possibility or even the desirability of consensus. See 'Politics and Ethics', in Rabinow 1984, pp.377–80.
42. Ariès, 'L'Histoire des mentalités, 1978, p.412.
43. Bourdieu 1987, pp.43–5. See also 'Heidegger par Pierre Bourdieu', 1988, p.vi and *L'ontologie politique* 1988. Like Foucault, Bourdieu situates the production of truth firmly in history.
44. Foucault, 'Space, Knowledge and Power', in Rabinow 1984, p.246.
45. Ibid, p.249.
46. Foucault, 'Structuralism and Post-Structuralism', 1983, p.202. Foucault makes this remark in the context of a discussion about Max Weber, the Frankfurt School and Habermas.
47. Foucault, 'What is Enlightenment?', in Rabinow 1984, p.43.
48. Foucault, 'Structuralism and Post-Structuralism', 1983, pp.201, 208; cf. 'Space, Knowledge and Power', in Rabinow 1984, p.249; 'What is Enlightenment?', in Rabinow 1984, pp.43–5.
49. Foucault, 'Structuralism and Post-Structuralism', 1983, p.206; cf. 'What is Enlightenment?', in Rabinow 1984, pp.33–4.
50. Foucault, 'Space, Knowledge and Power', in Rabinow 1984, p.250.
51. Foucault, 'On the Genealogy of Ethics', in Rabinow, pp.349–50.
52. Ibid, p.347.
53. Ibid, p.346.
54. See for example UP:20–1, 44–5 and SS:269–74.
55. Foucault, 'Le retour de la morale', 1984, p.41.
56. Cf. SS Chapter 2 'The culture of self', pp.53–85. See also 'On the Genealogy of Ethics', in Rabinow 1984, pp.371–2 and above, Chapter 4.
57. Foucault, 'Politics and Ethics', p.374. Cf. SS:79.
58. For a discussion on Nietzsche's views on aesthetics in these terms, see Habermas, 'The Entwinement', 1982, pp.25–6.
59. Bernauer 1988.
60. One might refer here to the classic analyses of Pierre Bourdieu on style and social distinction (1979, pp.50–1, 60–1). In his discussion

of life as a form of art, Bourdieu is concerned with an entirely different set of problems to those raised later by Foucault. It is unfortunate that some commentators, misled perhaps by the similarity in some of the terms, appear to confuse these two different sets of issues.

61. Rochlitz 1988.
62. See, for example, Pizzorno 1988, Bodei 1986, pp.916–17.
63. Rorty 1988; cf. Rorty 1986, pp.895–6.
64. Hadot 1987, p.231.
65. Veyne 1986, p.939.
66. Foucault, 'On the Genealogy of Ethics', in Rabinow 1984, p.362.
67. Foucault, 'Politics and Ethics', in Rabinow 1984, p.377.
68. Foucault remarks: 'Every time I have attempted to do theoretical work, it has been on the basis of elements from my experience – always in relation to processes that I saw taking place around me. It is in fact because I thought I recognised something cracked, dully jarring, or disfunctioning in things I saw, in the institutions with which I dealt, in my relations with others, that I undertook a particular piece of work, several fragments of an autobiography.' Foucault, 'Est-il important donc de penser?', *Libération* 30 May 1981, cited in Rajchman, *The Freedom of Philosophy*, 1985, pp.35–6.
69. Veyne 1986, p.937.
70. Veyne comments: 'Philosophy itself, in becoming a radical historicism, engulfs, recuperates or transforms history and this is at the heart of the meaning of the Foucault phenomenon.' Bellour 1977, p.21.

Bibliography

WORKS BY MICHEL FOUCAULT

Only works consulted for this study have been referred to. Hence a number of the English translations of Foucault's work are not listed. Works have been listed by category and chronologically.

I. Books

French
Maladie mentale et psychologie, 1st edition, 2nd edition, 3rd edition (Paris: Presses Universitaires de France, 1954, 1962, 1966).
Folie et déraison: histoire de la folie à l'âge classique (Paris: Plon, 1961).
Folie et déraison: histoire de la folie à 'âge classique, Abridged by Foucault (Collection 10/18, Paris: Union Générale d'Editions, 1964).
Histoire de la folie à l'âge classique, 2nd edition (Paris: Gallimard, 1972).
Histoire de la folie à l'âge classique (Collection Tel, Paris: Gallimard, 1976).
Naissance de la clinique: une archéologie du regard médical (Collection Galien, Paris: Presses Universitaires de France, 1963).
Naissance de la clinique: une archéologie du regard médical, 4th edition (Collection Galien, Paris: Presses Universitaires de France, 1978).
Raymond Roussel (Le Chemin, Paris: Gallimard, 1963).
Les Mots et les choses: une archéologie des sciences humaines (Paris: Gallimard, 1966).
L'Archéologie du savoir (Paris: Gallimard, 1969).
L'Ordre du discours: leçon inaugurale au Collège de France prononcée le 2 décembre 1970 (Paris: Gallimard, 1971).
Ceci n'est pas une pipe: deux lettres et quatre dessins de René Magritte (Montpellier: Fata Morgana, 1973).
Foucault, Barret-Kriegel, Blandine et al. (ed. Foucault), *Moi, Pierre Rivière, ayant égorgé ma mère, ma soeur et mon frère . . . un cas de parricide au XIXᵉ siècle*, (Paris: Gallimard, 1973).
Surveiller et punir: naissance de la prison (Paris: Gallimard, 1975).
Histoire de la sexualité, Vol. 1: *La Volonté de savoir* (Paris: Gallimard, 1976).
Histoire de la sexualité, Vol. 2: *L'Usage des plaisirs* (Paris: Gallimard, 1984).
Histoire de la sexualité, Vol. 3: *Le Souci de soi* (Paris: Gallimard, 1984).

English translations
Mental Illness and Psychology. Translated by A. M. Sheridan-Smith (New York: Harper & Row, Colophon Books, 1976).

Madness and Civilisation: A History of Insanity in the Age of Reason.
Translated by Richard Howard, Introduction by David Cooper (London:
Tavistock, 1970).
The Birth of the Clinic: An Archaeology of Medical Perception. Translated by
A. M. Sheridan-Smith (London: Tavistock, 1973).
The Order of Things: An Archaeology of the Human Sciences. Translated
anonymously; including Foreword to the English Edition (London:
Tavistock, 1970).
The Archaeology of Knowledge. Translated by A. M. Sheridan-Smith
(London: Tavistock, 1972).
Discipline and Punish: The Birth of the Prison. Translated by A. M.
Sheridan-Smith (London: Allen Lane, 1977).

II. Collections

The articles contained in each collection are listed here. The title and date
of the French original are also included. In cases where the original is not
listed in Sections III and IV, the full reference is given.

Language, Counter-Memory, Practice. Selected Essays and Interviews. Edited
by Donald F. Bouchard, translated by Donald F. Bouchard and Sherry
Simon, Preface and Introduction by Donald F. Bouchard (Ithaca, New
York: Cornell University Press, 1977).
'Preface', pp.7–14.
'Introduction', pp.15–28.
'A Preface to Transgression', pp.29–52. Translation of 'Préface à la
transgression' (1963).
'Language to Infinity', pp.53–68. Translation of 'Le langage à l'infini'
(1963).
'The Father's No', pp.69–86. Translation of 'Le "Non" du père' (1962).
'What is an author?', pp.113–38. Translation of 'Qu'est-ce qu'un auteur?'
(1969).
'Nietzsche, Genealogy, History', pp.139–64. Translation of 'Nietzsche, la
généalogie, l'histoire' (1971).
'Theatrum Philosophicum', pp.165–98. Translation of 'Theatrum Philo-
sophicum' (1970).
'History of Systems of Thought', pp.199–204. Translation of a summary of
a course given at the Collège de France, 1970–71. *Annuaire du Collège de
France* 71 (1971), 245–9.
'Intellectuals and Power', pp.205–17. Translation of 'Les Intellectuels et le
pouvoir' (1972).
'Revolutionary Action: "Until Now" ', pp.218–34. Translation of 'Par delà
le bien et le mal', *Actuel* 14 (1971), 42–7.

Michel Foucault: Power, Truth and Strategy. Edited with a Preface by
Meaghan Morris and Paul Patton (Sydney: Feral, 1979).
'Preface', pp.7–12.
'Truth and Power', pp.29–48. Translation of 'Vérité et pouvoir' (1977).
'Powers and Strategies', pp.49–58. Translations of 'Pouvoirs et stratégies',
Révoltes logiques 4 (1977).

Power and Norm: Notes', pp.59–66. Translation of Notes on a lecture delivered by Foucault at the Collège de France, 28 March 1973.

Interview with Lucette Finas', pp.67–75. Translation of 'Les Rapports du pouvoir passent à l'intérieur du corps' (1977).

The Life of Infamous Men', pp.76–91. Translation of 'La Vie des hommes infâmes', *Cahiers du chemin* (1977), 12–29.

Articles by authors other than Foucault in this collection, are referred to in the list of other works cited.

Power/Knowledge: Selected Interviews and Other Writings, 1972–1977. By Michel Foucault, edited with an Afterword by Colin Gordon (London: Harvester, 1981).

Preface', p.vii.

On Popular Justice: A Discussion with Maoists', pp.1–36. Translation of 'Sur la justice populaire: débat avec les maos', *Les Temps Modernes* 310 *bis* (1972). Discussion with Pierre Victor and Philippe Gavi.

Prison Talk', pp.37–54. Translation of 'Entretiens sur la prison: le livre et sa méthode' 1975.

Body/Power', pp.55–62. Translation of 'Pouvoir et corps', *Quel corps?*, September/October 1975.

Questions on Geography', pp.63–77. Translation of 'Questions à Michel Foucault sur la géographie' (1976).

Two Lectures', pp.78–108. Translation of 'Corso del 7 gennaio 1976' and 'Corso del 14 gennaio 1976'. In *Microfisica del potere: interventi politici*. Edited and translated by Alessandro Fontana and Pasquale Pasquino. (Turin: Einaudi, 1977).

Truth and Power', pp.109–33. Translation of 'Vérité et pouvoir' (1977).

Power and Strategies', pp.134–45. Translation of 'Pouvoirs et stratégies', *Révoltes logiques* 4 (1977).

The Eye of Power', pp.146–65. Translation of 'L'Oeil du pouvoir' (1977).

The Politics of Health in the Eighteenth Century', pp.166–82. Translation of 'La Politique de la santé au XVIIIe siècle' (1976).

The History of Sexuality', pp.183–93. Extract.

The Confession of the Flesh', pp.194–228. Translation of 'Le Jeu de Michel Foucault', *Ornicar* 10 (1977). Interview with Alain Grosrichard *et al.*

'Afterword', pp.229–60.

Rabinow, Paul, ed. *The Foucault Reader* (New York: Pantheon, 1984).

'Introduction', pp.3–29.

'What is Enlightenment?', pp.32–50. Translated from an unpublished manuscript.

'Truth and Power', pp.51–75. Translation of 'Vérité et pouvoir' (1977).

'Nietzsche, Genealogy, History', pp.76–100. Translation of 'Nietzsche, la généalogie, l'histoire' (1971).

'What is an Author?', pp.101–20. Translation of 'Qu'est-ce qu'un auteur?' (1969).

'*Madness and Civilization*', pp.124–67. Extracts.

'Disciplines and Science of the Individual', pp.169–238. Extracts from *Discipline and Punish*.

'Space, Knowledge, and Power', pp.239–56. Originally published in *Skyline* (March 1982). Translated by Christian Hubert.

'The Right of Death and Power over Life', pp.258–72. Extract from *The History of Sexuality*, Vol. 1: *An Introduction*.
'The Politics of Health in the Eighteenth Century', pp.273–89. Translation of 'La Politique de la santé au XVIIIe siècle' (1976).
'Sex and Truth', pp.291–329. Extracts from *The History of Sexuality*, Vol. 1: *An Introduction*.
'Preface to *The History of Sexuality*, Vol 2', pp.333–9. Translated by William Stock. This text is in fact an early version and does not appear in *L'Usage des plaisirs*.
'On the Genealogy of Ethics: An Overview of Work in Progress', pp.340–72. Discussion with Paul Rabinow and Hubert Dreyfus conducted in 1983.
'Politics and Ethics: An Interview'. Translated by Catherine Porter, pp.373–80. Interviews conducted by Rabinow et al. in 1984.
'Polemics, Politics and Problemizations: An Interview with Michel Foucault'. Translated by Lydia Davis, pp.381–90. Interviews conducted by Rabinow in May 1984.

III. Translations, Prefaces, Books edited

Binswanger, Ludwig, *Le Rêve et l'existence*, translated by Jacques Verdeaux, Introduction by Foucault (Paris: Desclée de Brouwer, 1954), pp.9–128.
Weizsaecker, Viktor von, *Le Cycle de la structure*, translated by Foucault and Daniel Rocher, Bibliothèque neuropsychiatrique de langue française (Paris: Desclée de Brouwer, 1958).
Rousseau, Jean-Jacques, *Rousseau Juge de Jean Jacques. Dialogues*, edited with introduction by Michel Foucault (Paris: Colin, 1962), pp.vii–xxiv.
Spitzer, Leo, *Etudes de style*, translated by Elaine Kaufholz, Alain Couchon and Michel Foucault, Preface by Jean Starobinsky (Paris: Gallimard, 1962, reprinted 1970).
Kant, Emmanuel, *Anthropologie du point de vue pragmatique*, translated with an introduction and notes by Michel Foucault (Paris: Vrin, 1964, reprinted 1970).
Arnauld, Antoine and Lancelot, Claude, *Grammaire générale et raisonnée, contenant les fondements de l'art de parler . . .*, Preface by Michel Foucault (Paris: Paulet, 1969).
Bataille, Georges, *Oeuvres complètes*, Vol 1: *Premiers écrits (1922–40)*, edited and annotated by Denis Hollier, Preface by Michel Foucault (Paris: Gallimard, 1970), pp.5–6.
Brisset, Jean-Pierre, *La Grammaire logique, suivi de la science de Dieu*, Preface by Michel Foucault, '7 propos sur le 7e ange' (Paris: Tchou, 1970), pp.vii–xix.
Bachelard, Suzanne, Georges Canguilhem, Michel Foucault et al. *Hommage à Jean Hyppolite*, Introductory Note by Michel Foucault (Paris: Presses Universitaires de France, 1971).
Livrozet, Serge, *De la prison à la révolte: essai-témoignage*, Preface by Michel Foucault (Paris: Mercure de France, 1973), pp.7–14.

Fromanger: le désir est partout, Introduction by Michel Foucault, 'La peinture photogenique' (Paris: Galerie Jeanne Bucher, 1975).

Jackson, Bruce, *Leurs prisons. Autobiographies de prisonniers et d'ex-détenus américains*, translator unknown, Preface by Michel Foucault (Paris: Plon, 1975).

Cuau, Bernard, *L'Affaire Mirval ou comment le récit abolit le crime*, Preface by Michel Foucault, 'Une mort inacceptable', Additional Preface by P. Vidal-Naquet (Paris: Les Presses d'Aujourd'hui, 1976), pp.vii–xi.

Wiaz, *En attendant le grand soir*, Preface by Michel Foucault, 'Les Têtes de la politique' (Paris: Denoël, 1976).

'La Politique de la santé au XVIIIe siècle'. *Les Machines à guérir: aux origines de l'hôpital moderne*. 'Dossiers et documents d'architecture' (Institut de l'Environnement, Paris, 1976).

Bentham, Jeremy, *Le Panoptique*, Preface/interview by Michel Foucault; L'Oeil du pouvoir', interview with Jean-Pierre Barou and Michelle Perrot (Paris: Belfond, 1977).

Debard, Mireille and Hennig, Jean-Luc, *Les Juges khaki*, Preface by Michel Foucault (Paris: Alain Moreau, 1977), pp.7–10.

Deleuze, Gilles and Guattari, Félix, *Anti Oedipus: Capitalism and Schizophrenia*, translated by Robert Huxley, Mark Seem and Helen R. Lane, Preface to the English edition by Michel Foucault (New York: Viking Press, 1977), pp.xii–xiv.

Ma vie secrète, translated by Christine Charnaux *et al.* Preface to the abridged French edition by Michel Foucault (Paris: Les formes du secret, 1978), pp.5–7.

Canguilhem, Georges, *On the Normal and the Pathological*, translated by Carolyn R. Fawcett, Introduction to the English Edition by Michel Foucault. Studies in the History of Modern Science, Vol. 3 (Boston: D. Reidel Publishing Co., 1978).

Herculine Barbin, dite Alexina B, edited with a Note by Michel Foucault (Paris: Gallimard, 1978).

Knobelspiess, Roger, *Q.H.S. Quartier de haute sécurité*. Preface by Michel Foucault (Paris: Lutter/Stock, 1980).

Daniel, Jean, *L'Ere des ruptures*, Preface by Michel Foucault (Paris: Le livre de poche, 1980).

IV. Articles, Reviews and Interviews

[Review of *La Révolution astronomique* by Alexander Koyré], *Nouvelle Revue Française* 18 (1961): 1123–4.

'La Folie n'existe que dans une société', *Le Monde*, 22 July 1961, p.9. Interview with Jean-Paul Weber.

'Le Cycle des grenouilles', *Nouvelle Revue Française* 114 (1962), 1159–60.

'Dire et voir chez Raymond Roussell', *Lettre ouverte* (Summer 1962), 38–51.

'Le "Non" du père', *Critique* 18 (1962), 195–209.

'Un si cruel savoir', *Critique* 18 (1962), 596–611.

[Review of *Hölderlin et la question du père* by Jean Laplanche (Paris: Laffont, 1962)], *Nouvelle Revue Française* 109 (1962), 125–7.

'Distance, aspect, origine', *Critique*, no. 198 (1963), 931–45.

'Le Langage à l'infini', *Tel Quel* 15 (1963), 44–53.

'La Métamorphose et la labyrinthe', *Nouvelle Revue Française* 124 (1963), 638–61.

'Préface à la transgression', *Critique* 15, no. 195 (1963), 751–69.

'Guetter le jour qui vient', *Nouvelle Revue Française* 11, no. 130 (1963), 709–16.

'La Folie, l'absence d'oeuvre', *Table ronde* 196 (1964), 11–21. Reprinted in *Histoire de la folie à l'âge classique*, pp.575–82 (Paris: Gallimard, 1972).

'Le Langage de l'espace', *Critique* 20 (1964), 378–82.

'Pourquoi réédite-t-on l'oeuvre de Raymond Roussel? Un précurseur de notre littérature moderne', *Le Monde*, 22 August 1964, p.9.

'La Prose d'Actéon', *Nouvelle Revue Française*, no. 135 (1964), 444–59.

'Le Mallarmé de J. P. Richard', *Annales: économies, sociétés, civilisations* 5 (1964), 996–1004.

'Débat sur le roman', *Tel Quel* 17 (1964), 12–54. With Jean-Louis Baudry, Jean Pierre Faye, Marcelin Pleynet, Philippe Sollers, Jean Thibaudeau *et al.* Directed by Foucault.

'Débat sur la poésie', *Tel Quel* 17 (1964), 69–82. With Jean-Louis Baudry, Jean Pierre Faye, Marcelin Pleynet, Philippe Sollers, Jean Thibaudeau *et al.* Directed by Foucault.

'L'Obligation d'écrire', *Arts: lettres, spectacles, musique*, 11 November 1964, p.7.

'L'Arrière-fable', *L'Arc* 29 (1966), 5–13.

'La Pensée du dehors', *Critique* 22 (1966), 523–46.

'Une histoire restée muette', *La Quinzaine Littéraire* 8 (1966).

'Entretien avec Madeleine Chapsal', *La Quinzaine Littéraire*, 15 May 1966, pp.14–15.

'Entretien: Michel Foucault, *Les Mots et les choses*', *Lettres françaises*, 31 March 1966. Interview with Raymond Bellour. Reprinted in Raymond Bellour, *Le Livre des autres*, pp.135–44. (Paris: Union Générale d'Editions, 1971).

'C'était un nageur entre deux mots', *Arts et loisirs*, 5 October 1966, pp.8–9. Interview with Claude Bonnefoy.

'L'Homme, est-il mort?', *Arts et loisirs*, 15 June 1966, pp.8–9. Interview with Claude Bonnefoy.

'Nietzsche, Freud, Marx', in *Cahiers du Royaumont: Nietzsche* (Paris, Minuit, 1967).

'La Bibliothèque fantastique', *Cahiers de la compagnie Madeleine Renaud – Jean-Louis Barrault* 59 (1967), 7–30.

'Deuxième entretien avec Michel Foucault: sur les façons d'écrire l'histoire', *Lettres françaises*, 15 June 1967. Interview with Raymond Bellour. Reprinted in Raymond Bellour. *Le Livre des autres*, pp.189–207. (Paris: Union Générale d'Editions, 1971).

'Les Déviations religieuses et le savoir médical'. In *Hérésies et sociétés dans l'Europe pré-industrielle XIe–XVIIIe siècles*. Collected papers from the Colloque de Royaumont, 27–30 May 1962. Edited by Jacques Le Goff (Paris: Mouton, 1968), pp.19–25; discussion pp.26–9.

'Réponse à une question', *Esprit* 36 (1968), 850–74.

'Sur l'archéologie des sciences: réponse au cercle d'épistémologie',

Généalogie des sciences, *Cahiers pour l'analyse* 9 (1968), 5–44.
'Correspondance à propos des *Entretiens sur Foucault'*, *La Penseé* 139 (1968), 114–19.
'Foucault répond à Sartre', *La Quinzaine Littéraire*, 1 March 1968, pp.20–22. Radio interview with Jean-Pierre Elkabbach edited for publication.
'Une mise au point de Michel Foucault', *La Quinzaine Littéraire*, 15 March 1968, p.21.
'Hommage à Jean Hyppolite (1907–1968)', *Revue de métaphysique et de morale* 74 (1969), 131–6.
'Médecins, juges et sorciers au XVIIᵉ siècle', *Médecine de France* 200 (1969), 121–8.
'Qu'est-ce qu'un auteur?', *Bulletin de la société française de philosophie* 63 (1969), 73–104. Followed by a discussion with Jacques Lacan, Lucien Goldmann *et al.*
'Ariane s'est pendue', *Le Nouvel Observateur*, 31 March 1969, pp.36–7.
'En bref', *Le Nouvel Observateur*, 31 March 1969, p.39.
'Michel Foucault explique son dernier livre', *Magazine littéraire* 28 (1969), 23–5. Interview with Jean-Jacques Brochier.
'La naissance d'un monde', *Le Monde*, 3 May 1969, p.viii. Interview.
'Linguistique et sciences sociales', *Revue tunisienne de sciences sociales* 6, no. 19 (1969), 248–55.
'La Situation de Cuvier dans l'histoire de la biologie: exposé de M. Michel Foucault', *Revue d'histoire des sciences et de leurs applications* 23 (1970), 62–9; discussion, pp.70–92.
'Theatrum philosophicum', *Critique* 26 (1970), 885–908.
'Croître et multiplier', *Le Monde*, 15 November 1970, p.13.
'Il y aura scandale, mais . . .', *Le Nouvel Observateur*, 7 September 1970, p.40.
'Une petition', *Le Monde*, 8 November 1970.
'Le Piège de Vincennes', *Le Nouvel Observateur*, 9 February 1970, pp.33–5. Interview.
'Le Discours de Toul', *Le Nouvel Observateur*, 27 December 1971, p.15.
'Monstrosities in Criticism'. Translated by Robert J. Matthews. *Diacritics* 1 (Fall 1971), 57–60.
'Foucault Responds/2', *Diacritics* 1 (Winter 1971), p.60.
'Mon corps, ce papier, ce feu', *Paideia* (September 1971). Reprinted in *Histoire de la folie à l'âge classique.* pp.583–603 (Paris: Gallimard, 1972).
'Nietzsche, la généalogie, l'histoire'. In *Hommage à Jean Hyppolite*, pp.145–72 (Paris: Presses Universitaires de France, 1971).
[A Letter], *La Pensée* 159 (1971), 141–4.
'Par delà le bien et la mal', *Actuel* 14 (1971), 42–7.
'A conversation with Michel Foucault', *Partisan Review* 38, no. 2 (1971), 192–201. Interview with J. K. Simon.
'Les Deux morts de Pompidou', *Le Nouvel Observateur*, 4 December 1972, pp.56–7.
'Gaston Bachelard, le philosophe et son ombre: piéger sa propre culture', *Figaro littéraire*, 30 September 1972, p.16.
'Histoire sociale et histoire des mentalités', *La Nouvelle Critique*, no. 49 (1972), 41–4. Interview with Robert Mandrou.

Foucault et les membres du GIS. 'Médecine et lutte de classes', *La Nef* 49 (1972), 67–73.

'Les Intellectuels et le pouvoir', *L'Arc* 49 (1972), 3–10. Discussion with Gilles Deleuze.

'Table ronde', Numéro spécial: Pourquoi le travail social? *Esprit* 40 (1972), 678–703. Discussion with J. M. Domenach, Jacques Donzelot, Philippe Meyer, Paul Thibaud *et al.*

Foucault, Landau, Alain and Petit, Jean-Yves, 'Convoqués à la P. J.', *Le Nouvel Observateur*, 29 October 1973, p.53.

'En guise de conclusion', *Le Nouvel Observateur*, 13 March 1973, p.92.

'Un parricide aux yeux roux: un crime fait pour être raconté', *Le Nouvel Observateur*, October 1973, pp.81–112.

'Pour une chronique de la mémoire ouvrière', *Libération*, 22 February 1973, p.6.

'Les Rayons noirs de Byzantios', *Le Nouvel Observateur*, 11 February 1974, pp.56–7.

'Anti-retro', *Cahiers du cinéma* 251–2 (1974), 5–17. Interview with Pascal Bonitzer and Serge Toubiana.

'Human Nature: Justice versus Power'. A debate between Noam Chomsky and Michel Foucault, directed by Fons Elders. In *Reflexive Water: The Basic Concerns of Mankind*, pp.133–97, edited by Fons Elders (London: Souvenir Press, 1974).

'Resumés des cours donnés au Collège de France sous le titre général 'Histoire des systèmes de pensée': Années 1970–1974'. In *Foucault et l'archéologie du savoir. Présentation, choix de textes, bibliographie*, by Angèle Krémer-Marietti (Paris: Seghers, 1974).

'Michel Foucault on Attica: An Interview', *Telos* 19 (1974), 154–61. Interview with J.K. Simon.

'Un pompier vend la mèche', *Le Nouvel Observateur*, 13 January 1975, pp.56–7.

'A propos de Marguerite Duras', *Cahiers Renaud-Barrault* 89 (1975), 8–22. Discussion with Hélène Cixous.

'Des supplices aux cellules', *Le Monde*, 21 February 1975, p.16. Interview with Roger-Pol Droit.

'Entretien sur la prison: le livre et sa méthode', *Magazine littéraire* 101 (1975), 27–33. Interview with Jean-Jacques Brochier.

[Excerpt from a letter to Maurice Clavel.] In Maurice Clavel, *Ce que je crois* (Paris: Grasset, 1975), pp.138–9.

'Sur la sellette: Michel Foucault', *Les Nouvelles littéraires*, 17 March 1975, p.3. Interview with Jean-Louis Ezine.

Foucault *et al*, 'L'Appel des sept', *Le Nouvel Observatuer*, 29 September 1975, p.41.

'Les Jeux du pouvoir', in *Politiques de la philosophie*, edited by Dominique Grisoni (Paris: Grasset, 1975).

'l'Occident et la vérité du sexe', *Le Monde*, 5 November 1976, p.24.

'La Politique de la santé au XVIIIᵉ siècle'. In *Les Machines à guérir (aux origines de l'hôpital moderne)*, pp.12–21 (Paris: Institut de l'Environment, 1976).

'Bio-histoire et bio-politique', *Le Monde*, 17 October 1976, p.5.

'Crimes et châtiments en URSS et ailleurs', *Le Nouvel Observateur*, 26 January 1976, pp.34–7. Interview with K. S. Karol.

'Des questions de Michel Foucault à *Hérodote*', *Hérodote* 3 (1976), 9–10.

'Entretien avec Michel Foucault', *Cahiers du cinéma* 271 (1976), 52–3. Interview with Pascal Kané.

'Questions à Michel Foucault sur la géographie', *Hérodote* 1 (1976), 71–85.

'Sorcellerie et folie', *Le Monde*, 23 April 1976, p.18. Interview with Roland Jaccard.

'Va-t-on extrader Klaus Croissant?', *Le Nouvel Observateur*, 14 November 1977, pp.62–3.

'L'Asile illimité', *Le Nouvel Observateur*, 28 March 1977, pp. 66–7.

'La Grande colère des faits', *Le Nouvel Observateur*, 9 May 1977, pp.84–6.

'De la psychiatrie comme moyen d'"invalider" toute pensée libre', *La Quinzaine Littéraire*, 16 October 1977, pp.17–20. Excerpt from a discussion with David Cooper, Victor Fainberg, J. P. Faye.

'Non au sexe roi', *Le Nouvel Observateur*, 12 March 1977, pp.92–130. Interview with Bernard-Henri Lévy.

'Vérité et pouvoir', *L'Arc* 70 (1977), 16–26. Interview with Alessandro Fontana and Pasquale Pasquino.

'Lettre à quelques leaders de la gauche', *Le Nouvel Observateur*, 28 November 1977, p.59.

'Les Rapports de pouvoir passent à l'intérieure des corps', *La Quinzaine Littéraire* 247 (1977), 4–6. Interview with Lucette Finas.

'Une mobilisation culturelle', *Le Nouvel Observateur*, 12 September 1977, p.49.

'L'Angoisse de juger', *Le Nouvel Observateur*, 30 May 1977, pp.92–126. Discussion with Jean Laplanche and Robert Badinter. Directed by Catherine David.

'The Political Function of the Intellectual', *Radical Philosophy*, no. 17 (Summer 1977), p.12.

'A quoi rêvent les iraniens?', *Le Nouvel Observateur*, 16 October 1978, pp.48–9.

'Attention: danger', *Libération*, 22 March 1978, p.9.

'Du bon usage du criminel', *Le Nouvel Observateur*, 11 September 1978, pp.40–42.

'Governmentality' trans. R. Braidotti, *Ideology and Consciousness* 6 (1979), 5–21. Lecture originally delivered at the Collège de France. Edited and translated into Italian by Pasquale Pasquine: 'La "governamentalità" ', *Aut aut* 167–8 (1978), 12–29.

'Le Citron et le lait', *Le Monde*, 21 October 1978, p.14.

'Eugène Sue que j'aime', *Les Nouvelles littéraires*, 12 January 1978, p.3.

Foucault, Sartre *et al.* 'Letter: In a Cuban Prison', *New York Review of Books*, 7 December 1978, p.42.

'l'Esprit d'un monde sans esprit: entretien avec Michel Foucault'. In Brière, Claire and Blanchet, Pierre, *Iran: la révolution au nom de Dieu*, pp.225–41 (Paris: Seuil, 1979).

'Inutile de se soulever?', *Le Monde*, 11 May 1979, pp.1–2.

'Lettre ouverte à Mehidi Bazargan', *Le Nouvel Observateur*, 14 April 1979, p.46.

'Manières de justice', *Le Nouvel Observateur*, 5 February 1979, pp.20–21.

'La Stratégie du pourtour', *Le Nouvel Observateur*, 28 May 1979, p.57.

'Notre ami Maurice Clavel. Vivre autrement le temps', *Le Nouvel Observateur*, 30 April 1979, p.88.

'Pour une morale de l'inconfort', *Le Nouvel Observateur*, 23 April 1979, pp.42–3.

'*Spiegel* interview with Michel Foucault on "Paris-Berlin" '. Translated by J. D. Steakley, *New German Critique* 16 (1979), 155–6.

Perrot, Michelle (ed.), *L'Impossible Prison: recherches sur le système pénitentiaire au XIXe siècle* (Paris: Seuil, 1980).

'Débat avec Michel Foucault: table ronde du 20 mai 1978', pp.29–56.

'La Poussière et le nuage', pp.59–63.

'Postface', pp.316–18.

'Georges Canguilhem: Philosopher of Error', *I&C* 7 (1980), 51–62.

Foucault *et al.* 'Letter: The Flying University', *New York Review of Books*, 24 January 1980, p.49.

'Des caresses d'hommes considerées comme un art', *Libération*. 1 June 1982, p.27.

'Sexual Choice, Sexual Act. An Interview with Michel Foucault', *Salmagundi* 58 (Fall 1982), 10–24. Interview with James O'Higgins.

'Le Terrorisme ici et là', *Libération*, 3 September 1982, p.12. Interview with Didier Eribon.

'Pierre Boulez ou l'écran traversé', *Le Nouvel Observateur*, 2 October 1982, pp.95–6.

'En abandonnant les polonais, nous renonçons à une part de nous-mêmes', *Le Nouvel Observateur*, 9 October 1982, p.52.

'Afterword: The Subject and Power' in Dreyfus, Hubert L. and Rabinow, Paul, *Michel Foucault: Beyond Structuralism and Hermeneutics* (Brighton: Harvester, 1982).

'Lawrence Stone and Michel Foucault: An Exchange', *New York Review of Books*, 31 March 1983, pp.41–3.

'Structuralism and Post-Structuralism: An Interview with Michel Foucault', *Telos* 55 (Spring 1983), 195–211. Interview with Gérard Raulet.

'Un cours inédit de Michel Foucault', *Magazine littéraire*, no. 207 (May 1984), 35–9.

'Le Retour de la morale', *Les Nouvelles*, 28 June 1984, pp.37–41. Interview with Gilles Barbedette and André Scala.

OTHER WORKS CITED

This list includes writings on Foucault's work in French and English as well as a number of general references.

Adamowski, T. H., 'Sex in the Head', *Canadian Forum* 59, no. 690 (June 1979), 40–42.

Adams, Michael Vannoy, 'Pillow Talk', *Commentary* 67, no. 3 (1979), 84–7.

Akoun, André, 'Entre l'existentialisme et la marxisme', in Brochier 1978, pp.11–22.

Albérès, R. M., 'L'Homme n'est plus dans l'homme', *Les Nouvelles littéraires*, 1 September 1966, p.3.

Albury, W. R., 'Michel Foucault and the Powers of Darkness', paper presented at a Conference on Culture and Ideology, Lorne, 1980.

_ _ _, 'Review of *The History of Sexuality*, Vol. 1: *An Introduction* by Michel Foucault', paper given on *The Science Show*, Australian Broadcasting Commission, Radio 1, 1980.

Albury, W. R. and Oldroyd, D. R., 'From Renaissance Mineral Studies to Historical Geology in the Light of Michel Foucault's *The Order of Things*', *British Journal for the History of Science* 10, no. 36 (1977), 187–215.

Alexander, George, 'Introduction: On Editorial strategies', in Foss and Morris 1978, pp.15–43.

Allio, René, 'Le Théâtre du père et de la mère', and 'Calibènes', *Cahiers du cinéma* 271 (1976), 49–51.

Althusser, Louis, *Pour Marx* (Paris; Maspero, 1965).

_ _ _, *Essays in Self Criticism*, translated by Graham Lock (London: NLB, 1976).

_ _ _, *Positions (1964–1975)* (Paris: Editions Sociales, 1976).

Althusser, Louis; Balibar, Etienne; and Establet, Roger, *Lire le Capital*, 2 vols (Paris: Maspero, 1966).

Altieri, Charles F., 'Northrop Frye and the Problem of Spiritual Authority', *Publications of the Modern Language Association of America* 87, no. 5 (1972), 964–75.

Amico Robert d', 'Introduction to the Foucault–Deleuze Discussion', *Telos* 6 (Summer 1973), 101–2.

_ _ _, 'The Contours and Coupures of Structuralist Theory', *Telos* (Fall 1973), 70–97.

_ _ _, 'Review of *Marxism and Epistemology: Bachelard, Canguilhem, Foucault* by Dominique Lecourt', *Journal of Modern History* 48, no. 2 (1976), 334–7.

_ _ _, 'Review of *Discipline and Punish, Language, Counter-Memory and Practice, La Volonté de savoir* by Michel Foucault and *Oublier Foucault* by Jean Baudrillard', *Telos* 36 (Summer 1978), 169–83.

Amiot, Michel, 'Le Relativisme culturaliste de Michel Foucault', *Les Temps Modernes* 22 (1967), 1271–98.

'Après Aron qui? . . .', *Pariscope-Parispoche*, 9 November 1983, pp.v–vii.

Ariès, Philippe, *Le Temps de l'histoire* (Monaco: Editions du Rocher, 1954).

_ _ _, 'La Singulière histoire de Philippe Ariès', *Le Nouvel Observateur*, 20 February 1978, pp.80–102. Interview with André Burguière.

_ _ _, 'L'Histoire des mentalités', in Le Goff 1978, pp.402–23.

_ _ _, 'A propos de *La Volonté de savoir*', *L'Arc* 70 (1977), 27–32.

_ _ _, *Un historien du dimanche*, with the collaboration of M. Winock (Paris: Seuil, 1980).

Armstrong, David, 'Coping', *London Review of Books*, 19 February 1981, p.6.

Aron, Raymond, *Introduction à la philosophie de l'histoire. Essai sur les limites de l'objectivité historique* (Paris: Gallimard, 1948).

_ _ _, *D'une sainte famille à l'autre: essais sur les marxismes imaginaires* (Paris: Gallimard, 1969). Reprinted and enlarged as *Marxismes imaginaires: d'une sainte famille à l'autre* (Paris: Gallimard 1970).

Aubral, François and Delcourt, Xavier, *Contre la Nouvelle Philosophie*

(Paris: Gallimard, 1977).

Auzias, Jean-Marie, *Clefs pour le structuralisme*, 2nd edition (Paris: Seghers, 1967).

___, *Michel Foucault*, Qui suis-je? (Paris: La Manufacture, 1986).

Balibar, Etienne, 'From Bachelard to Althusser: The Concept of "Epistemological Break" ', translated from Spanish by Elizabeth Kingdom, *Economy and Society* 7, no. 3 (1978), 207–37.

Bann, Stephen, 'Historical Text and Historical Object: The Poetics of the Musée de Cluny', *History and Theory* 17, no. 3 (1978), 251–66.

Barbadette, Gilles, 'La Culture de soi-même', *Les Nouvelles*, 28 June 1984, pp.53–4.

Barham, Peter, 'Sanctuaries of the Text', *Sociology: The Journal of the British Sociological Association* 13, no. 1 (1979), 111–15.

Barou, Jean-Pierre, 'Il aurait pu aussi bien m'arriver tout autre chose', *Libération*, 26 June 1984, p.4.

Barthes, Roland, *Mythologies* (Paris: Seuil, 1957).

___, 'Savoir et folie', *Critique* 17 (1961), 915–22.

___, *Critique et vérité* (Paris: Seuil, 1966).

___, *Image, Music, Text* translated by Stephen Heath (London: Flamingo, Fontana, 1977).

Baruk, Henri, *La Psychiatrie sociale*, 5th edition (Paris: Presses Universitaires de France, 1974).

___, 'La Condition du malade mentale en France de Pinel à nos jours', *Annales médico-psychologiques* 134, no. 1 (June 1976), 66–72.

___, 'Reflexions sur l'antipsychiatrie', *Revue internationale de philosophie* 32, no. 123 (1978), 26–45.

Baudrillard, Jean, *Oublier Foucault* (Paris: Galilée, 1977).

Beauvoir, Simone de, *Mémoires*, Vol. 3: *La Force des choses* (Paris: Gallimard, 1963).

Beigbeder, Marc, 'En suivant le cours de Foucault', *Esprit* 361 (1967), 1066–9.

Bellour, Raymond, 'Homme pour homme', *L'Arc* 30 (1966), 10–14.

___, 'L'Homme, les mots', *Magazine littéraire*, June 1975, pp.20–23.

Bellour, Raymond and Venault, Philippe (directors), 'L'Histoire, une passion nouvelle: table ronde avec Philippe Ariès, Michel de Certeau, Jacques Le Goff, Emmanuel Le Roy Ladurie, Paul Veyne', *Magazine littéraire* 123 (1977), 10–23.

Benamou, Georges-Marc and Pudlowski, Gilles, 'Où sont les intellos d'aujourd'hui?', *Parispoche-Pariscope*, 31 August 1983, pp.x–xi.

Bernauer, James W., 'Beyond Life and Death: On Foucault's Post-Auschwitz Ethic', paper presented at an International Conference, 'Michel Foucault, philosophe', Paris, 9–11 January 1988.

Bertrand, Pierre, *L'Oubli: révolution ou mort de l'histoire* (Paris: Presses Universitaires de France, 1975).

'Bibliographie', *Magazine littéraire*, May 1984, extract printed in *Libération*, 26 June 1984, p.10.

Blanchot, Maurice, 'L'Oubli, la déraison', *Nouvelle Revue Française* 18 (October 1961), 676–86. Reprinted in *L'Entretien infini*, pp.289–99 (Paris: Gallimard, 1969).

Bibliography 165

_____, *Foucault, tel que je l'imagine* (Montpellier, Fata Morgana, 1986).

Bloch, Marc, *The Historian's Craft*, translated by P. Putman (Manchester: Manchester University Press, 1954).

Bodei, Remo, 'Foucault: Pouvoir, politique et maîtrise de soi', *Critique* 52 (August 1986), 898–917.

B[onnefoy], C[laude], 'Un jeune philosophe Michel Foucault', *Arts et loisirs*, 25 May 1966, p.8.

Bonnet, Jean-Claude, 'Le Réseau culinaire dans l'Encyclopédie', *Annales: économies, sociétés, civilisations* 31, no. 5 (September 1976), 891–914.

Bossy, John, 'Abstract Acrobat', *New Statesman*, 4 June 1971, p.775.

Boulez, Pierre, 'Il s'étonnait de l'absence de dialogue entre intellectuels et monde musical', *Libération*, 26 June 1984, p.9.

Bourdé, Guy and Martin, Hervé, *Les Ecoles historiques* (Paris: Seuil, 1983).

Bourdieu, Pierre, *La Distinction: critique sociale du jugement* (Paris: Minuit, 1979).

_____, 'La Mort du philosophe Michel Foucault: Le plaisir de savoir', *Le Monde*, 27 June 1984, pp.1, 10.

_____, *Homo Academicus* (Paris; Minuit, 1984).

_____, *Choses dites* (Paris: Minuit, 1987).

_____, *L'Ontologie politique de Martin Heidegger* (Paris: Minuit, 1988).

_____, 'Heidegger par Pierre Bourdieu: le krach de la philosophie', *Libération*, 10 March 1988, pp.vi–vii.

Bourdieu, Pierre and Passeron, Jean-Claude, *Reproduction in Education, Society and Culture*, translated by Richard Nice (London: Sage Publications, 1977).

Bourgeois, Denis and Bouscasse, Sylvie, *Faut-il brûler les nouveaux philosophes?* (Paris; Nouvelles Editions Oswald, 1978).

Bouveresse, Jacques, 'Pourquoi pas des philosophes?', *Critique* 34, no. 369 (1978), 97–122.

Braudel, Fernand, *On History*, translated by Sarah Matthews (London: Weidenfeld and Nicolson, 1980).

Brochier, Jean-Jacques *et al.*, *Les Dieux dans la cuisine. Vingt ans de philosophie en France* (Paris: Aubier, 1978).

Brodeur, Jean-Paul, 'McDonell on Foucault: supplementary remarks', *Canadian Journal of Philosophy* 7, no. 3 (1977), 555–68.

Brown, P. L., 'Epistemology and Method: Althusser, Foucault, Derrida', *Cultural Hermeneutics* 3, no. 2 (1975), 147–63.

Brown, Robert, 'The Idea of Imprisonment', *The Times Literary Supplement*, 16 June 1978, p.658.

_____, 'The Institutions of Insanity', *The Times Literary Supplement*, 8 January 1982, pp.23–4.

Burgelin, Pierre. 'L'Archéologie du savoir', *Esprit* 35 (May 1967), 843–61.

Burguière, André. 'Histoire et structure', *Annales: économies, sociétés, civilisations* 26, no. 3 (May 1971), i–vii.

_____, 'Michel Foucault: la preuve par l'aveu', *Le Nouvel Observateur*, 31 January 1977, pp.64–6.

Burke, Peter, 'L'Histoire sociale des rêves', *Annales: économies, sociétés, civilisations* 28, no. 2 (March 1973), 329–42.

Butel, Michel, 'L'Absent', *Les Nouvelles*, 28 June 1984, p.13.

Canguilhem, Georges, 'Mort de l'homme ou épuisement du cogito?', *Critique* 24 (1967), 599–618.

___, *On the Normal and the Pathological*, translated by Carolyn R. Fawcett, Introduction to English Edition by Michel Foucault, Studies in the History of Modern Science, Vol. 3 (Boston: D. Reidel Publishing Co., 1978).

___, *Essai sur quelques problèmes concernant le normal et le pathologique* (Paris: Les Belles Lettres, 1951).

Carrol, David, 'The Subject of Archaeology or the Sovereignty of the Episteme', *Modern Language Notes* 93 (1978), 695–722.

Cassirer, Ernst, *The Logic of the Humanities*, translated by Clarence Smith Howe (New Haven: Yale University Press, 1961).

Castel, R., 'L'Institution psychiatrique en question', *Revue française de sociologie* 12 (1971), 57–92.

Castoriadis, Cornelius, 'Les Divertisseurs', *Le Nouvel Observateur*, 20 June 1977. Reprinted pp.285–9, Muchnik 1981.

Caws, Peter, 'Language as the Human Reality', *New Republic*, 27 March 1971, pp.28–34.

___, 'Review of *The Archaeology of Knowledge*', *New York Times Book Review*, 22 October 1972, pp.6, 22, 24.

___, 'Medical Change', *New Republic*, 10 November 1973, pp.28–30.

Certeau, Michel de, 'Les Sciences humaines et la mort de l'homme', *Etudes* 326 (1967), 344–60.

___, 'Une épistémologie de transition: Paul Veyne', *Annales: économies, sociétés, civilisations* 27 (November 1972), 1317–27.

___, *L'Absent de l'histoire* (Paris; Mame, 1973).

___, 'L'Opération historique', in Le Goff and Nora 1974, pp.3–41.

Chalumeau, Jean-Luc, *La Pensée en France de Sartre à Foucault* (Paris: Fernand Nathan, 1974).

Chapsal, Madeleine, 'La Plus Grande Révolution depuis l'existentialisme', *L'Express*, 23 May 1966, pp.119–21.

Chartier, Roger, 'Pauvreté et assistance dans la France moderne: l'exemple de la généralité de Lyon', *Annales: économies, sociétés, civilisations* 28, no. 2 (March 1973), 572–82.

Charvet, Dominique, 'Il savait dire qu'il ne savait pas', *Libération*, 26 June 1984, p.9.

Châtelet, François, 'L'Homme ce narcisse incertain', *La Quinzaine Littéraire*, 1 April 1966, pp.19–20.

___, 'Où en est le structuralisme?', *La Quinzaine Littéraire*, 1 July 1967, pp.18–19.

___, 'L'Archéologie du savoir', *La Quinzaine Littéraire*, 1 May 1969, pp.3–4.

___, 'Récit', *L'Arc*, no. 70 (1977), pp.3–15.

___, *Chronique des idées perdues* (Paris: Stock, 1977).

___, 'Suis-je un intellectuel?', *Lire*, no. 90 (February 1983), pp.32–3.

Chesneaux, Jean, *Pasts and Futures or What is History For?*, translated by Schofield Coryell (London: Thames and Hudson, 1978).

Chiari, Joseph, *Twentieth Century Thought: From Bergson to Lévi-Strauss* (New York: Gordian Press, 1975).

Clark, Michael, *Michel Foucault: An Annotated Bibliography. Tool Kit For a New Age* (New York: Garland, 1983).

Clavel, Maurice, 'La Fin du pur philosophe', *Le Nouvel Observateur*, 3 April 1968, p.42.

———, 'L'An zéro d'on ne sait quoi!', *Le Nouvel Observateur*, 7 June 1968. Reprinted Muchnik 1981, pp.106–8.

———, 'Un manifestant bien élevé', *Le Nouvel Observateur*, 23 December 1972, p.56.

———, *Ce que je crois* (Paris: Grasset, 1975).

———, 'Aujourd'hui la révolution culturelle', in Brochier 1978, pp.172–82.

Clavel, Maurice and Sollers, Philippe, *Delivrance: face à face* (Paris: Seuil, 1977).

Clifford, James, 'Review of *Orientalism* by Edward Said', *History and Theory* 19 (1980), 204–23.

Cohen, Sande, 'Structuralism and the Writing of Intellectual History', *History and Theory* 17, no. 2 (1978), 175–206.

Colombel, Jeannette, 'Les Mots de Foucault et les choses', *La Nouvelle Critique* (May 1967), 8–13.

Conrad, Peter, 'Syntax and Sin', *New Statesman*, 30 March 1979, pp.451–2.

'Contented Positivist: Michel Foucault and the Death of Man', *The Times Literary Supplement*, 2 July 1970, pp.697–8.

Cooper, David, 'Poetic Justice', *The Times Literary Supplement*, 27 July 1967, p.687.

Corvez, Maurice, *Les Structuralistes* (Paris: Aubier-Montaigne, 1969).

Cousins, Mark and Hussain, Athar, *Michel Foucault* (London: Macmillan, 1984).

Coutau-Begarie, Hervé *Le Phénomène 'nouvelle histoire'. Stratégie et idéologie des nouveaux historiens* (Paris: Economica, 1983).

Cranston, Maurice, 'Men and Ideas: Michel Foucault', *Encounter* 30 (June 1968), 34–42.

———, 'Les "Périodes" de Foucault', *Preuves* no. 209–10 (August 1968), 65–75.

Crémant, Roger, *Les Matinées structuralistes suivies d'un Discours sur l'écriture et précédées d'une Introduction critique par Albert K**** (Paris: Laffont, 1969).

Culler, Jonathan, 'Words and Things: Michel Foucault', *Cambridge Review*, 29 January 1971, pp.104–5.

———, 'Viewpoint', *The Times Literary Supplement*, 9 March 1973.

Dagognet, François, *Sciences de la vie et de la culture* (Paris: Hachette, 1953).

———, 'Archéologie ou histoire de la médecine', *Critique* 21 (1965), 436–47.

Daix, Pierre, 'Sartre est-il dépassé?', *Les Lettres françaises*, 2 February 1967, pp.1, 10.

———, 'Du structuralisme I: le divorce avec la philosophie', *Les Lettres françaises*, 20 March 1968, pp.5–7.

———, 'Du structuralisme (suite) II: Mort de l'homme ou fin de l'anthropocentrisme', *Les Lettres françaises*, 27 March 1968, pp.9–10.

———, 'Du journalisme de Flaubert de Foucault', *Les Lettres françaises*, 21

168   *Foucault*

May 1969, pp.11–12.

_ _ _, *Structuralisme et révolution culturelle* (Paris: Casterman, 1971).

_ _ _, *Le Socialisme du silence: de l'histoire de l'URSS comme secret d'état (1921–19..)* (Paris: Seuil, 1976).

Daniel, Jean, 'Quinze jours en images', *Le Nouvel Observateur*, 29 September 1975, pp.28–9.

_ _ _, *L'Ere des ruptures* (Paris: Grasset, 1977).

Daumézon, G. 'Lecture historique de *L'Histoire de la folie*', *L'Evolution psychiatrique* 36, no. 2 (June 1971), 227–41.

Davis, Nanette, J., *Sociological Constructions of Deviance: Perspectives and Issues in the Field* (Dubuque, Iowa: Wm C. Brown Company, 1975).

Debray, Régis, *Le Pouvoir intellectuel en France* (Paris: Ramsay, 1979).

Deleuze, Gilles, 'L'Homme une existence douteuse', *Le Nouvel Observateur*, 1 June 1966, pp.32–4.

_ _ _, *Un Nouvel Archiviste* (Paris: Fata Morgana, 1972).

_ _ _, 'Ecrivain non: un nouveau cartographe', *Critique* 31, no. 343 (December 1975), 1207–27.

_ _ _, 'Un Nouveau Cartographe', *Libération*, 26 June 1984, p.7.

_ _ _, *Foucault* (Paris: Minuit, 1986).

Derrida, Jacques, 'Cogito et histoire de la folie', *Revue de métaphysique et de morale* 68 (1963), 460–94. Reprinted in 1967.

_ _ _, 'A propos de "Cogito et histoire de la folie" ', *Revue de métaphysique et de morale* 69 (1964), 116–19.

_ _ _, 'La Parole soufflée', *Tel Quel* 20 (1965). Reprinted pp.253–92, 1967.

_ _ _, 'Violence et métaphysique: essai sur la pensée d'Emmanuel Lévinas'. Reprinted pp.117–228, 1967.

_ _ _, *L'Ecriture et la différence* (Paris: Seuil, 1967).

Descombes, Vincent, *Le Même et l'autre. Quarante-cinq ans de philosophie française (1933–1978)* (Paris: Editions de Minuit, 1979).

Dews, Peter, 'The Nouvelle Philosophie and Foucault', *Economy and Society* 8, no. 2 (1979), 127–71.

_ _ _, 'The New Philosophers and the End of Leftism', *Radical Philosophy* 24 (Spring 1980), 2–11.

_ _ _, 'Regime of Truth', *New Statesman*, 2 January 1981, pp.20–21.

Dhoquois, Guy, *Pour l'histoire* (Paris: Anthropos, 1971).

Domenach, Jean-Marie, 'Une nouvelle passion,' *Le Nouvel Observateur*, 20 July 1966, pp.26–7.

_ _ _, 'Le Système et la personne', *Esprit* 5 (1967), 771–80.

_ _ _, *Enquête sur les idées contemporaines* (Paris: Seuil, 1981).

_ _ _, 'Un engagement sans prétention, ni manipulation', *Libération*, 26 June 1984, p.9.

Donzelot, Jacques, *La Police des familles*, Afterword by Gilles Deleuze (Paris: Minuit, 1977).

Dreyfus, Hubert L. and Rabinow, Paul, *Michel Foucault: Beyond Structuralism and Hermeneutics*, Afterword by Michel Foucault (Brighton: Harvester, 1982).

_ _ _, 'Habermas et Foucault. Qu'est-ce que l'âge d'homme?', *Critique* 52 (August 1986), 857–72.

Bibliography

169

Droit, Roger-Pol, Michel Foucault et la naissance des prisons', *Le Monde*, 21 February 1975, p.16.

___, ' "Hérodote" et Michel Foucault', *Le Monde*, 23 January 1976, p.14.

___, 'Le Pouvoir et le sexe', *Le Monde*, 16 February 1977, pp.1, 18.

___, 'Un relativisme absolu', *Le Monde*, 27 June 1984, p.10.

Dufrenne, Mikel, 'La Philosophie du néo-positivisme', *Esprit* 5 (1967), 781–800.

___, 'Le Structuralisme et l'antihumanisme', *Le Monde [des livres]*, 28 December 1968, p.iii.

___, *Pour l'homme* (Paris: Seuil, 1968).

Dumur, Guy, 'Ces lieux où souffle l'esprit', *Le Nouvel Observateur: Spécial Littérature*, May 1981, pp.10–16.

Elders, Fons (ed. with an afterword), *Reflexive Water: The Basic Concerns of Mankind* (London: Souvenir Press, 1974).

Elkabbach, Jean-Pierre [Lettre], *La Quinzaine Littéraire*, 15 March 1968, p.21.

El Kordi, Mohamed. 'L'Archéologie de la pensée classique selon Michel Foucault', *Revue de l'histoire économique et sociale* 51 (1973), 309–35.

Ewald, François, 'Anatomie et corps politique, *Critique* 343 (December 1975), 1228–65.

___, 'Foucault: une pensée sans aveu', in Brochier 1978, pp.45–52.

___, 'Une expérience foucaldienne: les principes généraux du droit', *Critique* 52 (August 1986), 788–93.

Ey, Henri, 'Introduction aux débats', *Evolution psychiatrique: cahiers de psychologie clinique et de psychopathologie générale* 36, no. 2 (1971): La Conception idéologique de L'Histoire de la folie de Michel Foucault: Journées annuelles de l'Évolution psychiatrique 6 et 7 décembre 1969, 225–6.

___, 'Commentaires critiques sur l'histoire de la folie de Michel Foucault', *Evolution psychiatrique* 36 (June 1971), 243–58.

___, *Naissance de la médecine* (Paris: Masson, 1981).

Fanon, Frantz, *Les Damnés de la terre* (Paris: Maspero, 1961).

Farias, Victor, *Heidegger et le nazisme* (Paris: Lagrasse, Verdier, 1987).

Febvre, Lucien, *Le Problème de l'incroyance au XVIᵉ siècle: la religion de Rabelais* (Paris: Albin Michel, 1947).

Finkielkraut, Alain, *La Défaite de la pensée* (Paris: Gallimard, 1987).

Flynn, Bernard Charles, 'Michel Foucault and Comparative Civilizational Study', *Philosophy and Social Criticism and Cultural Hermeneutics* 5, no. 2 (1978), 145–58.

Forster, Robert and Ranum, Orest (eds), *Deviants and the Abandoned in French Society: Selections from the Annales: économies, sociétés, civilisations*, Vol. 4, translated by Elborg Forster and Patricia M. Ranum (Baltimore: Johns Hopkins Press, 1978).

Foss, Paul and Morris, Meaghan (eds), *Language, Sexuality and Subversion* (Sydney: Feral, 1978).

'Foucault comme des petits pains', *Le Nouvel Observateur*, 10 August 1966, p.29.

Friedrich, Otto and Burton, Sandra, 'France's Philosopher of Power', *Time*, 16 November 1981, pp.92–4.

Funt, D. P., 'The Structuralist Debate', *Hudson Review* 22, no 4 (1969–70), 623–46.

Furet, François, 'Les Intellectuels français et le structuralisme', *Preuves* 192 (February 1967), 3–12.

_ _ _, *L'Atelier de l'histoire* (Paris: Flammarion, 1982).

Gadamer, H. G., 'Historicité'. In *Encyclopaedia Universalis*, Vol. 8 (Paris, 1968).

Garaudy, Roger, *Perspectives de l'homme: existentialisme, pensée catholique, structuralisme, marxisme*, 4th edition (Paris: Presses Universitaires de France, 1969).

Gay, Peter, 'Chains and Couches', *Commentary* 40, no. 4 (1965), 93–5.

Geertz, Clifford, 'Stir Crazy', *New York Review of Books*, 26 January 1978, pp.3–6.

Giddens, Anthony, *A Contemporary Critique of Historical Materialism*, Vol. 1: *Power,Property and the State* (Berkeley: University of California Press, 1981).

Glucksmann, André. 'Un structuralisme ventriloque', *Les Temps Modernes*, no. 250 (March 1967), 1557–98.

_ _ _, *La Cuisinière et le mangeur d'hommes, essai sur les rapports entre l'Etat, le marxisme et les camps de concentration* (Paris: Seuil, 1975).

_ _ _, *Les Maîtres penseurs* (Paris: Grasset, 1977).

Godard, Jean-Luc, 'Lutter sur deux fronts. Conversation avec Jean-Luc Godard', *Cahiers du cinéma*, no. 194 (October 1967), 13–28, 66–70.

Gordon, Colin, 'Birth of the Subject', *Radical Philosophy*, no. 17 (Summer 1977), 15–25.

_ _ _, 'The Normal and the Biological: A Note on Georges Canguilhem', *I & C*, no. 7 (Autumn 1980), 33–6.

_ _ _, 'Episteme epitomized', *The Times Literary Supplement*, 27 March 1981, p.332.

_ _ _, 'Letter', *The Times Literary Supplement*, 15 May 1981, p.546.

_ _ _, 'Preface' and 'Afterword' to *Power/Knowledge: Selected Interviews and Other Writings 1972–1977 by Michel Foucault* (London: Harvester, 1981).

_ _ _, 'The Deviancy of Disease', *The Times Literary Supplement*, 16 July 1982, p.773.

_ _ _, 'Diagnosis as Disease', *The Times Literary Supplement*, 15 July 1983, p.761.

_ _ _, 'Attacks on Singularity', *The Times Literary Supplement*, 6 June 1986.

_ _ _, 'Reassessing Foucault', *The Times Literary Supplement*, 4 July 1986, p.735.

_ _ _, 'Foucault en Angleterre', *Critique* 52 (August 1986), 826–39.

Greene, John C., 'Les Mots et les choses', *Social Science Information* 6, no. 4 (1967), 131–8.

Grisoni, Dominique (ed.), *Politiques de la philosophie* (Paris: Grasset, 1976).

Guédez, Annie, *Foucault* (Paris: Editions Universitaires, 1972).

Guédon, Jean-Claude, 'Michel Foucault: The Knowledge of Power and the Power of Knowledge', *Bulletin of the History of Medicine* 51 (1977), 245–77.

Gutman, Claude, 'L'Avant mai des philosophes', in Brochier 1978, pp.23–32.

Habermas, Jürgen, 'Modernity versus Postmodernity', *New German Critique*, no. 22 (1981), pp.3–14.

_ _ _, 'A Reply to My Critics', in *Habermas: Critical Debates*, edited by John B. Thompson and David Held (Cambridge, Massachusetts: MIT Press, 1982).

_ _ _, 'The Entwinement of Myth and Enlightenment: Rereading *Dialectic of Enlightenment*', *New German Critique*, no. 26 (1982), pp.13–30.

_ _ _, *The Theory of Communicative Action, Vol 1: Reason and the Rationalization of Society*, translated by Thomas McCarthy (Boston: Beacon Press, 1984).

_ _ _, 'Jürgen Habermas: A Philosophico-Political Profile', *New Left Review*, no. 151 (May–June 1985), pp.75–105.

_ _ _, 'Une flèche dans le coeur du temps présent', *Critique* (August 1986), 794–9.

_ _ _, 'Les Sciences humaines démasquées par la critique de la raison: Foucault', *Le Débat*, no. 41 (September 1986), 70–92.

Hacking, Ian M., 'The Archaeology of Foucault', *New York Review of Books*, 14 May 1981, pp.32–7.

Hadot, Pierre, 'Exercises spirituels et philosophie antique', *Etudes Augustiniennes* 1987, pp.229–33.

Hamon, Hervé and Rotman, Patrick, *Les Intellocrates: expédition en haute intelligentsia* (Paris: Ramsay, 1981).

Handlin, Oscar, *Truth in History* (Massachusetts: Belknap Press of Harvard Press, 1979).

Harari, Josué V. (ed.), *Textual Strategies: Perspectives in Post Structural Criticism* (Ithaca, New York: Cornell University Press, 1979).

Harding, D. W., 'Good-bye Man', *New York Review of Books*, 12 August 1971, pp.21–2.

Harkness, J., 'Rear-Guard Mutterings about Michel Foucault', *New Republic*, 25 November 1978, pp.3, 39.

Hayman, Ronald, 'Cartography of Discourse? On Foucault', *Encounter* 47 (December 1976), 72–5.

Hegel, Georg Wilhelm Friedrich, *Lectures in the Philosophy of World History. Introduction: Reason in History*, edited by Johannes Hoffmeister, translated by H. B. Nisbet (Cambridge: Cambridge University Press, 1975).

Hexter, J. H., 'The Rhetoric of History', *History and Theory* 6 (1967), 3–13.

Hill, Leslie, 'Shades of the Prison House', *The Times Higher Education Supplement*, 2 January 1981, p.7.

Hillier, Sheila, 'Anyman Goes Mad', *Sociology: The Journal of the British Sociological Association* 9 (1975), 323–8.

Hillyard, P., 'Review of *Discipline and Punish*', *Community Development Journal* 14, no. 2 (1979), 163–5.

Hollier, Denis. 'Le Mot de Dieu: "Je suis mort" ', paper presented at an International Conference 'Michel Foucault, philosophe', Paris, 9–11 January 1988.

Hondt, Jacques d', 'L'Idéologie de la rupture', *Revue de théologie et de philosophie* 21, no. 4 (1971), 253–62.

Hottois, G., 'La Secondarité: concept central de la métaphilosophie contemporaine', *Etudes philosophiques* 3 (July 1978), 373–6.

Howard, Richard, 'Our Sense of Where We Are', *Nation*, 5 July 1971, pp.21–2.

_ _ _, 'The Story of Unreason', *The Times Literary Supplement*, 6 October 1961, pp.653–4.

Howe, M., 'Open Up a Few Corpses', *Nation*, 26 January 1974, pp.117–19.

Hoy, David, 'After Foucault', *London Review of Books*, 1 November 1984, pp.7–9.

Huppert, George, '*Divinatio et Eruditio*: Thoughts on Foucault', *History and Theory* 13 (1974), 191–207.

Hussain, Athar, 'Review of *Discipline and Punish*', *Sociological Review* 26, no. 4 (1978), 932–9.

Iggers, Georg G., 'Historicism', in *Dictionary of the History of Ideas. Studies of Selected Pivotal Ideas*, Vol. 11, pp.456–65, edited by Philip P. Wiener (New York: Charles Scribner's Sons, 1973).

_ _ _, *New Directions in European Historiography* (Middletown: Connecticut Wesleyan University Press, 1975).

Ignatieff, Michael, *A Just Measure of Pain: The Penitentiary in the Industrial Revolution, 1750–1850* (New York: Colombia University Press, 1978).

_ _ _, 'Une Grande Audience dans le monde anglo-saxon', *Le Monde*, 27 June 1984, p.10.

_ _ _, 'Anxiety and Ascetism', *The Times Literary Supplement*, 28 September 1984, pp.1072–3.

Jaccard, Roland, *La Folie* (Paris: Presses Universitaires de France, 1979).

_ _ _, 'La Hantise du grand renfermement', *Le Monde*, 27 June 1984, p.11.

Jambet, Christian, 'L'Unité d'une pensée: une interrogation sur les pouvoirs', *Le Monde*, 21 February 1973, p.17.

_ _ _, 'Constitution du sujet et pratique spirituelle', paper presented at an International Conference 'Michel Foucault, philosophe', Paris, 9–11 January 1988.

Janicaud, Dominique, 'Rationalité, puissance et pouvoir. Foucault sous les critiques de Habermas', paper presented at an International Conference 'Michel Foucault, philosophe', Paris, 9–11 January 1988.

Jannoud, Claude, 'Loin des synthèses totalisatrices', *Le Figaro*, 26 June 1984, p.33.

Joly, Henri, 'Retour aux Grecs', *Le Débat*, no. 41 (September 1986), 100–120.

Jorion, Paul, 'Ethnologie et archéologie de l'anthropologie', *Revue de l'institut de sociologie*, no. 3–4 (1977), 469–83.

_ _ _, 'Letter: regard éloigné', *The Times Literary Supplement*, 4 May 1984, pp.495–6.

July, Serge, 'Le Démineur des lendemains', *Libération*, 26 June 1984, p.3.

Kahn, Jean-François, 'La Minutieuse Conquête du structuralisme', *L'Express*, 21 August 1967, pp.39–41.

Kanters, Robert, 'Tu causes, tu causes, est-ce tout ce que tu sais faire?', *Le Figaro littéraire*, 23 June 1966, p.5.

Kaplan, Roger, 'France's "New Philosophers" ', *Commentary* 65, no. 2 (February 1978), 73–6.

Kellner, Hans D., 'Time Out: The Discontinuity of Historical Conscious-ness', *History and Theory* 14, no. 3 (1975), 275–96.

Kemp, Peter, 'Review of *Michel Foucault: Beyond Structuralism and Herme-neutics* by H. L. Dreyfus and Paul Rabinow', *History and Theory* 23, no. 1 (1984), 84–105.

Kermode, Frank, 'Crisis Critic', *New York Review of Books*, 17 May 1973, pp.37–9.

Kiejman, Georges, 'Le Premier à reconnaitre s'être fourvoyé dans l'erreur khomeiniste', *Libération*, 26 June 1984, p.9.

–– –– ––, 'Un combattant de rue', *Le Monde*, 27 June 1984, p.11.

Knibiehler, Yvonne, 'Les Médecins et la "nature féminine" au temps du code civil', *Annales: économies, sociétés, civilisations* 31, no. 4 (July 1976), 824–45.

Kravetz, Marc, 'Qu'est-ce que le GIP?', *Magazine littéraire*, no. 101 (June 1975), 13.

Krémer-Marietti, Angèle, *Foucault et l'archéologie du savoir. Présentation, choix de textes, bibliographie* (Paris: Seghers, 1974).

–– –– ––, *Michel Foucault: Archéologie et généalogie*. Revised and expanded edition (Paris: Livre de poche, 1985).

Kriegel, Annie, 'Mort du philosophe Michel Foucault. La souffrance et l'honneur', *Le Figaro*, 26 June 1984, pp.1, 33.

Kurzweil, Edith, 'Law and Disorder', *Partisan Review* 44, no. 2 (1977), 293–7.

–– –– ––, 'Michel Foucault: Ending the Era of Man', *Theory and Society* 4, no. 3 (1977), 395–420.

La Capra, Dominique, *Rethinking Intellectual History. Texts, Contexts, Language* (Ithaca: Cornell University Press, 1983).

Lacharité, Normand, 'Les Conditions de possibilité du savoir: deux versions structuralistes de ce problème', *Dialogue: Revue canadienne de philosophie* 7 (December 1968), 359–73.

–– –– ––, 'Archéologie du savoir et structures du langage scientifique', *Dialogue* 9 (1970), 35–53.

Lacroix, Jean, *Panorama de la philosophie française contemporaine* (Paris: Presses Universitaires de France, 1968).

Laing, R. D., 'Sanity and Madness 1: The Invention of Madness', *New Statesman*, 16 June 1967, p.843.

Langlois, Jean, 'Structuralisme et métaphysique', *Science et esprit* 20 (May 1968), 171–93.

–– –– ––, 'Michel Foucault et la mort de l'homme', *Science et esprit* 21, no. 2 (1969), 209–30.

Lasch, Christopher, 'Review of *The Birth of the Clinic*', *New York Times Book Review*, 24 February 1974, p.6.

–– –– ––, 'Life in the Therapeutic State', *New York Review of Books*, 12 June 1980, pp.24–32.

Leary, D. E., 'Essay Review: Michel Foucault, an Historian of the *Sciences Humaines*', *Journal of the History of Behavioural Sciences* 12, no. 3 (1976), 286–93.

Le Bon, Sylvie, 'Un positiviste désesperé: Michel Foucault', *Les Temps Modernes* 22 (1967), 1299–319.

Lecourt, Dominique, 'Sur l'archéologie et le savoir (à propos de Michel Foucault)', *La Pensée*, no. 152 (August 1970), 69–87.

_ _ _, *Pour une critique d'épistémologie: Bachelard, Canguilhem, Foucault* (Paris: Maspero, 1972).

_ _ _, *Dissidence ou révolution?* (Paris: Maspero, 1978).

Lefebvre, Henri, *L'Idéologie structuraliste* (Paris: Editions Anthropos, 1971).

Lefort, Claude, 'Then and Now', *Telos*, no. 36 (Summer 1978), 29–42.

_ _ _, *Eléments d'une critique de la bureaucratie* (Paris: Gallimard, 1979).

Lefort, Gèrard, 'Au Collège de France: Un judoka de l'intellect', *Libération*, 26 June 1984, p.6.

Le Goff, Jacques (ed.), *La Nouvelle Histoire*, Les Encyclopédies du savoir modern (Paris: CEPL, 1978).

_ _ _, 'L'Histoire Nouvelle', in Le Goff 1978, pp.210–41.

Le Goff, Jacques and Nora, Pierre, *Faire de l'histoire*, Vol 1: *Nouveaux problèmes* (Paris: Gallimard, 1974).

Lemaigre, B., 'Michel Foucault ou les malheurs de la raison et les prospérités du langage', *Review des sciences philosophiques et théologiques* 51 (July 1967), 440–60.

Lemert, Charles C., 'Rear-Guard Mutterings About Michel Foucault', *New Republic*, 25 November 1978, p.39.

_ _ _ (ed. with an introduction), *French Sociology: Rupture and Renewal Since 1968* (New York: Columbia University Press, 1981).

Lemert, Charles and Gillan, G., 'The New Alternative in Critical Sociology: Foucault's Discursive Analysis', *Cultural Hermeneutics* 4, no. 4 (1977), 309–20.

Léonard, Jacques, 'L'Historien et le philosophe. A propos de *Surveiller et punir: naissance de la prison*', in Perrot 1980, pp.9–28.

Le Roy Ladurie, Emmanuel, 'Dix années de recherches historiques', *L'histoire*, no. 2 (June 1978), 60–65.

_ _ _, *Paris–Montpellier P. C.–P.S.U. 1945–1963* (Paris: Gallimard, 1982).

Lévi-Strauss, Claude, *Anthropologie structurale* I (Paris: Plon, 1958).

_ _ _, *Mythologiques: Le cru et le cruit* (Paris: Plon, 1964).

_ _ _, *Tristes tropiques* (Paris: Gallimard 10/18, 1966).

Lévy, Bernard-Henri. 'Le Système Foucault', *Magazine littéraire*, no. 101 (June 1975), 7–9.

La barbarie à visage humaine (Paris: Grasset, 1977).

Lindon, Mathieu, 'Les Editeurs malades de leurs livres', *Le Nouvel Observateur: Spécial littérature*, May 1981, pp.21–37.

Lipovetsky, Gilles, *L'Ere du vide: essais sur l'individualisme contemporain* (Paris: Gallimard, 1983).

_ _ _, *L'Empire de l'éphémère: la mode et son destin dans les sociétés modernes* (Paris: Gallimard, 1987).

Livrozet, Serge, 'Le Philosophe aux portes de la prison', *Libération*, 26 June 1984, p.8.

Lodge, David, 'Adventures Among Master-Theories', *The Times Literary Supplement*, 4 May 1984, p.487.

Lombard, Jacques. 'Systèmes sociaux et modes de répression', *Cahiers internationaux de sociologie* 66 (June 1979), 349–64.

Lucas, Colin, 'Power and the Panopticon', *The Times Literary Supplement*, 26 September 1975, p.1090.

Macherey, Pierre, 'Pour une histoire naturelle des normes', paper presented at an International Conference 'Michel Foucault, philosophe', Paris, 9–11 January 1988.

Macksey, Richard and Donato, Eugenio (eds), *Languages of Criticism and the Sciences of Man: The Structuralist Controversy* (Baltimore: Johns Hopkins Press, 1970).

Maggiori, Robert, 'Michel Foucault: une pensée sur les chemins de traverse', *Libération*, 26 June 1984, pp.2, 5.

Maire, Edmond, 'Une tristesse douce', *Libération*, 26 June 1984, p.9.

Major-Poetzl, Pamela, *Michel Foucault's Archaeology of Western Culture. Toward a New Science of History* (Brighton, Sussex: Harvester, 1983).

Mandrou, Robert, 'Trois clefs pour comprendre la folie à l'époque classique', *Annales: économies, sociétés, civilisations sociétés* 17 (1962), 761–71.

Marcus, Steven, 'In Praise of Folly', *New York Review of Books*, 3 November 1966, pp.6–8.

Margolin, Jean-Claude, 'L'Homme de Michel Foucault', *Revue des sciences humaines* 128 (1967), 497–522.

_ _ _, 'Tribut d'un antihumaniste aux études d'humanisme et renaissance: note sur l'oeuvre de Michel Foucault', *Bibliothèque d'humanisme et renaissance* 29 (1967), 701–11.

Matza, David, *Becoming Deviant* (Englewood Cliffs, New Jersey: Prentice-Hall, 1969).

_ _ _ 'Review of Madness and Civilisation', *American Sociological Review* 31, no. 4 (1966), 551–2.

Mauriac, Claude, *Le Temps immobile*, Vol. 2: *Les Espaces imaginaires* (Paris: Grasset, 1975).

_ _ _, *Le Temps immobile*, Vol. 3: *Et comme l'esperance est violente* (Paris: Grasset, 1976).

Mauriès, Patrick, 'Diary', *London Review of Books*, 16 November 1983, p.21.

_ _ _, 'Dans les pays anglo-saxons: une influence contestée', *Libération*, 26 June 1984, p.5.

Mazlish, Bruce, 'The Hysterical Personality', *Journal of Interdisciplinary History* 11 (1980), 105–14.

McDonell, Donald J., 'On Foucault's Philosophical Method', *Canadian Journal of Philosophy* 7, no. 3 (1977), 537–53.

Megill, Allan, 'Foucault, Structuralism, and the Ends of History', *Journal of Modern History* 51, no. 3 (1979), 451–503.

Mendel, Gérard. *La Révolte contre le père: une introduction à la sociopsychanalyse*, 2nd edition (Paris: Payot, 1969).

_ _ _, *La Crise des générations: étude sociopsychanalytique* (Paris: Payot, 1969).

_ _ _, 'Folie, antifolie et non-folie', *La Nef* 42 (January 1971), 193–200.

Merleau-Ponty, Maurice, *Signes* (Paris: Gallimard, 1961).

Merquior, J. G., *Foucault* (London: Fontana Press/Collins, 1985).

Midelfort, H. C. Erik, 'Madness and Civilization in Early Modern Europe: A Reappraisal of Michel Foucault', in *After the Reformation: Essays in*

Honor of J. H. Hexter, pp.247–65, edited by Barbara C. Malament (Philadelphia: University of Pennsylvania Press, 1980).

Miel, Jan, 'Ideas or épistémès? Hazard versus Foucault', *Yale French Studies* 49 (1973), 231–45.

Milhau, Jacques, 'Les Mots et les choses', *Cahiers du communisme*, no. 2 (1968), 52–70.

Minson, Jeffrey, 'Strategies for Socialists? Foucault's Conception of Power', *Economy and Society* 9, no. 1 (1980), 1–43.

___ , *Genealogies of Morals. Nietzsche, Foucault, Donzelot and the Eccentricity of Ethics* (London: Macmillan, 1985).

Misrahi, Robert, 'Le Rêve et l'existence selon M. Binswanger,' *Revue de métaphysique et de morale* 64, no. 1 (1959), 96–106.

Mordier, Jean Pierre, *Les Débuts de la psychanalyse en France 1895–1926* (Paris: Maspero, 1981).

Morot-Sir, Edouard, *La Pensée française d'aujourd'hui* (Paris: Presses Universitaires de France, 1971).

Morris, Meaghan and Patton, Paul (eds), *Michel Foucault, Power, Truth, Strategy* (Sydney: Feral, 1979).

Muchnik, Nicole (ed.), *Le Nouvel Observateur: témoin de l'histoire* (Paris: Pierre Belfond, 1981).

Nemo, Philippe, 'D'une prison à l'autre', *Le Nouvel Observateur*, 10 January 1972, pp.40–41.

___ , 'Le Pouvoir pris en flagrant délit par Foucault', *Les Nouvelles littéraires*, 15 January 1976, pp.6–7.

O'Brien, Patricia, 'Crime and Punishment as a Historical Problem', *Journal of Social History* 11, no. 4 (1978), 508–20.

O'Farrell, Clare, 'Foucault and the Foucaldians', *Economy and Society* 11, no. 4 (November 1982), 449–59.

'Old New Novelist', *The Times Literary Supplement*, 12 July 1963, p.511.

Ormesson, Jean d', 'Passage de l'homme ou les avatars du savoir', *Nouvelle Revue Française* 15, no. 171 (1967), 477–90.

Pace, David, 'Structuralism in History and the Social Sciences', *American Quarterly* 30, no. 3 (1978), 282–97.

Painton, Frederick and Burton, Sandra, 'France's New Thinkers', *Time*, 5 September 1977, pp.18–23.

Palmier, Jean-Michel, 'Le Glas de la réflexion historique. La mort du roi', *Le Monde*, 3 May 1969, p.viii.

___ , '"L'Histoire de la folie", de Michel Foucault', *Le Monde*, 15 September 1972, p.16.

Parain-Vial, Jeanne, *Analyses structurales et idéologies structuralistes* (Toulouse: Privat, 1969).

___ , *Tendances nouvelles de la philosophie* (Paris: Seuil, 1978).

Patton, Paul, 'Of Power and Prisons', in Morris and Patton 1979, pp.109–47.

Pelorson, J. M., 'Michel Foucault et l'Espagne', *La Pensée*, no 152 (August 1970), 88–99.

Perrot, Michelle, 'Délinquance et système pénitentiaire français au XIXe siècle', *Annales: économies, sociétés, civilisations* 30, no. 1 (1975), 67–80.

___ (ed.), *L'Impossible Prison: recherches sur le système pénitentiaire au XIXᵉ siècle et débat avec Michel Foucault* (Paris: Seuil, 1980).

Philp, Mark, 'Notes on the Form of Knowledge in Social Work', *Sociological Review* 27, no. 1 (1979), 83–111.

___, 'When Knowledge Becomes Power', *Listener*, 12 April 1984, pp.12–13.

Piaget, Jean, *Le Structuralisme* (Paris: Presses Universitaires de France, 1968).

Pichol, Michel, 'A propos des questions de Michel Foucault: nouvelles du front idéologique', *Hérodote* 6 (1977), 31–9.

Pinto, Louis, 'Politiques de philosophes (1960–1976)', *La Pensée*, no 197 (1978), 52–72.

Pizzorno, Alessandro, 'Foucault and the Liberal View of the Free Individual', paper distributed at an International Conference 'Michel Foucault, philosophe', Paris, 9–11 January 1988.

Plummer, Ken, 'Review of *The History of Sexuality*, Vol. 1: *An Introduction*', *Sociology: The Journal of the British Sociological Association* 14, no. 2 (1980), 313–14.

Poirot-Delpech, Bertrand, 'Une ascèse de l'égarement', *Le Monde*, 27 June 1984, p.10.

Popper, Karl R., *The Poverty of Historicism* (London: Routledge & Kegan Paul, 1957).

Poster, Mark, 'Review of *The Archaeology of Knowledge*', *Library Journal* 97 (1972), 2736.

___, *Foucault, Marxism and History: Mode of Production versus Mode of Information* (Cambridge: Polity Press, 1984).

___, 'Foucault, the Present and History', paper delivered at an International Conference 'Michel Foucault, philosophe', Paris 9–11 January 1988.

Pratt, Vernon, 'Foucault and the History of Classification Theory', *Studies in the History and Philosophy of Science* 8, no. 2 (1977), 163–71.

Proust, J. (director), 'Entretiens sur Foucault', *La Pensée*, no. 137 (February 1968), 3–37.

Quétel, Claude, 'Une histoire de l'internement de Ramsès II à mardi en huit', *Magazine littéraire*, no. 175 (July 1981), 17–21.

Quétel, Claude and Morel, Pierre, *Les Fous et leurs médecins de la Renaissance au XXᵉ siècle* (Paris: Hachette, 1979).

Racevskis, Karlis, *Michel Foucault and the Subversion of Intellect* (Ithaca: Cornell University Press, 1983).

Rajchman, John, 'Nietzsche, Foucault and the Anarchism of Power', *Semiotexte* 3, no. 1 (1978), 96–107.

___, *Michel Foucault: The Freedom of Philosophy* (New York: Columbia University Press, 1985).

___, 'Ethics After Foucault', paper presented at the symposium 'Hommage à Michel Foucault', Columbia University, March 1985; also distributed at an International Conference 'Michel Foucault, philosophe', Paris, 9–11 January 1988.

___, 'L'Ethique et l'oeuvre', paper delivered at an International Conference on 'Michel Foucault, philosophe', Paris, 9–11 January 1988.

'Rendre à Sartre ce qui est à Sartre . . .', *Le Monde des livres*, 23 March 1968, p.ii.

'La Rentrée des vrais parisiens', *Parispoche-Pariscope*, 7 September 1983, pp.ix–xii.

Revault d'Allonnes, Olivier, 'Michel Foucault: les mots contre les choses', *Raison présente* 2 (1967), 19–41.

Revel, Jacques, 'Foucault et les historiens', *Magazine littéraire*, no. 101 (June 1975), 10–13.

Revel, Jean-François, *Pourquoi des philosophes? suivi de La Cabale des dévots et précédé d'une étude inédite sur la philosophie depuis 1960* (Paris: Julliard, 1971).

Robbe-Grillet, Alain, 'Enigmes et transparence chez Raymond Roussel', *Critique* 19 (1963), 1027–33.

Robinson, Paul, 'Review of *The History of Sexuality*, Vol. 1: *An Introduction*', *New Republic*, 28 October 1978, pp.29–32.

Rochlitz, Rainer, ' "Esthétique de l'existence". Morale postconventionnelle et théorie du pouvoir chez Michel Foucault', paper presented at an International Conference 'Michel Foucault, philosophe', Paris, 9–11 January 1988.

Rorty, Richard, 'Beyond Nietzsche and Marx', *London Review of Books*, 19 February 1981, pp.5–6.

___, 'What's It All About?', *London Review of Books*, 17 May 1984, pp.3–4.

___, 'Méthode science sociale et espoir social', *Critique* 52 (August 1986), 873–97.

___, 'Moral Identity and Private Autonomy', paper presented at an International Conference 'Michel Foucault, philosophe', Paris, 9–11 January 1988.

Roth, Michael S., 'Foucault's "History of the Present" ', *History and Theory* 20 (1981), 32–46.

Rothman, David J., *The Discovery of the Asylum: Social Order and Disorder in the New Republic* (Boston: Little, Brown, 1971).

___, 'Society and its Prisons', *New York Times Book Review*, 19 February 1978, pp.1, 26.

Rousseau, G. S., 'Whose Enlightenment? Not Man's: The Case of Michel Foucault', *Eighteenth-Century Studies* 6 (1972–73), 238–56.

___, 'Review of *The Birth of the Clinic*', *Philological Quarterly* (1975), 790–94.

___, 'Literature and Science: The State of the Field', *Isis* 69, no. 249 (1978), 583–91.

Roy, Claude, 'Claude Mauriac miroir ébloui', *Le Nouvel Observateur*, 29 March 1976, pp.52–3.

___, 'Un animal mal vu', *Le Nouvel Observateur*, 14 June 1976, pp.68–70.

Russell, Bertrand, *The Art of Philosophizing and Other Essays* (New York: The Philosophical Library, 1968).

Russo, François. 'L'Archéologie du savoir de Michel Foucault', *Archives de philosophie* 36 (1973), 69–105.

Said, Edward W., 'An Ethics of Language', *Diacritics* 4, no. 2 (Summer 1974), 28–37.

——, *Beginnings: Intention and Method* (New York: Basic Books, 1975).

——, 'Raymond Schwab and the Romance of Ideas', *Daedalus* 105 (Winter 1976), 151–67.

——, *Orientalism* (London: Routledge & Kegan Paul, 1978).

——, 'The Problem of Textuality: Two Exemplary Positions', *Critical Inquiry* 4, no. 4 (1978), 673–714.

——, 'The Text, the World, the Critic', in Harari 1979, pp.161–88.

Samuelson, F. M., *Il était une fois 'Libération', Reportage historique* (Paris: Seuil, 1979).

Sartre, Jean-Paul, *Situations VII* (Paris: Gallimard, 1965).

——, Jean-Paul Sartre répond', *L'Arc* 30 (1966), 87–96.

'Sartre répond', *La Quinzaine Littéraire*, 15 October 1966, pp.4–5.

'De Sartre à Foucault', *Le Monde*, 8 November 1974, p.18.

Schiwy, Günther, *Les nouveaux philosophes*, translated by Jeanne Etoré (Paris: Denoël/Gonthier, 1978).

Schmitt, Jean-Claude, 'Le suicide au Moyen Age', *Annales: économies, sociétés, civilisations* 31, no. 1 (1976), 3–28.

Scholes, Robert, 'A Discourse on Sex and Power', *Washington Post Book World*, 7 January 1979, pp. E1, E4.

Scruton, Roger, 'On Madness and Method', *Spectator*, 9 October 1971, p.513.

Serres, Michel, 'Géométrie de la folie', *Mercure de France* (Part 1), no. 1188 (August 1962), 683–96; (Part 2), no. 1189 (September 1962), 63–81.

——, *Hermès I: La Communication* (Paris: Minuit, 1968).

Sharratt, Bernard, 'Notes after Foucault', *New Blackfriars* 53 (June 1972), 251–64.

Sheehan, Thomas, 'Paris: Moses and Polytheism', *New York Review of Books*, 24 January 1980, pp.13–18.

Sheridan, Alan, *Michel Foucault: The Will to Truth* (London: Tavistock, 1981).

——, 'Letter', *The Times Literary Supplement*, 17 April 1981, p.437.

'Six volumes de Michel Foucault: une histoire de la sexualité', *Le Monde*, 5 November 1976, pp.1, 18.

Smart, Barry, *Foucault, Marxism and Critique* (London: Routledge & Kegan Paul, 1983).

——, *Michel Foucault*, Key Sociologists (Chichester: Ellis Horword; London: Tavistock, 1985).

'Soil Science', *The Times Literary Supplement*, 9 June 1972, p.663.

Sokolov, Raymond A., 'Inside Mind', *Newsweek*, 25 January 1971, pp.48–9.

Solé, Jacques, 'Un exemple d'archéologie des sciences humaines: l'étude de l'égyptomanie du XVIᵉ au XVIIIᵉ siècle', *Annales: économies, sociétés, civilisations* 27, no. 1 (January 1972), 473–82.

Sollers, Philippe, 'Aller-retour dans le système Sollers', *Le Nouvel Observateur*, 19 January 1981, pp.14–18: interview with Jean-Paul Enthoven.

Starobinski, Jean, 'Review of *Birth of the Clinic*', *New York Review of Books*, 22 January 1976, pp.18–22.

Steiner, George, 'Steiner Responds to Foucault', *Diacritics* 1 (Winter 1971), 59.

Steinert, Heinz, 'The Development of "Discipline" According to Michel Foucault: Discourse Analysis vs Social History', *Crime and Social Justice*, no. 20 (1984), 83–98.

Stock, Brian, 'Literary Discourse and the Social Historian', *New Literary History* 8 (1977), 183–94.

Stoianovich, Traian, *French Historical Method: The Annales Paradigm* (Ithaca: Cornell University Press, 1976).

Stone, Lawrence, 'Madness', *New York Review of Books*, 16 December 1982, pp.28–30.

___, 'An Exchange with Michel Foucault', *New York Review of Books*, 21 March 1983, pp.41–3.

Storr, Anthony, 'Bourgeois Sex', *Spectator*, 31 March 1979, pp.20–22.

Sztulman, Henri, 'Folie ou maladie mentale? Etude critique psychopatho-logique et épistémologique des conceptions de Michel Foucault', *Evolution psychiatrique: cahiers de psychologie clinique et de psychopathologie générale* 36, no. 2 (1971): 'La conception de la folie de Michel Foucault', *Journées annuelles de l'évolution psychiatrique 6 et 7 décembre 1969*, 259–78.

___, 'Anti-psychiatrie et psychiatrie', *Evolution psychiatrique: cahiers de psychologie clinique et de psychopathologie générale* 37, fasc. 1 (January 1972), 83–109.

Tricart, Jean-Paul, 'Génèse d'un dispositif d'assistance: les "cités de transit" ', *Revue française de sociologie* 18, no. 4 (1977), 601–24.

Turkle, Sherry R., 'Sound over Sense', *Nation*, 27 January 1979, pp.92–4.

Verley, Etienne, 'L'Archéologie du savoir et le problème de la périodisation', *Dix-huitième siècle* 5 (1973), 151–62.

Versele, S. C. and Van de Velde-Graff, Dominique, 'Marginalité ou marginalisation? Accident ou fonction?', *Revue de l'institut de sociologie*, no. 1–2 (1976), 23–49.

Veyne, Paul, *Comment on écrit l'histoire suivi de Foucault révolutionne l'histoire*, 2nd edition (Paris: Seuil, 1978).

___, 'La Fin de vingt-cinq siècles de métaphysique . . .', *Le Monde*, 27 June 1984, p.11.

___, 'Le Dernier Foucault et sa morale', *Critique* 52 (August 1986), 933–41.

Veyron, Martin, 'Cartoon', *Lire* February 1983

Von Bülow, Catherine and Ben Ali, Fazia, *La Goutte d'Or ou le mal des racines* (Paris: Seuil, 1979).

Wahl, François (gen. ed.), *Qu'est-ce que la structuralisme?* 5 vols (Paris; Seuil, 1968). Vol. 5: *Philosophie. La Philosophie entre l'avant et l'après du structuralisme* by François Wahl.

___, 'Hors ou dans la philosophie?', paper presented at an Inter-national Conference 'Michel Foucault, philosophe', Paris, 9–11 January 1988.

White, Hayden, V., 'Foucault Decoded: Notes from Underground', *History and Theory* 12, no. 1 (1973), 23–54.

— — —, 'Review of *Surveiller et punir*', *American Historical Review* 82, no. 3 (1977), 605–6.

— — —, 'The Archaeology of Sex', *The Times Literary Supplement*, 6 May 1977, p.565.

— — —, *Tropics of Discourse: Essays in Cultural Criticism* (Baltimore: Johns Hopkins University Press, 1978).

Williams, Karel, 'Problematic History', *Economy and Society* 1, no. 4 (1972), 457–81.

— — —, 'Unproblematic Archaeology, *Economy and Society* 3, no. 1 (1974), 41–68.

— — —, 'Facing Reality: A Critique of Karl Popper's Empiricism', *Economy and Society* 4, no. 3 (1975), 309–58.

Wolton, Dominique. 'Qui veut savoir?', *Esprit* 78 (1977), 36–47.

Wright, Iain, 'The Suicide of the Intellectuals', *The Times Higher Education Supplement*, 24 October 1986, p.16.

Wright, Peter and Treacher, Andrew (eds), *The Problem of Medical Knowledge. Examining the Social Construction of Medicine* (Edinburgh: Edinburgh University Press, 1982).

Wuthnow, Robert, Hunter, James Davison, Bergesen, Albert, and Kurzweil, Edith, *Cultural Analysis: The work of Peter L. Berger, Mary Douglas, Michel Foucault and Jürgen Habermas* (London: Routledge & Kegan Paul, 1984).

Ysmal, Colette, 'Histoire et archéologie: note sur la recherche de Michel Foucault', *Revue française de science politique* 22, no. 4 (August 1972), 775–805.

Zeldin, Theodore, 'An Archaeologist of Knowledge', *The New Statesman*, 7 December 1973, pp.861–2.

— — —, 'The Clerk from the Convent', *The Times Literary Supplement*, 13 October 1978, pp.1155.

Zoila, Adolfo Fernandez, 'Une archéologie du regard médical d'après Michel Foucault', *Hygiene mentale* 53 (1964), 150–58.

— — —, 'Michel Foucault anti-psychiatre?', *Revue internationale de philosophie* 123, no. 1 (1978), 59–74.

Index

aesthetics of existence 122, 127–9
Age of Confinement see Great
    Confinement
Akoun. A. 131
Alexander, G. 149
Algerian War 3,4
Allio, R. 133
Althusser, L. 3, 6, 10, 25, 31, 99,
    131, 132, 136, 137, 138
Annales School 35, 37–8, 49–50
anthropological sleep 32, 88
anti-history 11–12, 37, 51, 58
anti-humanism 10
anti-psychiatry movement 8, 17,
    50
a priori 33 (see also historical a
    priori)
archaeology 53, 59, 63, 80, 94, 96,
    100, 105, 136, 144, 145, 147
Archéologie du savoir, L' 14, 26–7,
    36, 46–7, 50, 59–62, 68, 93–4,
    96–9, 107, 132, 133, 144, 145,
    146
'archive' 60
Arguments 5
Ariès, P. 7, 27–8, 35, 43, 124, 132,
    135, 137, 151
Aron, R. 12, 32, 53, 99, 136, 139,
    146
arts of existence 127
Artaud, A. 68, 69, 73, 78, 89, 91
asceticism 122, 127
Auzias, J. M. 140, 150

Bachelard, G. 37
Balibar, E. 138, 146
Barbedette, G. 113
Barnham, P. 22, 134
Barthes, R. 7, 9–10, 12, 16, 24, 50,
    132
Baruk, H. 8, 132, 143

Bataille, G. 69, 91
Baudrillard, J. 92, 107, 138, 144,
    147
Beauvoir, Simone de 2, 31, 131
Benamou, J. M. 18, 134
Bernauer, J. 128, 151
Bertrand, P. 136
Bichat 68, 81–2
Birth of the Clinic see Naissance
    de la clinique
Blanchot, M. 7, 70, 113, 132, 133,
    142, 143, 149
bio-power 106
Bodei, R. 152
body 100–3, 105–7
Bonnet, J-C. 62, 140
Borges, J. L. 53
Bourdé, G. 137
Bourdieu, P. 13, 20, 124, 133, 134,
    136, 140, 143–4, 151–2
Bouveresse, J. 24–5, 45, 133, 134,
    135, 138
Braudel, F. 7, 27, 132, 135
Brodeur, J. P. 134, 140
Broussais 51
Burgelin, P. 139
Burguière, A. 37, 137
Burke, P. 29, 135

Cabanis, P. J. G. 77
Camus, A. 3, 5, 23
Canguilhem, G. 7, 12, 37, 58, 67,
    134, 141
Cassirer, E. 137
Castoriadis, G. 4, 5, 108, 131,
    147–8
cause 35–6, 49, 51–2, 58–9
Caws, P. 132, 140
Ceci n'est pas une pipe 15
Certeau, M.de 11, 27, 53, 132,
    136, 139, 141

change 34–7, 48–9, 57–8
change, in Foucault's work 40–2, 44–8, 92, 113, 116–17
Chartier, R. 139
Châtelet, F. 5, 12, 100, 135, 145–6
Chomsky, N. 98, 146
Christian philosophy 120–1, 127
Clark, M. 11, 132, 133, 149
class 98–9, 109
Classical Age 53–7, 61, 63, 65, 68, 73–6, 85–6, 113
classification, tables of 53, 55–6
classification of Foucault's work viii, 20–2, 26–8
Clavel, M. 16, 45, 92, 101, 133, 138, 144, 146
Clifford, J. 44, 114, 138, 148, 149
cogito see Descartes
Collège de France, courses at 15–16, 18, 113
Colombel, J. 146, 149
Comité Djellali 15
commentary 87, 144
confession 106
consensus 124, 151
continuity see discontinuity
Cooper, D. 8
Cousins, M. 147, 149
Coutau-Begarie, H. 137
Cranston, M. 22, 56, 134, 139
criticism viii, ix, 21, 62, 114
   English language viii, 9–10, 14–15, 17, 18, 20, 49, 58, 60, 70, 83, 99–101, 110–13, 131
   French 10–14, 22, 58, 70, 83, 99–101, 135
   Foucault's replies to 58–9

Daix, P. 140
D'Amico, Robert, 22, 134
Daumézon, G. 143
Davis, N. 149
death 30, 42, 72, 79–85, 88–9, 94, 103, 105
Debray, R. 133
Deleuze, G. 15, 108–10, 145, 148
Derrida, J. 136, 142
Descartes, R. 48, 73–4, 123, 142
Descombes, V. 94, 145
determinism, historical 39, 41, 43

deviancy 67, 70
Dews, P. 27–8, 135
D'Hondt, J. vii, 131, 54, 139
diachrony 58
dialectics 31–2, 41, 99
Diderot 77
difference vii, 30, 55–6, 59, 88–9, 93–4, 110–11, 114
disciplinary classification 20–2, 36
discipline 16, 91–2, 103–6, 112
Discipline and Punish 96 (*see also Surveiller et punir*)
discontinuity 35–37, 43, 47, 51, 54, 56–7, 59, 63, 65, 69, 94, 97, 111
discourse 50, 61, 85–7, 90, 93–7, 110, 121, 145
   and exclusion 9, 96
discursive formation 47–8, 59
discursive practice 60–61, 107
document as monument 62
dogmatism 3–6, 42, 111
Domenach, J. M. 13, 22, 132, 133, 134, 138, 146, 149
Don Quixote 68, 73, 88
Dostoievsky, F. 74
Dreyfus, H. 141, 150
Droit, R. P. 46, 138
Dufrenne, M. 139, 57
Dumézil, G. 37, 144

Elders, F. 138, 144
Enlightenment 125
empiricism 22, 94, 100, 111, 135
emptiness 32, 38, 78–9, 83, 142, 143
episteme 11, 47, 54–7, 59–62, 69, 89, 138–40
epistemological break see discontinuity
essence 33, 35–6, 43, 76, 123, 137
ethical substance 121
ethics 38, 41, 73–4, 76, 91, 102, 116, 120–3, 126–7, 129
ethos 38, 42, 135
events 31, 33, 58–9, 62, 96–7, 136, 140
Ewald, F. 46, 138, 144
examination 105

exclusion   49, 65, 68–72, 75, 96–7,
    146
existentialism   1–4, 12–14, 31, 40,
    98
explanation, historical   57–8
exteriority, exterior   32, 41, 44, 68,
    70, 75, 84, 88, 91, 98, 107, 119,
    144
Ey, H.   52, 132, 139, 143

facts   23–4, 29, 58, 94, 96, 111
Fanon, F.   131
Farias, V.   24, 134
fashion, intellectual   12–16
fiction, history as   29, 92, 94, 96,
    135–6, 145
finitude   30, 32–3, 72, 82–3, 87–9,
    115, 129, 136
Finkielkraut, A.   134
Folie et déraison   see *Histoire de la
    folie*
Forster, R.   13, 141
foundations   32, 87–8, 91, 98, 103,
    107–8, 114–15, 118, 124–25,
    129, 149
freedom   32, 35, 40, 57, 93, 116,
    118–19, 124–5, 127, 130
French Communist Party   *see*
    Parti Communiste Français
Freud, S.   91
Friedrich, O.   132, 141
Furet, F.   1, 6, 131, 132, 135

Gadamer, H. G. 137
Garaudy, R.   46, 146
genealogy   26, 39, 63, 112
geometry, Foucault's work as   58,
    62, 69
Giddens, A.   148
Glucksmann, A.   16–17, 134
Godard, J. L.   11, 132
Gordan, C.   10, 96, 111, 132, 135,
    136, 138, 145, 147, 149
Great Confinement   48–9, 70,
    74–5, 139
Grisoni, D.   110, 148–9
Groupe d'Information sur les
    Prisons (GIP)   15, 67, 133
Groupe Information Santé   15

Habermas, J.   101, 114–15, 149,
    150, 151
Hadot, P.   128–9, 152
Hallier, J. E.   46
Hamon, H.   133–4
Handlin, O.   29, 135
Hayman, R.   149
Hegel, W. H.   29, 31–34, 36, 91,
    126, 137
Heidegger, M.   3, 25, 32, 34, 134
Hillyard, P.   146
*Histoire de la folie à l'âge
    classique*   viii, 6–9, 33, 40,
    48–52, 59, 67–79, 81–85, 88,
    94–5, 102–3, 105, 110, 116, 132,
    139, 143
historians and Foucault
    Anglo-Saxon   28, 49
    French   26, 28, 49
historical *a priori*   51–2, 55, 60, 98
historicism   14, 34–6, 112, 149
historiography   37–8, 48–9, 51, 56,
    90, 137
history   99, 110, 125–6
    definitions of   33–5, 37, 134,
    139
    philosophy of   34–5
history of ideas   14, 52
history of science   49–50, 52
history versus philosophy   vii,
    22, 27–30, 43, 114–15, 124, 130,
    135, 152
Histoire de la sexualité   106, 113,
    116, 118, 126–7, 143
Hölderlin   68, 77, 83
Hollier, D.   143
Hottois, G.   134
Howard, R.   7, 132
Howe, M.   10, 21, 132, 134, 143
humanism   6, 11, 29, 32, 35, 51,
    57–8, 69, 77, 85, 87–8, 92, 98,
    101–3, 115, 125
human nature   76, 114
human sciences   6, 9, 11, 24, 28–9,
    39, 42, 60, 76, 81–2, 105
Huppert, G.   17, 134
Hyppolite, J.   33

ideology   92, 99, 111, 148
identity   30–1, 55–6, 88–9, 123

Iggers, G.   136–7
Ignatieff, M.   149
individual   30, 33, 39, 42, 68–9,
    77, 81–2, 103–5, 107, 116–17,
    120–2, 127, 129, 149
influence   35–6, 52
influences on Foucault   34, 136,
    142, 143
institutions   26, 39, 98, 110, 119
intellectuals, French   12–16, 22–4,
    45, 133, 135
  Foucault's theories of   37, 109,
    148
  and the media   12–13, 23–5, 134
  and politics   1–6, 27, 110–11,
    148
interpretation   84–5, 94
Iran   74
irrationalism   51, 114, 125, 149

Jambet, C.   102, 142, 147
Janicaud, D.   150
jargon   ix, 17
Joly, H.   121, 150
Jorion, P.   111, 149
July, S.   137

Kahn, J. F.   12, 133
Kanapa, J.   3
Kant, I.   29, 32–3, 123, 136
Kemp, P.   27, 40, 135, 138
Kiejman, G.   147
Kniebiehler, Y.   139
knowledge   30, 77
Kravetz, M.   133
Koestler, A.   4
Kuhn, T. S.   57
Kurzweil, E.   140

Lacan, J.   9–10, 16, 50
Laing, R. D.   8
language   41–2, 77–9, 82–3, 85–6,
    88–9, 144
  being of   40, 57, 80, 84–5, 87,
    89, 94, 144, 145
Leary, D. E.   140
Le Bon, S.   57–8, 139, 140, 146
Lecourt, D.   99, 140, 146
Lefebvre, H.   5
Lefort, Cl.   3, 4, 131

Lefort, G.   15–16, 133, 135
Le Goff, J.   27–9, 38, 135, 137, 141
Lemaigre, B.   84, 142, 144
Lemert, G.   133, 146
Léonard, J.   36, 62, 92, 108, 137,
    144, 146, 148
Le Roy Ladurie, E.   2–5, 27, 66,
    131, 141
Lévinas, E.   27, 31
Lévi-Strauss, Cl.   9–10, 21, 50,
    132, 134
Lévy, B. H.   16, 134
limits   31–3, 38–44, 47, 65–8, 70,
    72, 74, 79, 82–5, 87–91, 94–5,
    98, 107, 112, 115–19, 123,
    125–6, 129–30, 136, 143, 144,
    150
  history of   vii–viii, 91, 136
Lindon, M.   132
Lipovetsky, G.   134
Livrozet, S.   146
literature   73, 77–78, 83, 87–90,
    143
Lodge, D.   149
Lucas, C.   148

Macherey, P,   123, 146, 151
madness   42, 48–51, 68–86, 88–9,
    94–5, 97, 103, 105, 140, 142,
    143, 145
  tragedy of   68, 71–3, 77, 81
  absence of   75
  see also mental illness
Madness and Civilization   9, 95 (*see
    also Histoire de la folie*)
Maggiori, R.   102, 134, 147
Major-Poetzl, P.   147
Maladie mentale et psychologie   6,
    51, 71, 75–6
Mallarmé   50, 68
Man, death of   12, 87–8, 101
Maoism   15, 26, 45–6, 98, 101
Marcus, S.   78, 143
margins, social   8, 65–70, 98, 101,
    105, 136, 141
Marx, K.   10–11, 29, 54, 91,
    99–101, 146
Marxism   1–6, 10, 12, 34–5, 95,
    99–101, 146

Marxism (*cont'd*)
 and Foucault   viii, 12, 25, 95,
  99–101
materialism   100
Mauriac, Cl.   67, 133, 141, 144,
  146
Mauriac, F.   3
May 1968   25, 41, 133
Mazlish, B.   78, 143
meaning   115
medicine   81–2
Mendel, G.   86, 135, 144, 149
mental illness   50, 75, 77, 88 (*see
  also* madness)
mentality   35–6
Merleau-Ponty, M.   1, 3, 131, 109
Merquior, J. G.   114, 139, 149
metaphysics   22, 28–9, 33–5, 97,
  100, 115, 123, 136
methodology   14, 37, 49, 62–3, 95,
  121
Middle Ages   48, 71–2, 75, 142
Midelfort, H.C.   49, 139, 141, 142
Milhau, J.   100, 139, 146
Minson, J.   96, 102, 111–12, 138,
  145, 146, 149
Misrahi, R.   135
mode of subjectivation   121–3,
  127
Modern Age   48–9, 76
modernity   43, 66
Moi, Pierre Rivière...   15
moral behaviour   120–1
 laws   74, 120–2
 subject   116, 120, 122
morality   38, 64, 91, 102, 115,
  120–1, 124, 150
Mots et les choses, Les   7, 9–11,
  13–14, 40, 47, 53–60, 68, 81,
  84–6, 88–9, 91–2, 95, 99, 103–4,
  116, 126, 145–6
mutation   *see* discontinuity

Naissance de la clinique   9, 14, 30,
  40, 51–2, 55–6, 68, 79, 81–5, 87,
  103, 116, 141
Nemo, P.   110, 133, 148
Nerval, G. de   73, 77
'New History'   38

new novelists   46, 79, 85
new philosophers   16–17, 25,
  45–6, 101
Nietzsche, F.   23, 29, 33–4, 41,
  68–9, 73–4, 77–8, 83, 91, 94,
  102, 114, 126, 136, 139, 141,
  142, 145, 151
nihilism and Foucault   viii, 33,
  50–1, 94, 114, 130
normalisation   75, 92, 104–6, 123
nothingness   45, 72, 76, 84, 88, 93

objects (in history)   41–2, 48,
  50–1, 73, 107
order   40, 42, 44, 52–3, 55–7, 86,
  93, 97–8, 116, 118–19, 129, 139
Order of Things, The   58, 61 (*see
  also Les Mots et les choses*)
Ordre du discours, L'   14, 41, 68–9,
  96, 138, 144
Other   vii, 30–5, 40–2, 44, 49, 53,
  55, 61, 65–6, 71, 73, 74, 76, 78,
  80, 81, 84, 88–91, 93–4, 98, 103,
  107, 115–16, 127, 130, 136, 142,
  143

Pace, D.   50, 139
Panopticon   104
paradigm   57, 61, 140
Parti Communiste Français
  (PCF)   1–5
Patton, P.   133
Pelorson, J. M.   142
periodisation   36, 47–9, 51–3, 63,
  65
Perrot, M.   65
phenomenology   31, 51
philosophy
 Anglo-Saxon   22–4
 as an ascesis   117
 definitions of   14, 36, 122–4,
  126, 133
 French   22–4
Philp, M.   111, 114, 140, 146, 149
Pinel   8, 70, 75, 79
Pizzorno   152
pleb   98, 107–8
Plummer, K.   108, 148
poetry (Foucault as poet)   78, 80

politics 37, 41, 48, 63, 91–2, 96–8, 101, 106–7, 109, 112, 114, 128
Popper, K. 24, 34, 136–7
positivism 51, 58, 94
and Foucault 58, 96
Poster, M. 44–5, 100, 108, 135, 138, 146, 148, 149
power viii, 14, 16–18, 37, 62–3, 69, 90–2, 95–6, 98, 102–3, 105–10, 112–20, 128–30, 138, 147, 148
genealogies of 41, 96
macropower 102
microphysics of 102–4
power-knowledge 61, 95, 103, 105, 114
relations of 107, 110, 118–19, 147
technologies of 106, 145
see also discipline
post-modernism 25
practices 39, 109, 121, 123, 125, 127
present 36, 126, 137
prisons 101–5
progress 34–5, 50–1, 53, 75, 115
prohibition 97
proletariat 2, 98, 107
psychiatry 49, 78–9, 102
Proust, J. 17, 40, 134, 139
psychological sleep 88
psychology 49, 52, 75, 78, 82
punishment 101–3, 105

Quétal, Cl. 135

Racevskis, K. 134, 138, 149
Rajchman, J. 136, 149, 150, 152
Rancière, J. 146
Raymond Roussel 9, 79–80
rationalism 65, 73, 115, 122–3
rationality 34, 76, 108, 115, 125
Reason 34–5, 38, 49, 59, 70, 73–4, 76, 79, 85, 91, 97, 115, 125, 142, 144
relativism 27, 33–5, 50, 114–15
Renaissance 48, 53–6, 68, 72–5, 77, 82, 86, 88–9, 127
representation 56–7, 85–6

resemblance 55–6, 88–9
resistance 37, 107, 114, 118, 125, 130, 148
Revault d'Allonnes, O. 146, 149
Revel, J. 26, 131, 135
Revel, J. F. 1, 13–14, 100, 133, 146
rhetoric (Foucault's) 39, 99, 100, 115, 117, 138
Robinson, P. 146
Robbe-Grillet, A. 9, 11, 132
Rochlitz, R. 128, 150, 152
Rorty, R. 92, 114–15, 128, 144, 149, 152
Roth, M. S. 50, 139–40
Rothman, D. 140, 148
Rousseau, G. S. 22–4, 134, 138, 143
Roussel, R. 68, 77, 80–1, 89, 143
Roy, Cl. 146
rupture *see discontinuity*
Russell, B. 23–4, 134

Sade, Marquis de 56, 68–9, 82, 89, 91, 139
Said, E. 41, 111, 138, 140, 149
Same vii, 30–5, 40–2, 44, 53, 55, 65, 71, 74, 78, 80–81, 84, 89, 90, 93, 98, 107, 115–16, 119, 130, 136, 143, 144
Sarraute, N. 11
Sartre, J. P. 1–5, 11–13, 23, 27, 29, 31, 40, 99, 101, 109, 131, 132–3, 139, 140
Schmitt, J. C. 139
Scholes, R. 133
science 22–4, 62, 134
scientism 23, 58
self 40, 116, 121–4, 129, 149
techniques of 18, 106, 121, 127
as a work of art 40, 128–9
Serres, M. 7, 12, 69, 132, 136, 141
sexuality 16, 42, 63–4, 83, 96, 105–6, 118, 143, 145
in Antiquity 18, 63, 118, 120, 127
Shakespeare, W. 68, 73
Sheridan, A. 20, 132, 134, 138, 140, 146, 149

Ship of Fools 72
Smart, B. 100, 146
Socialisme ou barbarie 5
Socrates 18
Solé, J. 135
Sollers, P. 11, 46
Souci de soi, Le 18, 63, 106, 113, 116
'soul' 101–2, 107
spirit of the age *see* *Weltanschauung*
spirituality 18, 72–4, 107, 124, 127, 142, 147
Stalinism 3–5, 13, 131
Steiner, G. 58, 140
Steinert, H. 108, 148
Stoianovich, T. 135
Stone, L. 38, 49, 59, 79, 137, 139, 141, 143
Storr. A. 75, 108
structures 37, 40, 57–8
structuralism vii, 6, 9–11, 13, 17, 25, 37, 58, 92
style (literary) 17, 23, 148–9
Foucault's 23, 44, 79, 113–14, 117, 138, 149
stylisation of existence 120, 127–8
subject 6, 10, 29, 31, 34, 37, 39, 73–4, 85, 97, 106, 113–14, 116–17, 120–3, 125, 127, 142, 144
subjectivity 18, 39, 42, 74, 76–7, 102, 114, 118, 123, 127
surveillance 104–5
Surveiller et punir 16–17, 26, 61, 63, 67, 92–3, 101, 103–5, 107–8, 110, 116
synchrony 58
systems(s) vii, 6, 41, 51, 53–7, 59, 60, 84, 91–2, 98, 100, 108–12, 122–4, 130, 146, 148

tables 88, 104, 132–3
teleology 36, 49, 51
and the self 122

theory 17, 42, 135, 94, 100, 109, 111, 145
as a 'tool-box' 41, 44–5, 90, 110–12, 148
tragedy *see* madness
transcendentals *see* universals, foundations
transformation 59, 69, 97
transgression 32, 40, 67–8, 76, 83–5, 88–90, 115, 136
Tricart, J. P. 139
truth 14, 30, 37–8, 61, 71, 73–7, 79, 86, 88, 90–1, 97, 106–9, 111, 115–18, 123–4, 126–7, 129, 145, 148, 151
regimes of 103
Tuke 70, 75–6

unities of discourse 37, 97
'universals' 123–4
unreason *see* madness
Usage des plaisirs, L' 18, 30, 39, 63, 106, 116–17, 120–1

Van Gogh, V. 68, 77–8
Volonté de savoir, La 16–18, 61, 63–64, 69, 93, 96, 105–8, 118–19
Verley, E. 139
Veyne, P. 27, 29, 38, 51, 115, 128–9, 134, 135, 137, 139, 142, 150, 152
Veyron, M. 25, 135
void *see* nothingness

Wahl, F. 79, 136, 143
Weissman, G. 79
Weltanschauung 35–6, 52, 59, 61
White, H. 50, 84, 86, 136, 139, 140, 143, 144
will to power 102
will to truth 69, 97
Wolton, D. 147
Wright, I. 114–15, 132, 149
writing, Foucault and 92–3
Wuthnow, R. 28, 100, 135, 140, 141, 145, 146, 150